Project Management Excellence

The Art of Excelling in Project Management

Project Management Excellence

The Art of Excelling in Project Management

Book 2 in the five-part series
The Five Pillars of Organizational Excellence

H. James Harrington, Ph.D.
and
Thomas McNellis

Foreword by Spencer Hutchens Jr.

Paton Press LLC
Chico, California

Most Paton Press books are available at quantity discounts when purchased in bulk. For more information, contact:

Paton Press LLC
P.O. Box 44
Chico, CA 95927-0044
Telephone: 1-888-377-5480
Fax: (530) 342-5471
E-mail: *books@patonpress.com*
Web: *www.patonpress.com*

© 2006 H. James Harrington. All rights reserved. Printed in the United States of America. Except as permitted under the U.S. Copyright Act of 1976, no part of this publication may be reproduced or distributed in any form or by any means, or stored in a database or retrieval system, without the prior written permission from Paton Press LLC.

Printed in the United States of America

10 09 08 07 06   5 4 3 2 1

ISBN-13: 978-1-932828-07-8
ISBN-10: 1-932828-07-9

Library of Congress Cataloging-in-Publication Data
Harrington, H. J. (H. James)
  Project management excellence: the art of excelling in project management / by H. James Harrington and Thomas McNellis.
    p. cm. — (The five pillars of organizational excellence; 2)
  ISBN 1-932828-07-9
  1. Project management. 2. Industrial management. I. McNellis, Thomas, 1949- II. Title.
    HD69.P75H363 2006
    658.4'04—dc22
                    2006000233

Notice of Liability
The information in this book is distributed on an "as is" basis, without warranty. Although every precaution has been taken in the preparation of the book, neither the authors nor Paton Press LLC shall have any liability to any person or entity with respect to any loss or damage caused or alleged to be caused directly or indirectly by the information contained in this book.

Staff
Publisher: Scott M. Paton
Editor: Taran March
Book design: David Hurst

CONTENTS

About the Authors ix
Other Books By H. James Harrington xi
Dedication xiii
Acknowledgments xv
Foreword xvii
Preface xix

    Pillar I—Process Management Excellence xxii
    Pillar II—Project Management Excellence xxiv
    Pillar III—Change Management Excellence xxv
    Pillar IV—Knowledge Management Excellence xxvii
    Pillar V—Resource Management Excellence xxviii
    The Sky Is Not the Limit xxx
    Why Do You Need Organizational Excellence? xxxi
    Organizational Excellence Summary xxxiv

CHAPTER I
Introduction to Process Management Excellence 1

    Why Projects Historically Fail 4
    Why Is Project Management So Important? 6
    How Much Could an Effective Project Management System
        Save Your Organization 7
    The New Project Management 9
    Project Management Body of Knowledge (PMBOK) 11
    The PRINCE Project Management Approach 18
    The Project Management Model 19
    Why Use a Six-Phase Project Life Cycle? 22

CHAPTER II
Project Operating Structure 25

    Steering Committee's Role 26

    The Project Sponsor's Role 27
    The Project Manager's Role. 28
    The Team Leader's Role. 32
    The Process Owner's Role 32
    The Project Team Member's Role 33
    The Resource Manager's Role 34
    The Project Office's Role 35
    Project Office Duties and Responsibilities 37
    Project Office Types and Styles. 38
    Project Office Staffing 40
    Myths Versus Truths 40

CHAPTER III
Project Management Knowledge Areas. 43
    Project Integration Management 43
    Project Scope Management. 45
    Project Planning and Estimating Management 50
    Project Time Management 64
    Project Financial (COST) Management. 64
    Project Quality Management 65
    Project Human Resource Management. 66
    Project Communications Management 66
    Project Risk Management 67
    Project Procurement Management. 67
    Organizational Change Management. 68
    Project Portfolio Management 68
    Project Document/Configuration Management 80

CHAPTER IV
Project Selection. 83
    Subphases 85
    Project Selection 85

CHAPTER V
Project Initiation. 95
    Project Selection Activities 95

Project Portfolio 97
Sponsorship. 98
Charter. 99
Project Team Activities 100
Stages of Team Development 100
Project Team Performance. 102
Project Target Board 104
Project Initiation Summary. 104

CHAPTER VI
Project Planning 105

Requirements. 107
Conceptual Design 108
Detailed Design Document. 109
Risk Analysis 111
Change Strategy 111
Project Organizational Change Management. .113
Project Structure Based on Planning Phase Results 115
Project Office. 115
The Engagement Model 116
Project Planning Summary 117

CHAPTER VII
Project Execution 119

Rapid Application Development. 120
Prototype. 121
Testing Strategy 121
Linking Test Objectives to Business Requirements. 122
Setting Up the Test cycle. 122
Test Cases. 123
Unit Testing. 124
System Testing. 124
Defect Detection 125
Reporting Project Status 125
Project Execution Phase Summary 127

CHAPTER VIII
Project Control 129
- Continuous Improvement 129
- Project Control Framework..130
- Cost and Schedule Control-Variance Analysis 131
- Quality Control..133
- Information and Reporting Needs 133
- Earned Value Analysis..140
- Dashboard Reporting 143
- Project Control Phase Summary..145

CHAPTER IX
Project Closeout 147
- Rewards and Recognition 147
- Project Closeout Phase Summary 149

CHAPTER X
Project Management Life Cycle Summary 151
- How Three Organizations Improved Their Project Management 151

Appendix A: Definitions 155
Appendix B: PMBOK Tools and Techniques 169
Index 173

ABOUT THE AUTHORS

In the book *Tech Trending* (Capstone, 2001) by Amy Zuckerman, H. James Harrington was referred to as "the quintessential tech trender." The *New York Times* referred to him as having a ". . . knack for synthesis and an open mind about packaging his knowledge and experience in new ways—characteristics that may matter more as prerequisites for new-economy success than technical wizardry . . . "

H. James Harrington, Ph.D.
CEO, Harrington Institute Inc.

Present Responsibilities

Harrington now serves as the chief executive officer for the Harrington Institute. He also serves as the chairman of the board for a number of businesses and as the U.S. chairman of Technologies for Project Management at the University of Quebec.

Harrington is recognized as one of the world leaders in applying performance improvement methodologies to business processes.

Previous Experience

In February 2002, Harrington retired as the COO of Systemcorp ALG, a leading supplier of knowledge management and project management software solutions. Prior to this, he served as a principal and one of the leaders in the Process Innovation Group at Ernst & Young. He was with IBM for more than thirty years as a senior engineer and project manager.

Harrington is past chairman of the prestigious International Academy for Quality and past president of the American Society for Quality. He is also an active member of the Global Knowledge Economics Council.

Credentials

The Harrington/Ishikawa Medal, presented yearly by the Asia Pacific Quality Organization, was named after Harrington to recognize his many contributions to the region. In 1997, the Quebec Society for Quality named their quality award "The Harrington/Neron Medal," honoring Harrington for his many contributions to Canada's quality movement. In 2000, the Sri Lanka national quality award was named after him.

Harrington's contributions to performance improvement around the world have brought him many honors and awards, including the Edwards Medal, the Lancaster Medal, ASQ's Distinguished Service Medal, China's Magnolia Award, and many others. He was appointed the honorary advisor to the China Quality Control Association, and he was elected to the Singapore Productivity Hall of Fame in 1990. He has been named lifetime honorary president of the Asia Pacific Quality Organization and honorary director of the Chilean Association of Quality Control.

Harrington has been elected a Fellow of the British Quality Control Organization and the American Society for Quality. He was also elected an honorary member of the quality societies in Taiwan, Argentina, Brazil, Colombia, and Singapore. He is listed in *Who's Who Worldwide* and *Men of Distinction Worldwide*. He has presented hundreds of papers on performance improvement and organizational management structure at local, state, national, and international levels.

Harrington is a prolific author, having published hundreds of technical reports and magazine articles. He has authored twenty-eight books and ten software packages.

Thomas McNellis is recognized as an international trainer in the fields of project management, e-business, and quality. He is also a well-known advisor to corporate leaders interested in bridging the gap between project management and e-business opportunities. McNellis currently serves as director of operations for the Association for E-business Research, a research-based consulting firm that focuses on cutting-edge e-business best practices. He's also a founding member of Angels on the Internet, a program that introduces Internet education into inner-city grade schools, and a principal consultant for The CRM Institute, which specializes in customer relationship management workshops.

Thomas McNellis
Dean, Harrington Academy

McNellis' background in computer science, project management, quality, e-business, and management provided the foundation for his unique approach to creating customer- and e-business-centered organizations. McNellis holds five degrees, numerous certifications, and is the author of many articles on project management and e-business. He's served as interim vice chairperson-at-large for the Project Management Institute's E-business Specific Interest Group.

OTHER BOOKS BY H. JAMES HARRINGTON

- *The Improvement Process* (McGraw-Hill, 1987, a best-selling business book that year)
- *Poor-Quality Cost* (Marcel Dekker, 1987)
- *Excellence—The IBM Way* (American Society for Quality, 1988)
- *The Quality/Profit Connection* (American Society for Quality, 1988)
- *Business Process Improvement* (McGraw-Hill, 1991, the first book about process redesign)
- *The Mouse Story* (Ernst & Young, 1991)
- *Of Tails and Teams* (American Society for Quality, 1994)
- *Total Improvement Management* (McGraw-Hill, 1995)
- *High Performance Benchmarking* (McGraw-Hill, 1996)
- *The Complete Benchmarking Implementation Guide* (McGraw-Hill, 1996)
- *ISO 9000 and Beyond* (McGraw-Hill, 1996)
- *The Business Process Improvement Workbook* (McGraw-Hill, 1997)
- *The Creativity Toolkit—Provoking Creativity in Individuals and Organizations* (McGraw-Hill, 1998)
- *Statistical Analysis Simplified—The Easy-to-Understand Guide to SPC and Data Analysis* (McGraw-Hill, 1998)
- *Area Activity Analysis—Aligning Work Activities and Measurements to Enhance Business Performance* (McGraw-Hill, 1998)
- *Reliability Simplified—Going Beyond Quality to Keep Customers for Life* (McGraw-Hill, 1999)
- *ISO 14000 Implementation—Upgrading Your EMS Effectively* (McGraw-Hill, 1999)
- *Performance Improvement Methods—Fighting the War on Waste* (with Kenneth C. Lomax, McGraw-Hill, 1999)
- *Simulation Modeling Methods—An Interactive Guide to Results-Based Decision Making* (McGraw-Hill, 2000)
- *Project Change Management—Applying Change Management to Improvement Projects* (with Daryl R. Conner and Nicholas L. Horney, McGraw-Hill, 2000)
- *E-Business Project Manager* (American Society for Quality, 2002)
- *Project Management Excellence: The Art of Excelling in Process Management* (Paton Press, 2006)
- *Change Management Excellence: The Art of Excelling in Change Management* (Paton Press, 2006)
- *Knowledge Management Excellence: The Art of Excelling in Knowledge Management* (Paton Press, 2006)
- *Resource Management Excellence: The Art of Excelling in Resource Management* (Paton Press, 2006)
- *Making Teams Hum* (Paton Press, 2006)

DEDICATION

I dedicate this book to my son, James S. Harrington, whom I love with all my heart. He's turned out to be better than I ever hoped he would. And by the way, he's a better writer than I am. Jim, thanks for all you've given your mother and me.

ACKNOWLEDGMENTS

I want to acknowledge Candy Rogers, who transcribed and edited endless hours of dictation into the finished product. I could not have done it without her help. To my friends at the American Society for Quality and the International Academy for Quality, I want to thank you for your many contributions to the concepts expressed in this book.

I also want to recognize the contributions made by the team from Harrington Institute Inc. But most of all, I want to recognize the contributions made by my wife, Marguerite. She's always there when I need her.

FOREWORD

They say the road to hell is paved with good intentions. But to that dictum I think we need to add the painful truth that in today's organizations, the road is also littered with the debris of sloppy project management. That's why I was so delighted to learn that Jim Harrington and Thomas McNellis were turning their attention and experience to the subject of project management. That they were dealing with this topic within the systematic framework of their pillars of organizational excellence model further piqued my interest.

Despite efforts to slim down, project work is where much of the fat resides in today's organizations. Chances are we've all seen it in our own organizations in the high percentage of failed projects and resources poured into projects that produce little tangible payback. And those of us who have the opportunity to work with many different organizations have a clear appreciation for the magnitude of the problem as well as the great opportunities that await those who grasp the nature of the problem and are equipped to deal with it. This book provides both the understanding and tools needed to turn project management problems into successes.

Successful project managers are definitely change agents. They've learned to embrace the change that is inevitable in any contemporary undertaking of any consequence. But they are much more, as Harrington and McNellis point out. They are also leaders. The futures studies undertaken by the American Society for Quality challenged quality practitioners to find new ways to assume leadership roles within their organizations if they wish to remain relevant in the future—such as the leadership inherent in acting as an effective organizational change agent. Project management experience affords people such as quality practitioners, who are adept at process management, tremendous opportunities to exercise and develop their managerial talents and to assume new leadership positions.

The treatment Harrington and McNellis give to project management is thorough, systematic, and logical. For organizations facing the difficult decisions implementing organizational change, this book constitutes a compelling guide that can spell the difference between effective change and useless good intentions.

—Spencer Hutchens Jr.
Senior vice president, RAM Consulting

PREFACE

"No person or company should be content to stay where they are, no matter how successful they now seem to be."
—Stephen R. Covey, Ph.D.
The Seven Habits of Highly Effective People

This series was written for a small group of organizations. It's not for traditionalists, the weak of heart, or for organizations that believe winning a national quality award is their ultimate objective. This series was written for organizations that aren't content with being anything less than the best they can be. It's for organizations that want to stand out from the crowd and that hunger to obtain optimum results in the five Ps:

- *Pride.* Employees are proud of their work and their organization.
- *Performance.* The entire organization operates at high levels of efficiency and effectiveness.
- *Profit.* The organization is profitable, able to pay its employees good salaries, and pay higher-than-average dividends to its investors.
- *Prestige.* The organization is considered an admirable place to work for and is known for its highly desired products and services.
- *Pleasure.* Employees enjoy coming to work because they're doing something worthwhile in a friendly, supportive environment.

Good is no longer good enough. Doing the right thing "right" isn't good enough. Having the highest quality and being the most productive doesn't suffice today. To survive in today's competitive environment, you must excel. To excel, an organization must focus on all parts of itself, optimizing the use and effectiveness of all of its resources. It must also provide "knock their socks off" products and services. An organization must be so innovative and creative that customers say, "I didn't know they could do that!"

> "To compete and win, we must redouble our efforts, not only in the quality of our goods and services, but in the quality of our thinking, in the quality of our response to our customers, in the quality of our decision making, in the quality of everything we do."
> —E. S. Woolard
> Chairman and CEO, Dupont

After years of working with all types of organizations and using many different approaches to improve performance, I've come to realize that five key elements must be managed for an organization to excel. I call them the "five pillars of organizational excellence." All five must be managed creatively and simultaneously. Top

xix

Figure P.1   **Organizational Excellence**

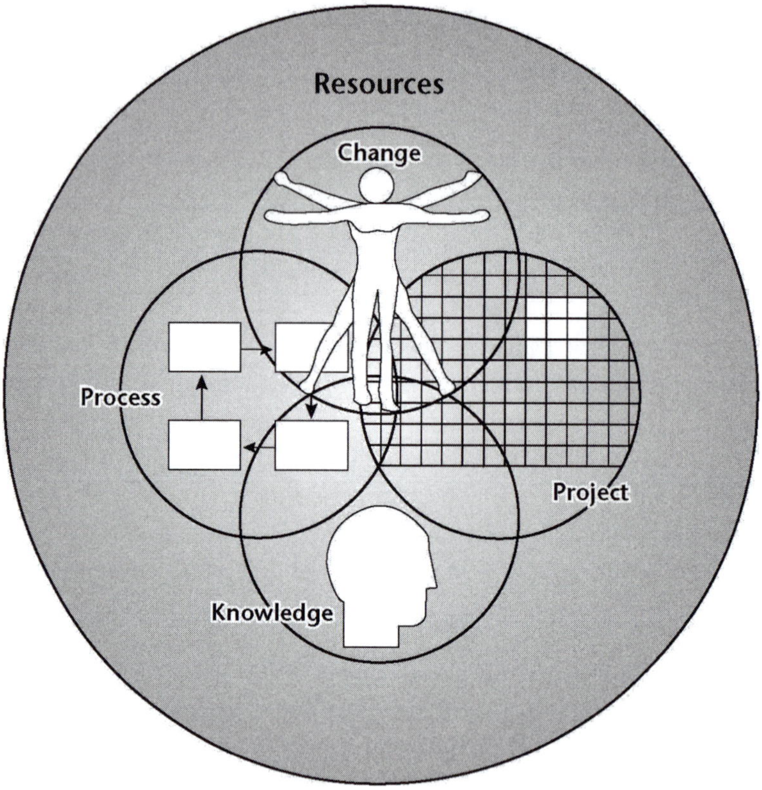

management's job is to keep all these elements moving ahead simultaneously. To concentrate on one or two alone is a surefire formula for failure. Priorities might shift, causing an individual pillar to move from "very important" to simply "important," but it should never shift lower than that.

The processes discussed in this series are designed to permanently change an organization by skillfully managing its five key pillars. Each of these management pillars is not new by itself, but by combining and managing them together, a holistic approach to improving an organization's performance is possible. (See figure P.2)

The five pillars of organizational excellence are:

- *Process management excellence.* We must manage our processes and continuously improve them because they are the way we do business.
- *Project management excellence.* We must manage our projects because they are the way we obtain major improvements in our processes.

- *Change management excellence.* We must manage the organization so that it can cope with the chaos it will be subjected to by the magnitude and quantity of necessary changes.
- *Knowledge management excellence.* We must manage the organization's knowledge, its most valuable asset. (Knowledge gives an organization its competitive advantage, as technology can easily be reverse-engineered and transferred to any place in the world almost overnight.)
- *Resource management excellence.* We must manage our resources and assets because they're what drive our business results.

By effectively managing these five key pillars and leveraging their interdependencies and reactions, an organization can bring about a marvelous self-transformation. It will emerge from its restricting cocoon and float on the winds of success and self-fulfillment.

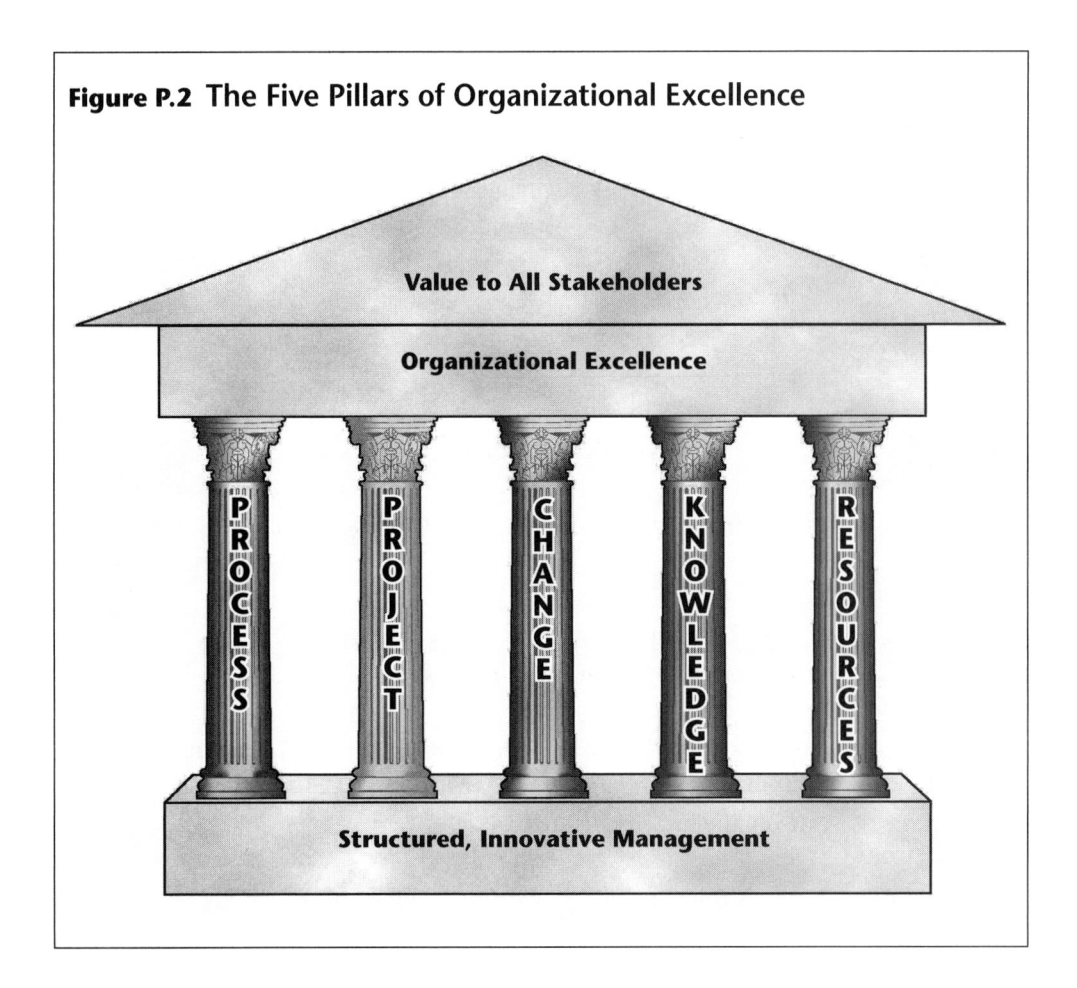

Figure P.2 The Five Pillars of Organizational Excellence

Project Management Excellence

Organizational excellence is designed to permanently change an organization by focusing on the five pillars of excellence. Learning to manage the pillars together is the key to success in the endless pursuit of improved performance. To help you in this endeavor, each volume in this five-book series addresses one of the pillars. The series consists of the following books:

- *Process Management Excellence: The Art of Excelling in Process Management*
- *Project Management Excellence: The Art of Excelling in Project Management*
- *Change Management Excellence: The Art of Excelling in Change Management*
- *Knowledge Management Excellence: The Art of Excelling in Knowledge Management*
- *Resource Management Excellence: The Art of Excelling in Resource Management*

None of the five pillars can individually support organizational excellence. All of them must be present and equally strong to support the weight of success for all of its stakeholders. The challenge that excellent organizations face today is how to nurture an innovative learning culture while maintaining the procedures and structure to ensure optimum performance as well as customer and investor satisfaction. The Five Pillars of Organizational Excellence series was designed to help you solve this dilemma.

Because it's important to understand how the five pillars interact with and support each other, a short discussion about each of them follows.

> **"These companies [excellent organizations] implement their results through effectiveness in developing and deploying management capital's intellectual, technical, human, information, and other resources in integrating a company's hard and soft assets."**
> —Armand V. Feigenbaum and Donald Feigenbaum
> *The Power of Management Capital*

PILLAR I—PROCESS MANAGEMENT EXCELLENCE

"Your processes manage the organization, not your managers."
—HJH

The process management concept certainly isn't new to management professionals; it's the basis of most improvement methodologies.

Definition: A *process* is a series of interconnected activities that takes input, adds value to it, and produces output. It's how organizations work their day-to-day routines. Your organization's processes define how it operates.

To manage a process, the following must be defined and agreed upon:
- An output requirement statement between process owners and customers

- An input requirement statement between process owners and suppliers
- A process that can transform suppliers' input into output that meets customers' performance and quality requirements
- Feedback measurement systems between process and customers, and between process and suppliers
- The method by which people are trained to understand the process
- A measurement system within the process

These six key factors should be addressed when designing a process. However, the problem facing most organizations is that many of their support processes were never designed in the first place. They were created in response to a need without understanding what a process is.

> "Most individuals, teams, and groups within an organization will take the path of least resistance. Inevitably, over time, they will function at the lowest level of acceptability."
> —William J. Schwarz
> CEO, CEO Alliance and the Center for Inspired Performance

The Two Approaches to Process Management

There are two basic approaches to managing processes:

- The micro-level approach, which is directed at managing processes within a natural work team or an individual department
- The macro-level approach, which is directed at managing processes that flow across departments and/or functions within the organization.

Most of the work that quality professionals do involves continuously improving processes. Some of the tools they use include design of experiments, process capability studies, root cause analysis, document control, quality circles, suggestion systems, Six Sigma, Shewhart's cycles, ISO 9001, and just-in-time manufacturing and supplier qualification.

In excellent organizations, management requires each natural work team (or department) to continuously improve the processes it uses.

> "If you [management] create an expectation of continuous product or service improvement but fail to deliver on that expectation, you will see a buildup of fear and negative forecasting."
> —Stephen R. Covey, Ph.D.
> *The Seven Habits of Highly Effective People*

Refining a process is an ongoing activity. If the refinement process is working as it should, the total process's efficiency and effectiveness should be improving at a rate of 10 to 15 percent a year. In most cases, the project team focuses on the major problems that reflect across departments and reap such a harvest within three to twelve months. At that time, the project team can be disbanded and the process-refinement activities turned over to the natural work teams involved in the process. Area activity analysis methodology, which is discussed later on in this book, is the most effective approach to process refinement.

Figure P.3 What Different Types of People Have to Say About a Half-Full Glass

- The optimist: It's half full.
- The pessimist: It's half empty.
- The process manager: We have twice the number of glasses as we need.

By focusing on its processes and working with its suppliers, IBM reported that, "Between 1997 and 2001, the hardware reliability of our high-end servers improved by more than 200 percent while computing power increased by a factor of four."

PILLAR II—PROJECT MANAGEMENT EXCELLENCE

"How can you compete when more than 70 percent of your improvement efforts are unsuccessful?"

—HJH

According to the *Chaos Report* compiled by the Standish Group International:
- Only 26 percent of all projects are successful.
- Forty percent of all information technology (IT) projects fail or are canceled.

Definition: A *project* is a temporary endeavor undertaken to create a unique product or service.

Projects in most organizations are mission-critical activities, and delivering quality products on time is non-negotiable. Even for IT projects, things have changed. Benchmark organizations are completing 90 percent of their projects within 10 percent of budget and schedule. Information systems organizations that establish standards for project management, including a project office, cut their major project cost overruns, delays, and cancellations by 50 percent. This book will discuss these changes in detail.

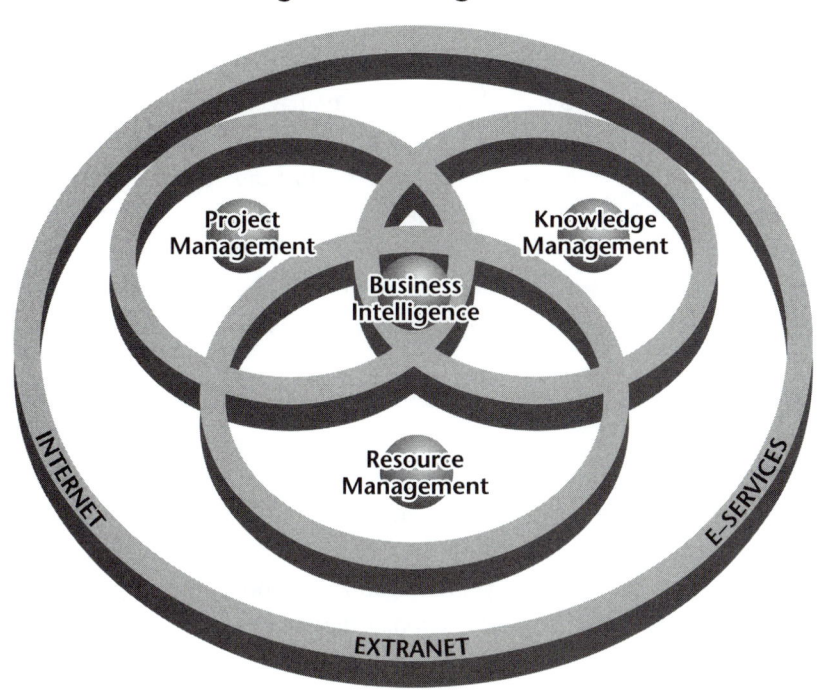

Figure P.4   **Integrated Management Tools**

(Diagram: concentric and overlapping rings labeled INTERNET, EXTRANET, E-SERVICES surrounding interlocking circles for Project Management, Knowledge Management, Resource Management, with Business Intelligence at the center.)

PILLAR III—CHANGE MANAGEMENT EXCELLENCE

> "Research confirms that as much as 60 percent of change initiatives and other projects fail as a direct result of a fundamental inability to manage their social implications."
>
> —Gartner Group

We all like to think of ourselves as change masters, but, in truth, we're change bigots. Everyone in the management team supports change. They want to see others change, but when it comes to the managers themselves changing, they're reluctant to move away from past experiences that have proven successful for them. If an organization is going to change, top management must be the first to do so.

Change is inevitable, and we must embrace it if we're going to be successful in the challenging world in which we live. In *Change Management Excellence: The Art of Excelling in Change Management*, book three in this series, we discuss a change management system made up of three distinct elements:

- Defining what will be changed
- Defining how to change
- Making the change happen

Most of the books written to date about change management have been theoretical in nature. They talk about black holes, cascading sponsorships, and burning platforms, but these are only the last phase of the change process. Most organizations don't understand or follow a comprehensive change management system. An effective change management system requires that the organization step back and define what will be changed. It's not about reducing stock levels, increasing customer satisfaction, or training people; it's about the fundamentals. Which of the key business drivers must be changed, and how do they need to be changed?

An organization must develop crisp vision statements that define how key business drivers will be changed over time. This requires that the organization have an excellent understanding of what its business drivers are and how they're currently operating. Then the organization must define exactly how it wants to change these key business drivers over a set period of time. Once the organization has defined what it wants to change, it can then define how to change. During this stage, the organization looks at the more than 1,100 different improvement tools that are available today, determines which tools will bring about the required changes to these key business drivers, and schedules the implementation of these tools and methodologies. This schedule makes up a key part of the organization's strategic business plan.

The last phase in the change management process is making the change happen. This is the area where behavioral scientists have developed a number of excellent approaches to break down resistance and build up resiliency throughout the organization. It's this phase that most change management books have concentrated on, but it's the last phase in the total change management system. Book three of this series focuses on all three phases of the change management system, discussing in detail how to define what will be changed, defining how to change it, and how to make the change happen.

PILLAR IV—KNOWLEDGE MANAGEMENT EXCELLENCE

> "When a person dies, a library is lost."
> —HJH

Today, more than ever before, knowledge is the key to organizational success. To fulfill this need, the Internet and other information technologies have provided all of us with more information than we can ever consume. Instead of having one or two sources of information, the Internet provides us with hundreds, if not thousands, of inputs, all of which must be researched for that key nugget of information. We're overwhelmed with so much information that we don't have time to absorb it.

To make matters worse, most of an organization's knowledge is still undocumented; it rests in the minds and experiences of its employees. This knowledge disappears from the organization's knowledge base whenever an individual leaves an assignment. In *Knowledge Management Excellence: The Art of Excelling in Knowledge Management*, book four in this series, we define how to establish a knowledge management system (KMS) that will be designed to sort out unneeded and/or false information and capture the "soft" knowledge needed to run an organization.

Because an almost endless amount of information clouds our computers, desks, and minds, a KMS must be designed around the organization's key capabilities and competencies.

What Is Knowledge?

Knowledge is a mixture of experiences, practices, traditions, values, contextual information, expert insight, and sound intuition that provides an environment and framework for evaluating and incorporating new experiences and information.

There are two types of knowledge: explicit and tacit.

Explicit knowledge is defined as knowledge that is stored in a semistructured medium, such as in documents, e-mail, voicemail, or video media. We like to call this hard or tangible knowledge. It is conveyed from one person to another in a systematic way.

Tacit knowledge is defined as knowledge that is formed around intangible factors embedded in an individual's experience. It is personal, content-specific knowledge that resides in an individual. It is knowledge that an individual gains from experience or skills that he or she develops. It often takes the form of beliefs, values, principles, and morals. It guides the individual's actions. We like to call this soft knowledge. It's embedded in the individual's ideas, insights, values, and judgment. It is only accessible through direct corroboration and communication with the individual who has the knowledge.

Knowledge management is defined as a proactive, systematic process by which value is generated from intellectual or knowledge-based assets and disseminated to the stakeholders. In *Knowledge Management Excellence* we'll discuss the six phases required to implement

an effective KMS. These are: *(Knowledge management system)*
- Phase I—Requirements definition (seven activities)
- Phase II—Infrastructure evaluation (sixteen activities)
- Phase III—Knowledge management system design and development (twelve activities)
- Phase IV—Pilot (fifteen activities)
- Phase V—Deployment (ten activities)
- Phase VI—Continuous improvement (one activity)

"Knowledge takes us from chance to choice"
—HJH

The true measure of success for knowledge management is the number of people who access and implement ideas from the knowledge networks. These networks bring state-of-the-art ideas and/or best practices into the workplace. This allows the organization to develop areas of critical mass to implement standards that work. It also provides access to all employees—allowing them to make comments to improve those standards. Even the newest employee can look at the materials and make recommendations based upon personal insight, creativity, and experience.

A big challenge related to implementing a KMS is transforming knowledge held by individuals, including process and behavioral knowledge, into a consistent technological format that can be easily shared with the organization's stakeholders. However, the biggest challenge is changing the organization's culture from a knowledge-hoarding culture to a knowledge-sharing one.

PILLAR V—RESOURCE MANAGEMENT EXCELLENCE

"Even the best ideas need resources to transform them into profit."
—HJH

Nothing can be accomplished without resources. They lie at the heart of everything we do. If we have too few, we fail; if there are too many, there's waste—hindering the organization's competitive ability. Too many organizations limit their definition of resources to people and money. These are important, but they're only a small part of the resources an organization must manage. In *Resource Management Excellence: The Art of Excelling in Resource Management*, book five in this series, we look at all of the resources available to an organization and how to manage them effectively.

When resource management is discussed, it's in the broadest sense—all the resources and assets that are available to the organization. This includes stockholders, management, employees, money, suppliers, inventory, boards of directors, alliance partnerships, real estate, knowledge, customers, patents, investors, goodwill, and brick and mortar. When all of these are considered, it quickly becomes apparent that effective resource management is one of the most critical, complex activities within any organization. Managers and employees must both examine their own performances to be sure they're doing the best they can.

Jack Welch, former CEO of GE, has created the following "Six Rules for Self-Examination":

1. Face reality as it is, not as it was or as you wish it were.
2. Be candid with everyone.
3. Don't manage; lead.
4. Change before you have to.
5. If you don't have a competitive advantage, don't compete.
6. Control your own destiny, or someone else will.

Each resource must be managed in its own special way to assist in building an excellent organization. The big question is, "How do you pull all these different activities and improvement approaches together and prioritize them?" To answer this, we'll present a thorough, total-involvement approach to strategic planning, one that involves everyone—from the chairman of the board to the janitor, from sales to personnel, from development engineering to maintenance. Yes, this is a total-involvement approach to strategic planning; it's both bottom up and top down.

A total strategic planning process (i.e., business plan) has three main objectives. (See figure P.5)

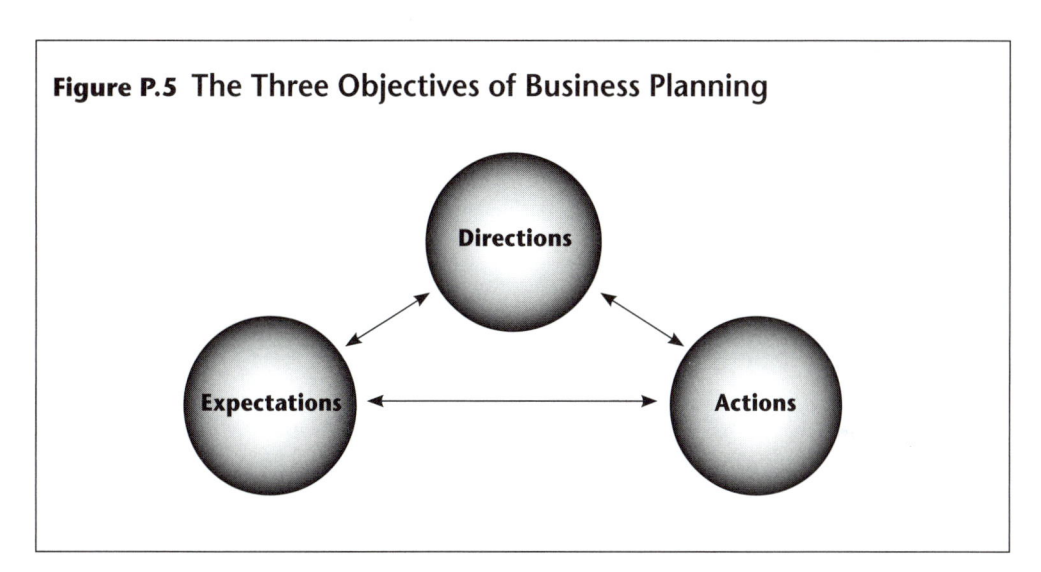

Figure P.5 The Three Objectives of Business Planning

Directions — Expectations — Actions

Eleven documents are needed in a comprehensive, strategic business plan:

- Mission statement
- Value statements
- Organization's vision statements
- Strategic focus
- Critical success factors
- Objectives
- Goals
- Strategies
- Tactics
- Budgets
- Performance plans

> "We expect a lot—highly motivated people consciously choosing to do whatever is in their power to ensure every customer is satisfied . . . and more. Every day. Without this concentrated effort, attempting a flawless service is really quite futile."
> —**Fred Smith**
> Founder and CEO,
> Federal Express

Resource management can't be an afterthought; all executive decisions must be based upon it. It requires a lot of planning, coordination, reporting, and continuous refining to do an excellent job. Too many organizations manage operations by simply throwing more resources into the pot. They may be successful with this approach as long as they have little competition, but even the giants fail if they don't do an outstanding job of resource management.

THE SKY IS NOT THE LIMIT

"You are only limited by what you can envision."
—HJH

We used to say, "The sky's the limit" when we were thinking of the limits of possibility. Today there's no limit—if you can dream it or imagine it, then you can do it, or there is someone out there that can do it for you.

We need to start thinking differently. The word "impossible" should be stricken from our vocabularies. Thinking outside of the box isn't good enough; we must tear down the walls of the box and build a culture without walls.

Our workforce is becoming more mobile. Organizations are cutting back by outsourcing all but their core capabilities and competencies. Business offices are shrinking as increasingly large numbers of people work from their homes. No organization can afford to pay its employees to do one-of-a-kind jobs when consultants can do them faster, better, and at reduced risk.

Preface

WHY DO YOU NEED ORGANIZATIONAL EXCELLENCE?

Times have changed, and our thinking about the way we manage our improvement activities must change with them. Only the very best organizations will attract customers in today's competitive environment. Producing excellent products isn't enough today; we must excel in all parts of our organization. Piecemeal approaches such as TQM, Six Sigma, and customer relationship management must give way to a holistic view of the organization and its improvement efforts. An organization should wow its customers, not just satisfy them. Customers should rate the total organization as outstanding, not just very good.

> "We must simply learn to love change as much as we have hated it in the past."
> —**Tom Peters**
> *Thriving on Chaos*

Customers remember an organization's name for two reasons and for two reasons only:

- If it produces a poor product or service
- When it produces an exceptional product or service that makes them say, "Wow! That was a great experience."

If you simply meet your customers' requirements, you don't build customer loyalty. They can be lured away from you if your competition undercuts you by a few cents. Your organization must radiate excellence in everything it does.

For the last fifty years, the quality professional, management professional, and consultant have tried—unsuccessfully—to impose improvement systems on business, government, and academia. Consider the following attempts:

- Quality control—failed
- Total quality control—failed
- Zero defects—failed
- Total quality management—failed
- Process reengineering—failed
- Six Sigma—failing
- ISO 9001:2000—added little real value

The question is, "Why, after great spurts of success, do these sound improvement systems fall into oblivion?" They're much like an old toy that gets put back in the dark corner of the closet when a new toy is found under the Christmas tree.

These exercises in futility stem from applying improvement initiatives to an organization as if they were bandages. What's really needed is fundamental organizational change. Treating symptoms usually doesn't affect a cure; it just prolongs the agony.

Project Management Excellence

These approaches failed because the initiatives were applied as separate activities instead of with the intention of making a total organizational transformation. It's similar to giving a person who has pneumonia an aspirin for his or her headache, thinking it will cure the disease.

From decade to decade, our business focus continually changes:
- 1970s—people
- 1980s—teams
- 1990s—processes
- 2000s—knowledge and adaptability

In keeping with these changes, the approaches to performance improvement have also changed:
- ISO 9001 and ISO 14001—process-driven, lacking in business focus
- Total quality management (TQM)—process-driven, with statistical analysis and teams that are customer-focused
- National quality awards—quality-driven, plus results
- Six Sigma—problem/solution-driven, with a customer focus
- Total improvement management (TIM)—performance-driven/total organization-driven sales, marketing development, personnel, and production. It included organizational change.
- Organizational excellence—performance-driven, including processes, projects, organizational change, information technology, resources, and knowledge management

"Only 5 percent of the organizations in the West truly excel. Their secret is not what they do, but how they do it."

—HJH

The following list gives a point score to these approaches' effectiveness in improving organizational performance.
- Casual—no recognized system .... 0 points
- ISO 9001 and ISO 14001—minimum requirements.................... 200 points
- Six Sigma—problem-focused .... 400 points
- TQM—"womb to tomb" quality and teams .... 500 points
- National quality awards—results-based............................. 600 points
- TIM—combined quality, reliability, performance, and results .... 800 points
- Organizational excellence—five pillars .... 1,000 points

"You can win the national quality award with 600 points out of a maximum of 1,000 points. That's 60 percent of the way to the goal."
—HJH

You might ask the question, "Where are we today?" A survey conducted by HI Europe for Dow Corning provides us with the 2003 status. It included sixty-nine executives from a wide range of industries in the Americas, Europe, and Asia. This survey revealed that TQM was the most important business innovation for these organizations during the last three years. Although Six Sigma has received a lot of press during the past eight years, it didn't rate in the top three most important business innovations. The top three, in descending order, are:

- TQM
- Process engineering
- Supply chain management

"We want to operate far more efficiently. We want to operate at a new level of excellence."
—**Robert J. Herbold
Former COO,
Microsoft**

The American Society for Quality recently sponsored a survey of 600 executives from manufacturing, service, government, health care, and education. The survey reported that 99 percent of the executives surveyed believe that quality contributed to the bottom line. Also, it indicated that 92 percent of the executives believe that an organizationwide effort to use quality techniques provides a positive return. Figure P.6 gives a breakdown of the most frequently used quality techniques.

The survey indicates that a wide gap exists between the executives' awareness of quality improvement processes and their implementation. Again, the survey reveals that TQM is used 300 percent more than Six Sigma. The quality profession suffers by continuously changing the name of its activities despite little change in content.

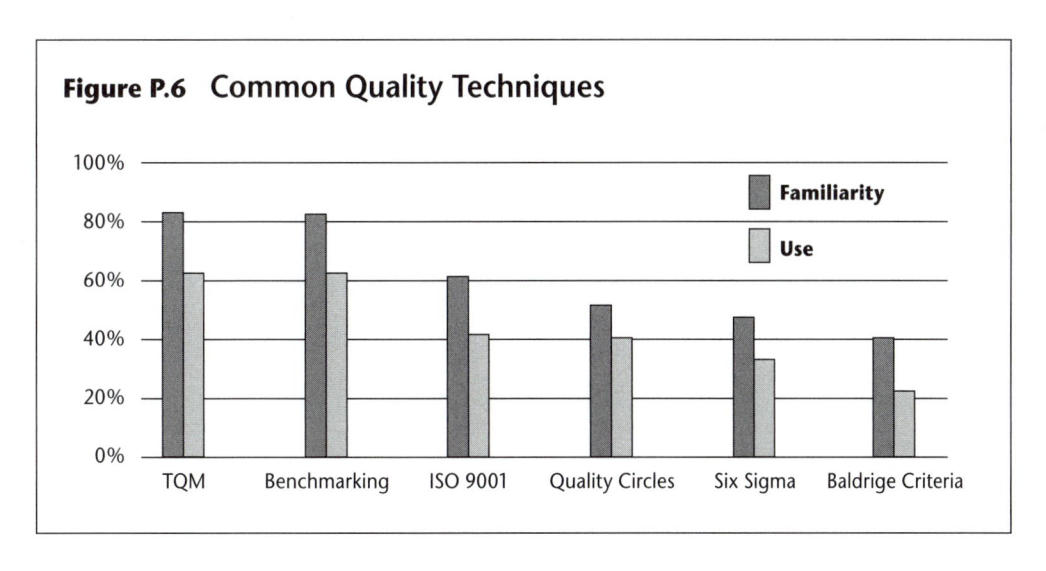

Figure P.6 Common Quality Techniques

Project Management Excellence

ORGANIZATIONAL EXCELLENCE SUMMARY

Lame "Being good is good. Being the best is great!"
—HJH

> "The sizeable gap between usage and awareness leads me to believe that businesses and organizations either don't use quality methodologies to improve their operations, or they just don't realize that the processes they have in place are attributable directly to the quality discipline."
> —Ken Case
> Former president,
> American Society for Quality

When we look at the five pillars that must be managed to achieve excellence, we see common threads that run through all of them:

- Communication
- Teamwork
- Empowerment
- Respect for one another
- Honesty
- Leadership
- Quality
- Fairness
- Technology

All of these key factors are built into the word "management." They turn an employee into an individual who owns his or her job, thereby bringing satisfaction and dignity to the individual for a job well done.

In today's worldwide marketplace, customers don't have to settle for second best. Overnight mail brings the best to everyone's doorstep. The Internet allows people to shop internationally, making it easy for them to get the best quality, reliability, and price, no matter who offers it. [*Not true, no way to test reliability over internet. Only price*] Customers are concerned about the products they buy, but they're equally or more concerned about dealing with organizations that care, are quick to respond, and that will listen and react to their unique needs. This means that to succeed in the 21st century organizations must excel in all parts of their businesses. Your organization must excel at what it does, but its stakeholders must also recognize your efforts as excellent. This will win over today's savvy customers.

> "The essence of competitiveness is liberated when we make people believe that what they think and do is important—and the get out of the way while they do it."
> —Jack Welch
> Former CEO,
> General Electric

CHAPTER 1

INTRODUCTION TO PROJECT MANAGEMENT EXCELLENCE

"Processes define how we operate. Projects are the way we improve our processes."

—HJH

In this section, we'll focus on the essentials of how to manage a project. However, before we begin, let's define a few concepts.

Definition: A *project* is defined as a temporary endeavor undertaken to create a unique product, service, or result.

Definition: Project management is defined as the application of knowledge, skills, tools, and technology to project activities to meet or exceed stakeholder needs and expectations from a project.

Definition: A *program* is a group of projects managed in a coordinated way to obtain benefits not available from managing them individually. Programs may include elements of related work outside the scope of the discrete projects in the program. Programs also involve a series of repetitive or cyclical undertakings.

Although they seem straightforward enough, the concepts can't be that simple or organizations would get better results from the projects they fund. In its 1999 report, *CHAOS: A Recipe for Success,* The Standish Group International states that "Corporate America spends more than $275 billion per year on application software development projects, many of which will fail due to lack of skilled project management. Only 26 percent of projects were successful (on time and on budget)." The Standish Group also notes that:

- 40 percent of all information technology (IT) projects fail or are cancelled.
- U.S. firms spend $75 billion annually on cancelled projects.
- 26 percent of projects will cost 189 percent of their original estimates.

Project Management Excellence

- More than 60 percent of the projects don't produce the projected return on investment.

> "Nobody is surprised that projects fail, but I don't think executive management is aware how bad these failures are."
> —Ted Smith
> Vice president of research products, Tech Republic

According to the *Wall Street Journal*, "The average cycle time for IT projects is twenty-seven weeks. The (average) ones that are cancelled are cancelled after fourteen weeks; at that point in time they are 52-percent complete. Many of the project teams know that the project is likely to fail six weeks before it's cancelled." ("Tech Project Inefficiencies Found in Corporate Study." The Wall Street Journal Report. November 14, 2000.)

The Gartner Group reports that as much as 20 percent of the money businesses spend globally on technology is a total waste. It noted at a 2002 conference in Montreal, Canada, that, "In a four-year period, an application development organization of 100 developers can expect to spend more than $10 million on cancelled contracts."

Enterprise resource planning (ERP) is one of the more popular and widely implemented IT concepts, and yet at least 90 percent of ERP projects end up late and/or over budget. Nearly half fail to achieve the desired results.

Let's look at a well-known example, the Hubble telescope, which was a $1.5 billion blunder. During its first six months of operation, project managers had to deal with the following failures:

- Two (out of six) faulty memory banks
- Flopping solar-energy panels
- Velocity-measurement system failure
- Chemistry-of-celestial-objects systems failure

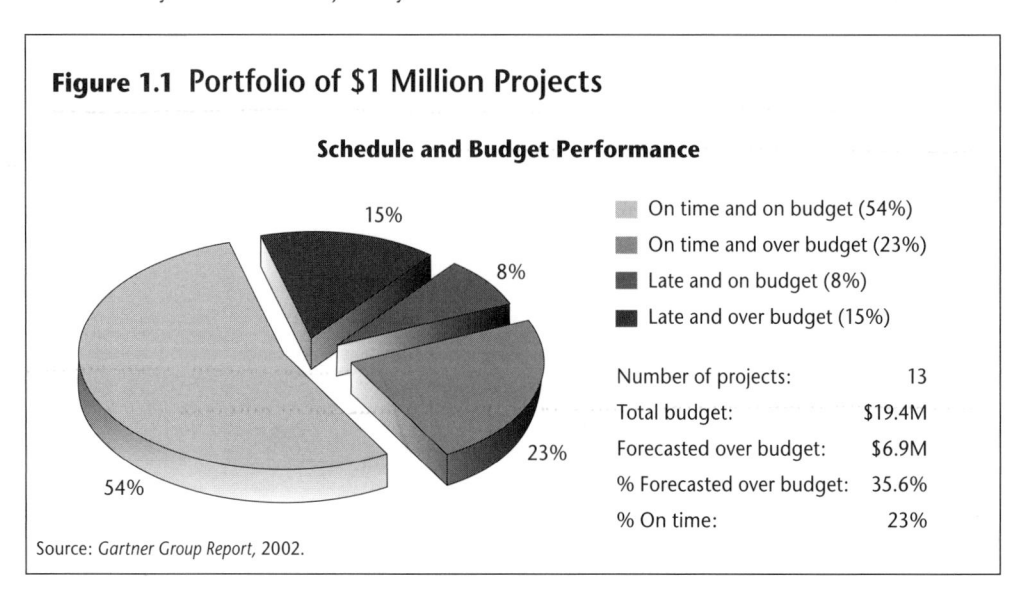

Figure 1.1 Portfolio of $1 Million Projects

Schedule and Budget Performance

- On time and on budget (54%)
- On time and over budget (23%)
- Late and on budget (8%)
- Late and over budget (15%)

Number of projects:	13
Total budget:	$19.4M
Forecasted over budget:	$6.9M
% Forecasted over budget:	35.6%
% On time:	23%

Source: *Gartner Group Report*, 2002.

- Three faulty gyroscopes
- Deformed mirror

As a result of these defects, four tons of repair parts were sent into space at a cost of hundreds of millions of dollars.

Is this a one-of-a-kind blunder? Unfortunately, no. NASA's Space Station Freedom originally was budgeted for $8 billion; it's now up to $32 billion and still climbing.

Projects in most organizations are mission-critical activities, and delivering quality products on time is non-negotiable. Even with IT projects, the old Microsoft paradigm of "Get it out fast, then fix the bugs as customers find them," no longer applies. The new paradigm is, "Get them out at Web speed and error-free." Benchmark organizations complete 90 percent of their projects within 10 percent of budget and schedule, although the norm for most projects is 54 percent on time and on budget. (See figure 1.1.) Information systems organizations that establish standards for project management, including a project office, cut their major project cost overruns, delays, and cancellations by 50 percent. (Gartner Group, August 2000.) "IBM has seen its project success rate improve since it implemented more structured project management training seven years ago," reports Carol Wright, head of IBM's Project Management Center of Excellence.

> "Projects are big business. Project Management Institute (PMI) estimates show that U.S. public and private sectors spend approximately $2.3 trillion a year on projects. That's equivalent to one-quarter of the nation's gross domestic product. Global estimates show that the world spends nearly $10 trillion (U.S. dollars) of the world's $40.7 trillion gross product on projects of all kinds."
>
> —HJH

PMI also estimates that about 4.5 million people in the United States are engaged in project management work, along with twelve million additional people elsewhere in the world. Is it any wonder that project management is one of the fastest-growing professions in the developed world?

Process redesign and process reengineering are two of the most important projects that organizations undertake, and yet the failure rate of such projects is estimated to be as high as 60 percent. There are two main causes for these high-cost failures: poor project management and poor change management. Companies that address those issues profit from their efforts. Those who don't face huge cash outflows with little in return.

> "Some 50 percent to 70 percent of reengineering attempts fail to deliver the intended dramatic results."
> —Michael Hammer and James Champy
> *Reengineering the Corporation*

Project Management Excellence

For example, beginning in 1993, IBM launched eleven reengineering projects that overhauled the way it manages internal information systems to the way it developed products and served customers. "We have reduced IT spending by 31 percent for a total savings of more than $2 billion, the company reported. "Since 1993, cycle time for large systems development has been slashed from fifty-six months to sixteen months today. For low-end systems, it's seven months—down from two years." ("We Rewired the Enterprise," IBM report, 2001.)

In 2000, Nike tried to implement a supply-chain management system. The project failed, which led the company's CEO, Phil Knight, to make the now-famous lamentation, "Is this what we get for our $400 million?"

WHY PROJECTS HISTORICALLY FAIL

The Standish Group International conducted a survey to define the success rate of IT projects. (See figure 1.2.) The company found that projects under $750,000 have the highest probability of success, although that's only a 55 percent success rate.

Another survey conducted by the Center for Business Practices indicated that the biggest project management challenges are:
- Taking a consistent approach
- Allocating resources
- Taking on too many projects
- Selecting the wrong projects

The following tools (listed in order of preference) are those most used to improve project performance:
- Software (78%)
- Methodology development (69%)
- Training (69%)

Figure 1.2 IT Project Success Rate

Project size	People	Time (months)	Success rate
Less than $750K	6	6	55%
$750K to $1.5M	12	9	33%
$1.5M to $3M	25	12	25%
$3M to $6M	40	18	15%
$6M to $10M	+250	+24	8%
Over $10M	+500	+36	0%

Source: *CHAOS: A Recipe for Success*. The Standish Group. 1999.

Introduction to Project Management Excellence

It's useful as well to note the following trends in project management:
- The average yearly spending to improve project management is $712,000 per organization.
- 95.6 percent of organizations that use software to help manage their projects use Microsoft Project.
- 39 percent of organizations outsource their project management activities to improve their performance.

("Project Management—The State of the Industry." Center for Business Practices. *www.cbponline.com*.)

Let's take a closer look at why projects fail. To begin with, organizations fail to adhere to their committed schedules. This is caused by:
- *Variances.* The project team doesn't execute the project as planned, often because the original plan isn't properly estimated.
- *Exceptions.* Things that aren't included in the original plan and are identified later on as the project progresses.
- *Poor planning.* Individuals who prepare the plan overcommit the organization.
- *Delays.* The status of interdependencies between other projects and/or suppliers isn't controlled.
- *Scope creep.* This is usually caused by poorly defined deliverables that are redefined as the project progresses.

> "I've been involved with way too many three-year projects that turned into five-year projects."
> —**Bill Zollars**
> **CEO, Yellow Roadway**

Projects also fail due to one or more of the following:
- Poor resource utilization:
  - ☐ Proper skills aren't available when they're needed.
  - ☐ Individuals' time isn't used wisely.
  - ☐ The right skills aren't available within the organization.
  - ☐ The best people aren't assigned to the most critical jobs.
  - ☐ Skills and assignments are misaligned.

- Poor management of the organization's portfolio of projects:
  - ☐ The wrong projects are selected.
  - ☐ The wrong resources are assigned to projects.
  - ☐ High-risk projects aren't identified.
  - ☐ Interdependencies between projects are poorly controlled.

- Loss of intellectual capital and/or knowledge capital:
  - ☐ No means exist to transfer knowledge from past to future projects (e.g., people leave the organization or are assigned to other activities).

Project Management Excellence

- Lack of implementation support:
  - People who will use the project's output aren't properly prepared to do so (i.e., no organizational change management).

Cross Functional Support [handwritten annotation]

Poor project management is one of the biggest problems facing most organizations today. It's therefore surprising that quality professionals haven't addressed ways to improve the quality of the project management process. Even ISO 9000 ignores this critical issue. In our knowledge-driven economy, the quality of an organization's project management process is key to the organization's success.

WHY IS PROJECT MANAGEMENT SO IMPORTANT?

Things are changing at an accelerating rate. More than ever before, projects must be completed quickly and at less cost, even as they become more complex and our customers more demanding. Product cycles used to be measured in years; today it's months, and in some cases the product cycle is measured in mere weeks. Let's look at some examples of this phenomenon that have occurred during the past fifty years:

- The home video camera you use contains more processing power than an old IBM 360—the wonder machine that gave birth to the mainframe computer age. (I helped set up the line that manufactured the IBM 360-20.)
- "Something on the order of 1,000 new products are introduced into American supermarkets every month." (Toffler, Alvin and Heidi. *Creating a New Civilization: The Politics of the Third Wave*. Turner Publishing, 1995.)
- "The number of different products actually on the shelves of the average store has doubled over the last ten years." (Morrison, Ian. *The Second Curve*. Diane Publishing Co., 1996.)
- "Let's say you're going to a party, so you pull out some pocket change and buy a little greeting card that plays "Happy Birthday" when it's opened. After the party, someone casually tosses the card into the trash, throwing away more computer power than existed in the entire world before 1950. The party gift you gave is a system called *Saturn*, made by Sega, the gamemaker. It runs on a higher-performance processor than the original 1976 Cray supercomputer, which in its day was accessible to only the most elite physicists." (Huey, John. "Waking Up to the New Economy," *Fortune*. June 27, 1994.)
- "In 1880 it took more than twenty man-hours to harvest an acre of wheat land. By 1916 the number of man-hours was reduced to 12.7. Just twenty years later only 6.1 man-hours were required. Now it can be done in a matter of minutes, but today's farmers are busier than ever." (Rifkin, Jeremy. *The End of Work: The Decline of the Global Labor Force and the Dawn of the Post-Market Era*. Jeremy P. Tarcher, 1996.)

Introduction to Project Management Excellence

- "In 1990, automobiles took six years from concept to production. Today they take two years." (Tapscott, Don. *The Digital Economy.* McGraw-Hill, 1997.)
- "Most of Hewlett-Packard's revenues come from products that didn't exist a year ago." (Tapscott, Don. *The Digital Economy.* McGraw-Hill, 1997.)
- "90 percent of Miller's revenues come from beer that didn't exist twenty-four months ago." (Tapscott, Don. *The Digital Economy.* McGraw-Hill, 1997.)

It's almost as though the world keeps spinning faster; I know my head is. Today's projects are time-boxed to decrease cycle time, but they produce much more sophisticated output. This accelerated project cycle is driven by a continuously changing technology, by increased demands and by quickly changing customer expectations. The "good old days" were yesterday. The game is different today, and your project is already behind schedule.

HOW MUCH COULD AN EFFECTIVE PROJECT MANAGEMENT SYSTEM SAVE YOUR ORGANIZATION?

A survey performed by Robbins-Gioia with senior project managers revealed that "for organizations that systematically align projects and programs to their overall business strategy, nearly 75 percent reported they are either very profitable (i.e., exceeding goals) or gaining momentum and increasing profitability." This confirms that organizations which prioritize and manage projects for maximum organizational value realize greater financial returns.

According to the Gartner Group, 68 percent of projects and/or programs are late and/or over budget. Inadequate work-execution tools that hamper real-time visibility of output and effort are chiefly responsible for this. Projects either take longer than initially predicted and/or they require more resources to complete.

Either way, the related losses are expected to worsen. In fact, outsourced projects and/or program provisioning has grown by more than 30 percent during the last five years. This increasing distribution of work within and across organizations has only exacerbated challenges in achieving deliverables-based visibility and control. As a result, even higher levels of late and/or over-budget outcomes—not to mention greater money leaks—are expected.

As an example of possible losses caused by missing expected schedules, let's consider a project with a budget of $1.8 million over a twelve-month period. Here, a schedule slippage of thirty days will generate losses of $150,000. Ask yourself the following questions about your current project management system, and you'll to get an idea of what you could save from implementing an improved one.

- Would real-time visibility of output and effort to date, coupled with simplified work execution tools, enable you to reduce your slippage by 50 percent?
- How much will you spend on projects during the next twelve months, and how much do you expect to improve your adherence to committed schedules?
- How will expected changes in how you use remote workers and/or brokered resources and contractors affect your ability to stay on schedule? For example, what percentage of your project and/or program budget goes to pay external resources and contractors rather than directly providing services?
- If you currently outsource 40 percent of your projects, and 60 percent of them come in at more than 100 percent of budget, what would your organization expect to save from improved visibility and control of your brokered and/or remote work? The Gartner Group estimates late and/or over-budget performance at 60 percent; we foresee opportunities of reducing this to 40 percent through real-time visibility of output and effort-to-date work, coupled with fact-based work execution tools.
- Could you drive down your company's late and/or over-budget performance from 60 percent to 30 percent?
- What's the annual savings realized from reducing your current late and/or over-budget percentage of total project expenditures during the next six months?

Another major source of money leaks occurs from cancelled IT development costs. How much do you lose from this source? This depends, of course, on the size of your internal IT development staff. How many developers do you employ? According to averages reported by The Standish Group International, $10 million is spent on cancelled contracts for a development staff of 100 during a four-year period. This equals $25,000 in lost revenues per developer per year. If we assume an annual expense of $100,000 per developer (for salary, benefits, etc.), then this developer's cost is not covered for three months out of the year, or 25 percent of every twelve months.

Let's adjust The Standish Group's estimated average loss experience to reflect the relative superiority of your management. Is your performance twice as good as the U.S. average? Let's say your experience is better than The Standish Group average by 20 percent. Therefore, we'll project an $8 million loss as a more likely experience in your case. If we assume an annual expense of $100,000 per developer, then the developer's cost is *not* covered for approximately two and one-half months of the year, or 20 percent of every twelve-month period.

> **"The whole discipline and art of project management is going to be the essence of management training, operational excellence, and value-added"**
> —**Tom Peters**
> **Business author and consultant**

THE NEW PROJECT MANAGEMENT

Project management has long been an accepted mode of doing business throughout the world. The building of the first atomic bomb during World War II (known as the Manhattan Project), which was sponsored by the U.S. government, is an excellent example of a full-length project team effort. Since that time project management has come a long way. Project tactics have penetrated the entire spectrum of business strategy, and project teams are involved in everything from placing transactional processes on the Web, to reducing customer turnover, to getting new products out the door.

> "I don't see how you can do a credible product solution without a project management discipline."
> —**Pamela Miller**
> **Vice president of enterprise strategy,**
> **Horizon Blue Cross Blue Shield**

Over time, project teams have become more nimble, project delivery time has shortened, and best practices for project managers have taken on a more structured approach. Many pharmaceutical companies credit project management with saving hundreds of millions of dollars in costs by simplifying new products' cycle times. The most recent innovations in project management have occurred in the quality arena, where a new type of project team is harnessing technological power to reduce error rates and cycle time, optimize operational efficiency, and increase customer satisfaction.

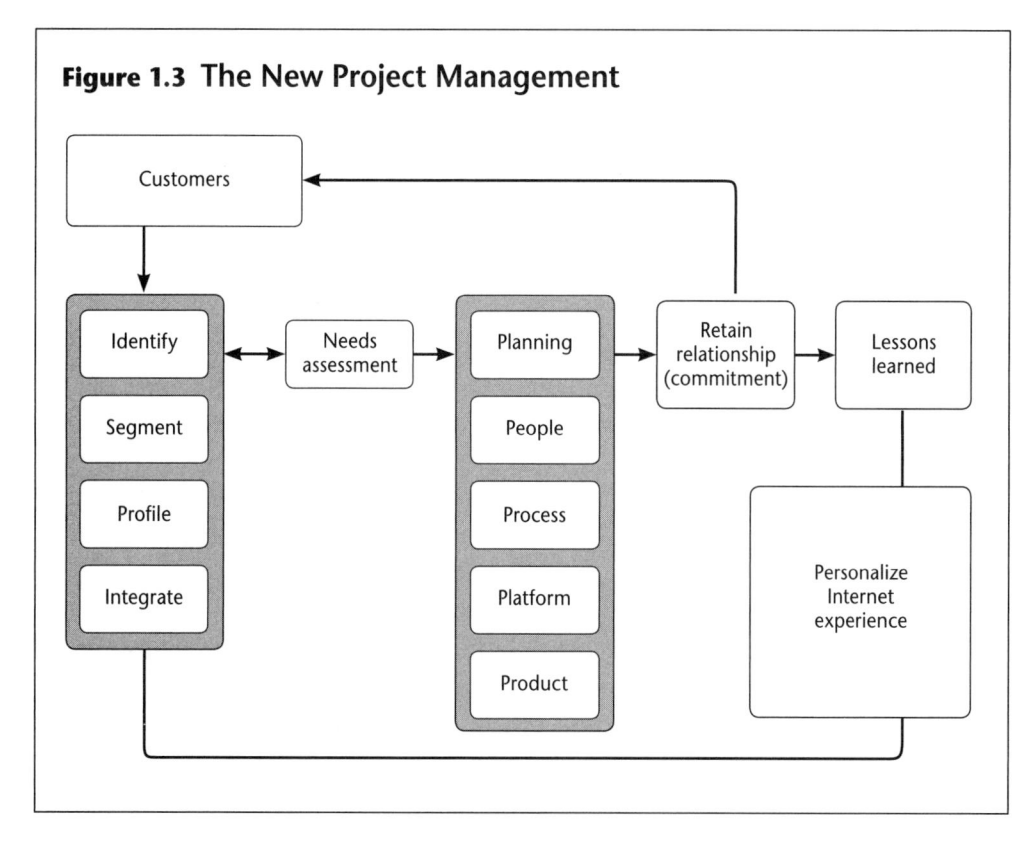

Figure 1.3 The New Project Management

Project management is no longer an exclusive strategy for public and private sectors. The complications associated with larger and more expensive work efforts have forced hospitals, charitable institutions, and community groups to adopt formal project management practices. The strongest indication that the technique has taken hold in numerous domains of influence around the globe is the phenomenal international growth rate of the Project Management Institute (for more information, visit the organization's Web site at *www.pmi.org.*) During the past ten years PMI's membership has tripled to more than 150,000, and the varieties of "specific interest groups" represented now run the gamut from software development to financial management to NASA contracting.

Adaptation requires change, and organizations with a vision of the future must adjust their focus from that of product quality to one of customer responsiveness. Do you remember the days when you stopped by the local grocery store, and the owner greeted you by name and knew you so well that you felt special? Much of that personal touch was lost as companies grew into larger and more streamlined, product-focused businesses.

Process improvement projects are becoming more commonplace in today's competitive marketplace. Because most companies designed and automated processes during the late 1980s and early 1990s (before the current focus on lean thinking), studies show that as much as 80 percent of all process steps either are redundant or nonvalue-added. Companies face tremendous competitive pressure to increase customer loyalty, reduce customer turnover, and focus on customer satisfaction. Thus, each project must be analyzed for its ability to provide value to both the organization and the customer. Process improvement is most effective when processes (including people, product, platform, and planning) are directly aligned with customer expectations. The following are some important guidelines to follow:

- Empower people to capture customer feedback.
- Constantly analyze customer perception of product and service quality.
- Use technology platforms for customer profiling.
- Plan carefully to optimize customer experience.

To meet the ever-changing customer demands in today's marketplace, organizations are also constantly changing. Increased organizational change equates to new products and services as well as streamlined operations to optimize organizational performance. Handling product and process improvements and/or innovations requires a structured approach to analyze, plan, develop, and implement the appropriate solutions. Projects should be the means by which the solutions are enacted.

To handle the ever-increasing number of projects in changing organizations, project management principles, processes, and best practices should be fully utilized. In the following section we present the best approach to managing projects, no matter what organizational effort you're launching.

PROJECT MANAGEMENT BODY OF KNOWLEDGE (PMBOK)

According to PMI, "the PMBOK is an inclusive term that describes the sum of knowledge within the profession of project management." PMI, the world's largest project management professional society, assembled the PMBOK and created a standard-writing body to develop it. In 2004, PMI published the most recent version (third edition) of a document it calls *The Guide to the Project Management Body of Knowledge* (or simply, *PMBOK Guide*). The primary purpose of the *PMBOK Guide* is to identify that subset of the Project Management Body of Knowledge that is generally recognized as good practice. PMBOK wisdom currently is published as the ANSI/PMI 99-001-2000 standard and continually updated based on the latest best practices. Many national standards boards, including the American National Standard Institute (ANSI), have approved ANSI/PMI 99-001-2000. It's the most used and referenced project management standard throughout the world. For this reason we use *PMBOK Guide* as the framework for this section.

We find the *PMBOK Guide* extremely useful in helping organizations develop a project management system because it organizes project management into a set of five process groups and nine knowledge areas which, in turn, are broken down into a total of forty-four processes. For example, project risk management is broken down into the following six processes:

- Risk management planning
- Risk identification
- Qualitative risk analysis
- Quantitative risk analysis
- Risk response planning
- Risk monitoring and control

Each of these processes is then examined to determine related inputs and outputs, and what tools and techniques are used to convert the inputs to outputs. Under the risk identification process, for example, you'll find the following inputs, tools, and outputs:

- Inputs
  - ☐ Enterprise environmental factors
  - ☐ Organizational process assets
  - ☐ Project scope statement
  - ☐ Risk management plan
  - ☐ Project management plan

- Tools and techniques
  - ☐ Document reviews

Project Management Excellence

- ☐ Information-gathering techniques
- ☐ Checklist
- ☐ Assumption analysis
- ☐ Diagramming techniques

■ Outputs
- ☐ Risk register

The new Project Management Body of Knowledge (PMBOK) has nine knowledge areas. (See figure 1.4.) These nine knowledge areas contain forty-four processes that are grouped into five process groups. (See figure 1.5.) During each phase of a project, the project manager and the project team will cycle through the five process groups. (See figure 1.6.) This cycle will be repeated over and over again in each phase of the project. (See figure 1.7.)

Figure 1.8 shows a typical project cycle—the five process groups that are repeated during the five main phases of the process and the typical six stage gates that are held during the project cycle.

Note: These figures were contributed by William Ruggles.

Introduction to Project Management Excellence

Figure 1.4 PMBOK Nine Knowledge Areas

PROJECT MANAGEMENT

4. Project integration management
- 4.1 Develop project charter
- 4.2 Develop preliminary project scope statement
- 4.3 Develop project management plan
- 4.4 Direct and manage project execution
- 4.5 Monitor and control project work
- 4.6 Integrated change control
- 4.7 Close project

5. Project scope management
- 5.1 Scope planning
- 5.2 Scope definition
- 5.3 Create work breakdown structure
- 5.4 Scope verification
- 5.5 Scope change control

6. Project time management
- 6.1 Activity definition
- 6.2 Activity sequencing
- 6.3 Activity resource estimating
- 6.4 Activity duration estimating
- 6.5 Schedule development
- 6.6 Schedule control

7. Project cost management
- 7.1 Cost estimating
- 7.2 Cost budgeting
- 7.3 Cost control

8. Project quality management
- 8.1 Quality planning
- 8.2 Perform quality assurance
- 8.3 Perform quality control

9. Project human resource management
- 9.1 Human resource planning
- 9.2 Acquire project team
- 9.3 Develop project team
- 9.4 Manage project team

10. Project communications management
- 10.1 Communications planning
- 10.2 Information distribution
- 10.3 Performance reporting
- 10.4 Manage stakeholders

11. Project risk management
- 11.1 Risk management planning
- 11.2 Risk identification
- 11.3 Qualitative risk analysis
- 11.4 Quantitative risk analysis
- 11.5 Risk response planning
- 11.6 Risk monitoring and control

12. Project procurement management
- 12.1 Plan purchases/acquisitions
- 12.2 Plan contracting
- 12.3 Request seller responses
- 12.4 Select sellers
- 12.5 Contract administration
- 12.6 Contract closure

Figure 1.5 Forty-Four Processes From *PMBOK Guide 2004*

Process Group / Knowledge area	Initiating (2)	Planning (21)	Executing (7)	Monitoring and controlling (12)	Closing (2)
Chapter 4: Integration	Develop project charter Develop preliminary project scope statement	Develop project management plan	Direct and manage project execution	Monitor and control project work Integrated change control	Close project
Chapter 5: Scope		Scope planning Scope definition Create work breakdown structure		Scope verification Scope control	
Chapter 6: Time		Activity definition Activity sequencing Activity resource planning Activity duration estimating Schedule development		Schedule control	
Chapter 7: Cost		Cost estimating Cost budgeting		Cost control	
Chapter 8: Quality		Quality planning	Perform quality assurance	Perform quality control	
Chapter 9: Human resources		Human resource planning	Acquire project team Develop project team	Manage project team	
Chapter 10: Communications		Communications planning	Information distribution	Performance reporting Manage stakeholders	
Chapter 11: Risk		Risk management planning Risk identification Qualitative risk analysis Quantitative risk analysis Risk response planning		Risk monitoring and control	
Chapter 12: Procurement		Plan purchases and acquisitions Plan contracting	Request seller responses Select sellers	Contract administration	Contract closure

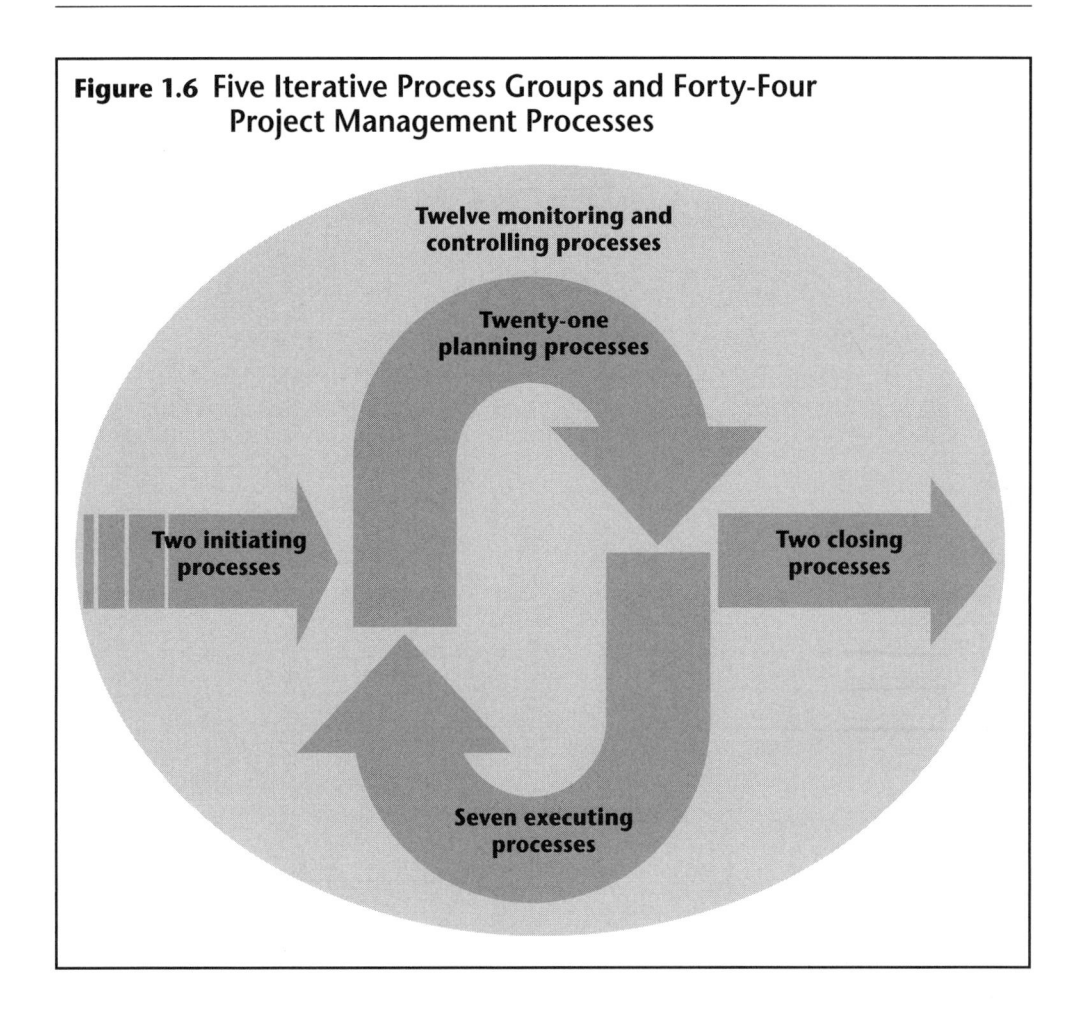

Figure 1.6 Five Iterative Process Groups and Forty-Four Project Management Processes

- Twelve monitoring and controlling processes
- Twenty-one planning processes
- Two initiating processes
- Two closing processes
- Seven executing processes

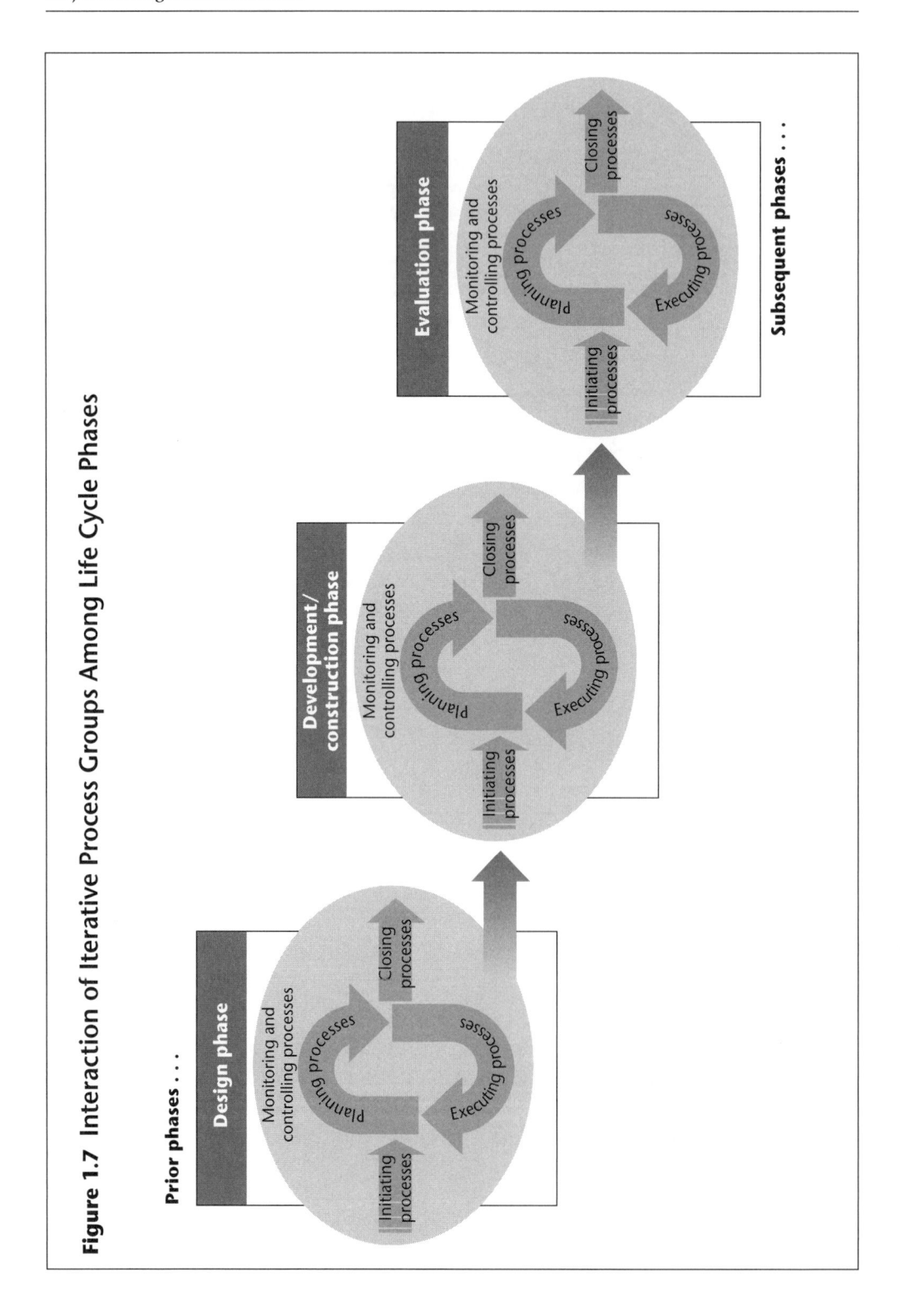

Figure 1.7 Interaction of Iterative Process Groups Among Life Cycle Phases

Wayyy too complicated.

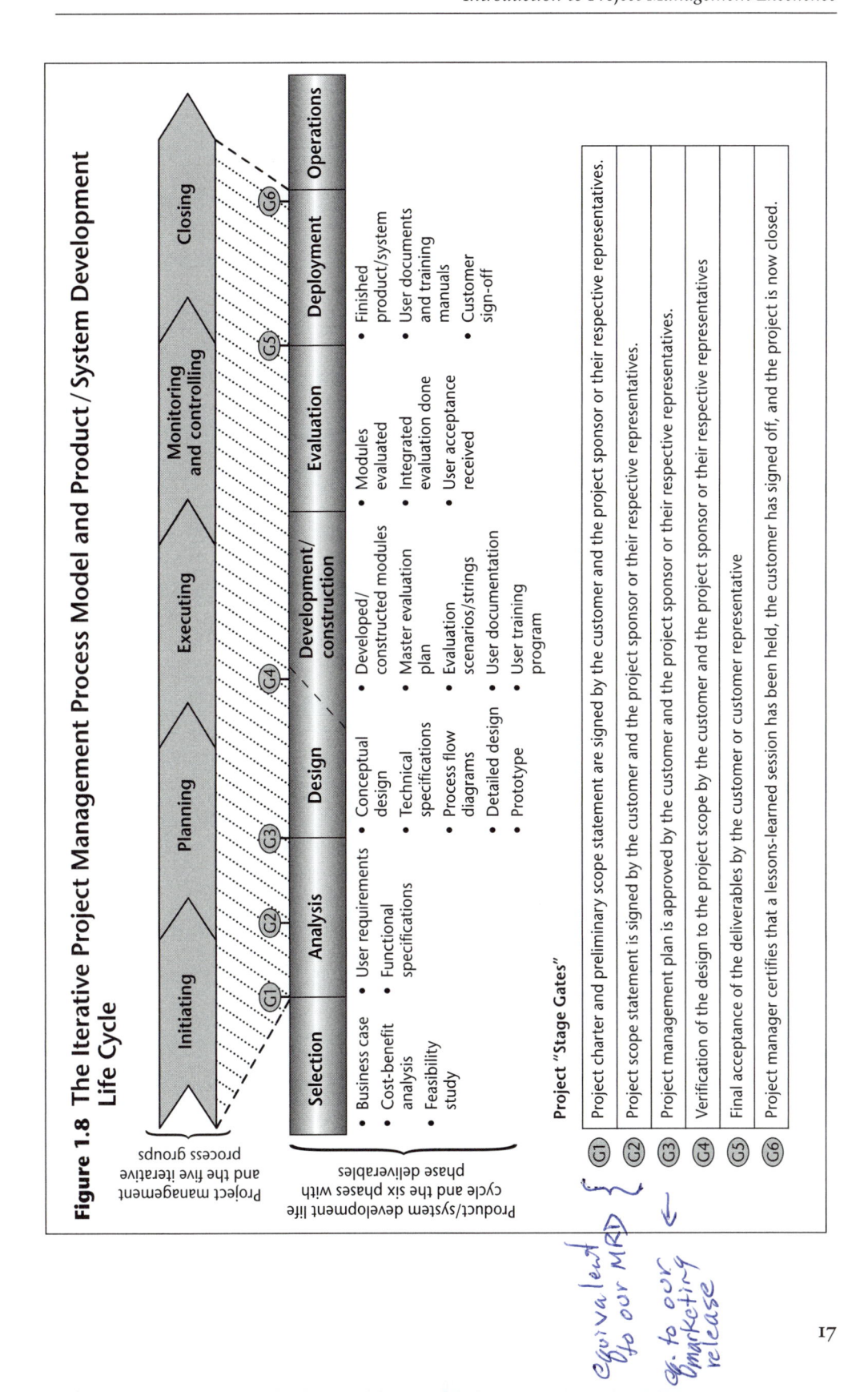

Introduction to Project Management Excellence

Figure 1.8 The Iterative Project Management Process Model and Product/System Development Life Cycle

Project management life cycle and the five iterative process groups:
- Initiating
- Planning
- Executing
- Monitoring and controlling
- Closing

Product/system development life cycle and the six phases with phase deliverables:

Selection	Analysis	Design	Development/construction	Evaluation	Deployment
• Business case • Cost-benefit analysis • Feasibility study	• User requirements • Functional specifications	• Conceptual design • Technical specifications • Process flow diagrams • Detailed design • Prototype	• Developed/constructed modules • Master evaluation plan • Evaluation scenarios/strings • User documentation • User training program	• Modules evaluated • Integrated evaluation done • User acceptance received	• Finished product/system • User documents and training manuals • Customer sign-off

Stage Gates: G1, G2, G3, G4, G5, G6

Project "Stage Gates"

- G1: Project charter and preliminary scope statement are signed by the customer and the project sponsor or their respective representatives.
- G2: Project scope statement is signed by the customer and the project sponsor or their respective representatives.
- G3: Project management plan is approved by the customer and the project sponsor or their respective representatives.
- G4: Verification of the design to the project scope by the customer and the project sponsor or their respective representatives.
- G5: Final acceptance of the deliverables by the customer or customer representative
- G6: Project manager certifies that a lessons-learned session has been held, the customer has signed off, and the project is now closed.

equivalent to our MRD

equiv. to our marketing release

17

THE PRINCE PROJECT MANAGEMENT APPROACH

PRINCE (projects in controlled environments) is a project management approach used in Europe. It's not intended to cover all subjects relevant to project management. Project management aspects that are effectively covered in proven technologies aren't included, such as:
- People management techniques
- Risk management techniques
- Business-case management, budgetary control, and earned-value analysis
- Planning techniques, such as critical path

The PRINCE process model contains eight components. They are:
- Organization
- Planning
- Controls
- Stages
- Risk management
- Quality in a project environment
- Configuration management
- Change control

The PRINCE process model has a variable number of stages based upon the application. Each stage defines a set of products or outcomes, activities, and outputs. The stage boundaries must be in keeping with the specific project. Figure 1.9 depicts the PRINCE process model.

Each of the blocks in the process model is broken down into subprocesses. For example, "Starting up a project" is subdivided into the following subprocesses:
- Appointing a project business executive and project manager
- Designing a project management team
- Appointing a project management team
    - Creating project management team structure and job definitions
    - Assembling a project management team

- Preparing a project brief
- Defining project approach
    - Planning quality

- Planning an initiation stage
- Authorizing initiation

Figure 1.9 PRINCE Process Model

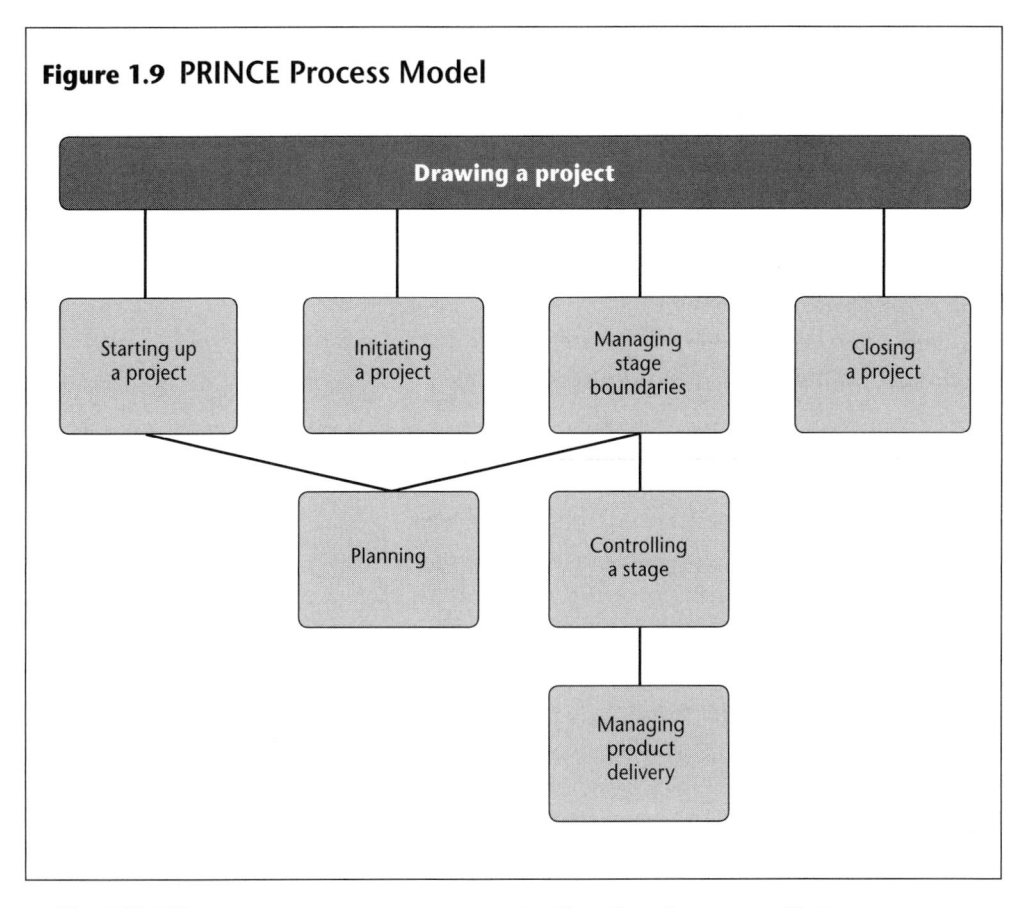

```
                    Drawing a project
    ┌──────────┬──────────┬──────────┬──────────┐
 Starting up  Initiating  Managing   Closing
 a project   a project    stage      a project
                          boundaries
        └─────────┬──────────┘
                Planning    Controlling
                            a stage
                              │
                           Managing
                           product
                           delivery
```

The PRINCE project management approach offers the advantage of being very process-focused, but we believe the PMBOK provides a more thorough approach. In actual implementation, they're quite similar.

THE PROJECT MANAGEMENT MODEL

According to *A Guide to Project Management Body of Knowledge,* published by the Project Management Institute and accepted as the standard for project management, there are nine project management knowledge areas:

- Project integration management
- Project scope management
- Project time management
- Project financial/cost management
- Project quality management

Project Management Excellence

- Project human resource management
- Project communications management
- Project risk management
- Project procurement management

We're also introducing four new critical areas for consideration:
- Project organizational change management
- Project portfolio management
- Project document/configuration management
- Project planning and estimating management

Project integration management is crucial in today's business environment because most organizations must manage many projects simultaneously. Each of these projects competes for limited resources. This requires the management team to manage not only the individual projects but the total portfolio of projects as well.

Project procurement management is an important project component today because most projects depend on other organizations for inputs that are crucial to their success. In other cases, major aspects of projects are subcontracted or outsourced to consulting or engineering firms. Imagine a project to build an eighty-story building without using subcontractors. Yes, it would be impossible. There are just too many special skills required, and no organization can do everything well.

Poor organizational change management is the biggest cause of project failure. Most projects are technically sound and take into consideration related processes, but project managers fail to recognize what's required to get people who will be effected by the projects to accept them. Organizational change management represents the people side of a project. It prepares people who are affected by the project to accept and commit to the change—even to look forward to it.

The project management model displayed in figure 1.10 combines the best practices of common processes and the project life cycle, divided into six phases. We believe that only by including the four new critical areas can a project manager integrate the necessary components of success.

The common processes represent work performed by the project management team over the entire project life cycle. The processes offer a road map that integrates both knowledge and practice, and enables a project manager to begin, track, direct, control, and end a project in an organized, efficient, and effective manner through its life cycle. The project manager's primary goal is to keep the project on track and within budget. These project management best-practice processes help project managers choose the appropriate tools to track and report progress, make decisions, remove obstacles, communicate, and keep the team focused.

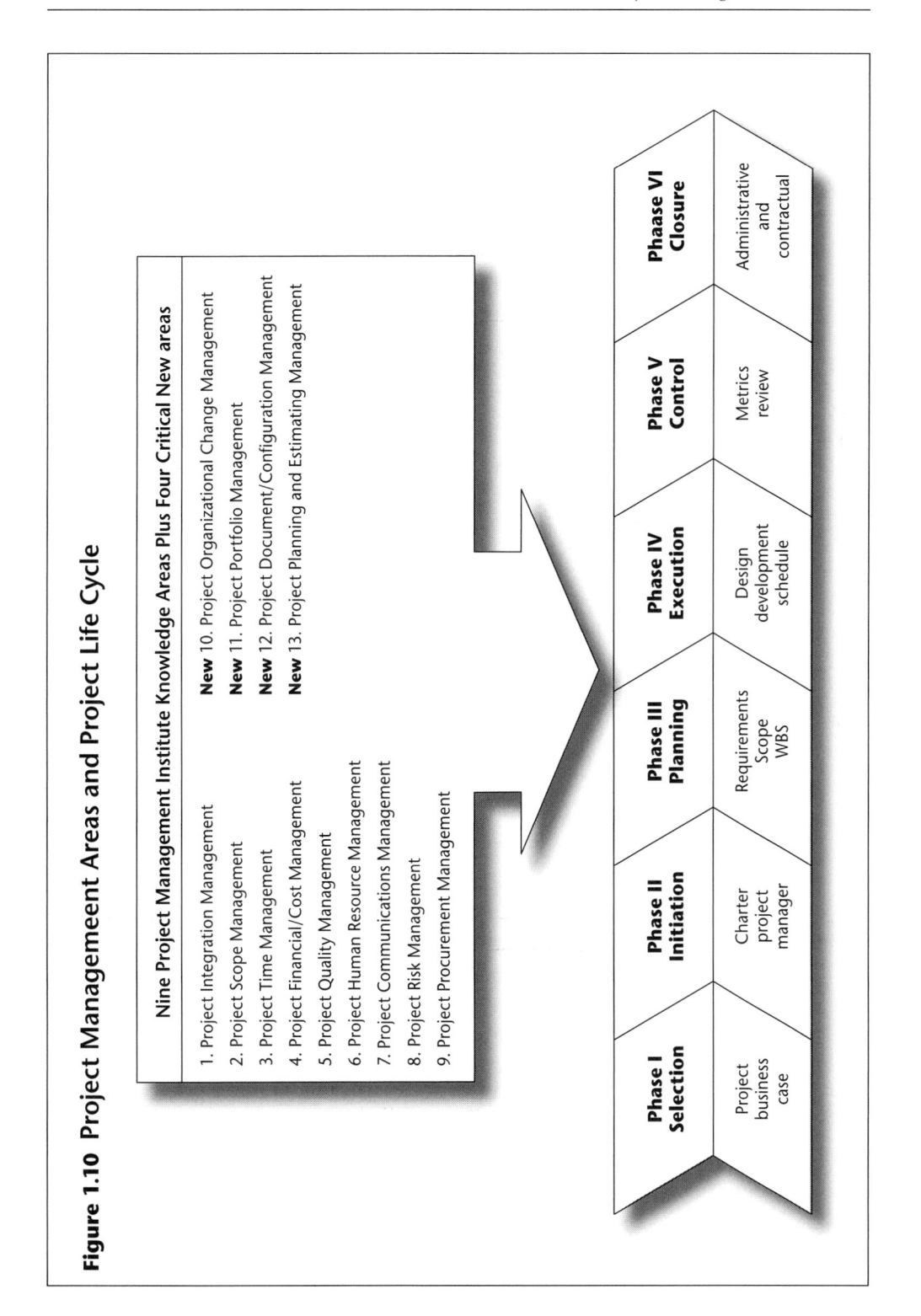

Introduction to Project Management Excellence

Figure 1.10 Project Management Areas and Project Life Cycle

Nine Project Management Institute Knowledge Areas Plus Four Critical New areas

1. Project Integration Management
2. Project Scope Management
3. Project Time Management
4. Project Financial/Cost Management
5. Project Quality Management
6. Project Human Resource Management
7. Project Communications Management
8. Project Risk Management
9. Project Procurement Management

New 10. Project Organizational Change Management
New 11. Project Portfolio Management
New 12. Project Document/Configuration Management
New 13. Project Planning and Estimating Management

Phase I Selection	Phase II Initiation	Phase III Planning	Phase IV Execution	Phase V Control	Phaase VI Closure
Project business case	Charter project manager	Requirements Scope WBS	Design development schedule	Metrics review	Administrative and contractual

21

The processes are closely integrated with the project life cycle, which not only shows how the project is started but also serves as a road map to the work that must be done, and who's responsible for doing it, in each phase of the project. By executing the phases in the project life cycle, a project manager with the project team can answer questions such as:

- Why are we doing this project?
- What are the business measures that indicate this project's success?
- How do I convert this idea into a solution?
- How do I get approval to commit resources to this project?
- How do I plan the project? To what level of detail?
- What are the day-to-day project management and execution activities?
- What did we learn from our experience on this project?

Projects represent a significant investment of strategic importance to any organization. The investment consists of resources, capital expenditure, time commitment, and individual dedication to make and embrace a change that will better enable the organization to improve business performance and strengthen competitive position.

WHY USE A SIX-PHASE PROJECT LIFE CYCLE?

We're using a six-phase cycle that includes selection, initiation, planning, execution, control, and closure. A phased approach not only provides a consistent and repeatable project-delivery framework that reduces project risk, but it also allows for project evaluation throughout each phase of the project life cycle. This approach is designed to apply to all types of projects. It ensures that the project team will maintain momentum from phase to phase while ensuring that the proper decisions are made to avoid committing resources to projects that have a high risk of failing. For example, it's critical that a project manager gets clear direction from the project sponsor when one phase has been completed prior to advancing the project team to the next phase.

The phases that make up a project start with project selection, which includes a draft project charter and the requirements definition. If the project manager and sponsor are confident about the project direction, funding is approved. The risk, which should be considered beforehand, is if the project's scope and objectives aren't clearly defined prior to starting a new phase, the project team could spend time and money on the wrong activities.

Business case and cost-benefit analysis (CBA) can also be more appropriately verified using a phased approach. This helps to properly facilitate the decision to either keep the team momentum going (as long as the project manager and project sponsor are confident that the CBA will support continuation of the project) or pull the plug on the project because benefits won't be realized.

These phased-decision points enable project managers and leaders to review and evaluate the business case, CBA, project progress, and plans for the remaining activities. Moreover, they also provide the juncture for project work plan refinement and realignment with customer satisfaction. This allows plan accuracy to improve as each phase is completed.

CHAPTER II

PROJECT OPERATING STRUCTURE

Figure 2.1 shows a typical project organizational structure:

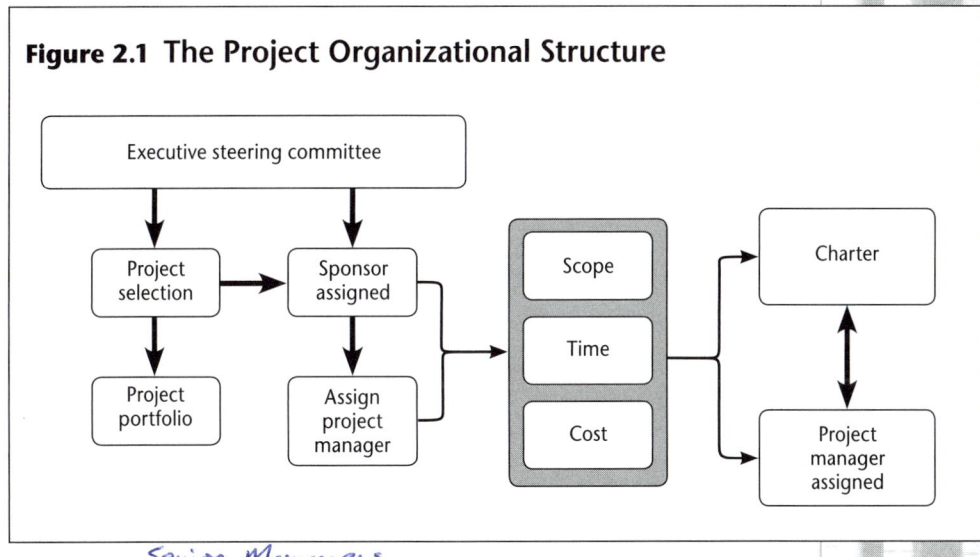

Figure 2.1 The Project Organizational Structure

Once the steering committee selects the right project and the sponsor is assigned, project initiation, phase two of the project life cycle, can begin. This phase brings together the decision-making body (or steering committee) and the project sponsor and manager, thereby solidifying the shared vision of success. The output of the project initiation phase is an approved project charter and an assigned project manager. The project charter defines the project's objectives and authorizes the project manager to move forward. It also outlines and models the high-level schedule and project size. During phase two initial work is started on the project plan.

> "Life . . . is about the development and execution of projects. All work can be converted to project's work. Train! Train! Train! The idea is to train everyone."
> —Tom Peters
> Author and motivational speaker

THE STEERING COMMITTEE'S ROLE

Senior Managers

The steering committee usually consists of senior managers from different areas within the organization (e.g., business and technical) that are affected by the projects. The committee is responsible for managing the portfolio of active projects and those proposed for selection. Because only a limited amount of resources are available to invest in projects, the committee must approve projects that will provide the highest added value to the organization. Along with this, the steering committee stops projects that aren't producing desired results and changes project priorities or shifts project resources to bring troubled projects back under control.

The steering committee provides guidance on the project's overall strategic direction. It aligns projects with corporate strategy and infuses a wider business perspective into project prioritization, particularly with projects within the same business sector. Consisting of key project decision makers, the steering committee has the final authority on project priority, change control, and issue escalation. The project manager, who as you recall provides the necessary team tactics to carry out the organization's strategy, relies heavily on the steering committee's active support and involvement in making strategic project decisions and ensuring management's commitment and understanding.

Some of the steering committee's responsibilities include but aren't limited to:

- Selecting projects to put into motion
- Reviewing and approving project charters (formal project approval)
- Selecting project managers with the right skills for a chosen project
- Participating in project tollgate activity (i.e., the pass/fail point for project deliverables)
- Providing recommendations to resolve project issues
- Approving changes that escalate beyond the project manager's authority
- Identifying interdependencies between customer readiness and operations
- Assessing project readiness to deliver project objectives
- Ensuring resource availability across the portfolio of projects and programs
- Building consensus and cooperation between all project stakeholders
- Determining when a project should be terminated

Organizations must do more than follow through with projects as they occur. They must manage their entire portfolio of projects simultaneously, selecting those that will succeed and provide the biggest return on investments.

THE PROJECT SPONSOR'S ROLE

Definition: A *project sponsor* is an individual in an organization whose support and approval is required for a project to continue.

> "More and more CIOs are saying, 'If I don't have a business sponsor, then I'm not doing the project."
> —**Erin Kinikin**
> **Vice president of research,**
> **Forrester Research**

The project sponsor usually "owns" the project. He or she provides overall leadership and acts as the project's vocal advocate. Generally delegated the authority by the steering committee, the project sponsor assists with business and project management issues that arise outside of the steering committee's formal charter. This individual is ultimately accountable for ensuring that business benefits are identified, validated, and delivered in a timely manner, and he or she should lead discussions with steering committee members on project issues and proposed changes to project scope.

[handwritten: A Marketing person]

The project sponsor should be actively engaged in the project and readily available to the project manager to aid in critical decision making. As the person responsible for leading project-related discussions, the project sponsor usually will chair these meetings and make the final decisions.

The project sponsor has several other important responsibilities. For example, he or she helps to develop and sustain the project's focus, obtain resources, and resolve issues that represent major barriers to success.

Some of the project sponsor's responsibilities include but aren't limited to:

- Understanding the business need for the project
- Initiating project requests
- Determining project priority against other project requests
- Evaluating the project business case (i.e., project justification)
- Assisting in the chartering process
- ✓ Assigning a project manager
- Ensuring that the project team agrees on clear and measurable metrics
- Approving major project deliverables
- Participating in project governance and business-issue resolution
- Approving user training and documentation
- Motivating and inspiring the project team
- Overseeing risk-mitigation planning
- Recognizing and rewarding project success
- Agreeing on the project and organizational alignment strategy
- Providing information on project effect, degree of change, organizational readiness, parallel/dependent projects, and constraints

Project Management Excellence

THE PROJECT MANAGER'S ROLE

> "The most valuable and least used word in a project manager's vocabulary is 'no'."
>
> —HJH

Definition: A *project manager* is the individual responsible for managing a project and its deliverables. This person acts as the customer's single point of contact for services delivered within the project's scope. He or she controls scope planning as well as the activities and resources required to meet established cost, time, and quality goals.

A project manager, according to business wisdom, is someone who accomplishes unique outcomes during critical timelines and with limited resources to meet organizational objectives. I liken project management to quality management. Just as a quality manager is a special type of professional with unique skills and training, so is a project manager. He or she must have special skills, training, and effective leadership specifically related to project management.

A selected project should have a project manager assigned immediately to ensure accountability. This individual usually reports, directly or indirectly, to the project sponsor. A project manager's primary role is to manage day-to-day project activities. These include leading, directing, and coordinating activities related to planning, executing, and implementing the project. Many of these activities must be managed simultaneously: scope, schedules, plans, budgets, process trends, project metrics, change requests, team dynamics, stakeholder relations, organizational change, and facilitating skills associated with root cause analysis and corrective action, as required. Therefore, it's vitally important that the project manager has senior management's support, particularly its total buy-in and trust. Such support authorizes the project manager to perform his or her duties accountably even if he or she has no direct authority over the resources involved in project activities.

Some of the project manager's day-to-day activities include but aren't limited to:

- Coordinating approval of project changes, risks, and issues
- Improving collaboration between teams throughout the project life cycle
- Implementing a consistent and repeatable approach for project delivery
- Leveraging scarce resources to best utilize valued skills and experience
- Attaining commitment from project team members to their assigned deliverables
- Providing reliable and timely distribution of information to project stakeholders
- Directing the project to completion in an orderly and progressive manner
- Ensuring that the tradeoffs between performance, scope, and costs are satisfactory
- Maintaining oversight of project performance, schedule, cost, and staffing

Project Operating Structure

- Delivering the proper amount of coaching and mentoring techniques to develop all the project team members' personal and professional skills
- Following the project sponsor's directions

Organizations rely on their project managers to help meet the incredible competitive challenge of our global marketplace. Its rapidly changing demands mean that companies must launch many projects simultaneously. Often project managers must oversee more than one project while balancing the resulting resource constraints across the entire organization. To prepare a project manager for the many challenges he or she must face during a project's life cycle, senior management must provide the training, practical methodology, tools, leadership strategy, and authority for the project managers to make wise and effective decisions.

As "agents of change," project managers are also expected to help the organization transition to a new operational status, which requires overcoming cultural resistance. Cross-enterprise cooperation is necessary to achieve this, and, because few people are born with essential leadership skills, most project managers must be properly trained in consulting and overcoming resistance and obstacles. Project management isn't just about work plans and milestones; it's mainly about leadership.

Some of the more important leadership attributes for project managers include the following:

- Listening skills
- Charisma
- Ability to motivate people
- Ability to get along with senior management
- Problem identification and solution
- Flexibility and adaptability
- Conflict resolution and negotiation skills
- Creativity
- Mentoring and coaching skills
- Financial ability
- Management ability
- Consulting skills

[Handwritten annotation: Required attributes for project managers]

How can project managers ensure that they deliver their projects on time and on budget? Statistics, unfortunately, are against them: Less than 26 percent of information technology projects are successfully completed on time and on budget; 46 percent are late, over budget, or fail to meet defined scope and quality; and 28 percent are cancelled. Here are some suggestions to keep projects on track:

Hints

Project Management Excellence

- Capture and share project intellectual capital.
  - ☐ Access, update, and store "post-project process review" reports, standard templates, sample projects and best-demonstrated practices.
  - ☐ Respect formalized project management methodology and flow.

- Establish integrated project documentation management to:
  - ☐ Control revisions and change.
  - ☐ Establish an audit trail of project documents.
  - ☐ Author, modify, store and retrieve templates.
  - ☐ Monitor concurrent access and modifications.

- Manage work-breakdown structures, both top-down and bottom-up.
  - ☐ Track projects globally through a single database repository across multiple functions within the organization.
  - ☐ Using generic profiles, request, negotiate, and accept resources scheduling in cooperation with the resource manager.
  - ☐ Roll up all budgets, incurred costs, work effort, resource allocation, and schedules to project, initiative, and portfolio levels.
  - ☐ Define links at multiple levels to reflect resource constraints or dependencies of deliverables and outputs.

- Identify and perform strategic trade-offs, including:
  - ☐ Scenario analysis across multiple projects to forecast results on timing, resource allocation, and project status
  - ☐ Critical-path project reviews to identify project milestones and deliverables
  - ☐ Performance reports against baseline at all levels

- Quantify, qualify, and respond to changes, risks, and issues (CRI).
  - ☐ Track CRIs through identification; assignment of responsibility, dates, classification, priority level, and response tasks; impact evaluation and resolution.
  - ☐ Store CRIs in central database and retrieve at multiple levels.

- Ensure that projects and portfolios perform within budget.
  - ☐ Estimate budgets by building on readily available historical data.
  - ☐ Capture internal and external staff effort, procurement, funds, and non-personnel costs.
  - ☐ Allocate and charge back expenditures across business units, functional groups, and cost centers, projects, and portfolios.

Hints

Project Operating Structure

- ☐ Plan, control, and monitor incurred and committed costs, payments, revenues, purchase orders, materials allocation, and shipping/receiving of project materials.
- ☐ Allow for fixed unit-costing and amortization of capital expenditures.

- Report to management on project development.
  - ☐ Schedule predefined, automatically broadcasted reports.
  - ☐ Generate an array of performance, project status, and executive summary reports at multiple levels.

The following is a project manager's typical weekly checklist:
- Validate project actual
- Update project work plan with actuals
- Update budget with actuals
- Update control plan with actuals
- Review issue log and address outstanding issues
- Review change request log
- Update project statistics/performance data
- Determine status
- Prepare weekly project status report
- Forecast project completion based on status
- Initiate action to keep/bring projects back to plan
- Update short-interval schedule in work plan
- Hold team meetings
- Meet with project sponsor

"If "no" is the least-used word in a project manager's vocabulary, the most valuable and least-used phrase in a project manager's vocabulary is, 'I don't know'."

—HJH

THE TEAM LEADER'S ROLE

For each group of special skills on the project team, there's usually a team leader, each of whom is accountable to the project manager. Although project team leaders have specific skills in a particular area of business or technology, they're not the same as subject matter experts because they accomplish specific objectives through successfully applying skills from other workers.

Project team leaders usually assist with coordinating and scheduling activities, preparing detailed work plans, participating in problem solving and conflict resolution, and identifying the resources best suited to performing required project tasks. They also act as the primary liaison between the project manager, other project team leaders, and their assigned team members.

Team leader responsibilities usually include the following activities:
- Select team members and identify their roles and responsibilities.
- Recommend meeting times and agendas.
- Oversee work assignments.
- Identify discrete team deliverables, accountability, timelines, and integration.
- Provide reliable and timely performance status to the project manager.
- Encourage, support, and tolerate team members when they make mistakes.
- Keep the team focused on tasks at hand.
- Take the necessary steps to keep team progress moving forward.
- Bring issues to the project manager's attention.
- Listen to and motivate team members.

THE PROCESS OWNER'S ROLE

The process owner is known by many names—gatekeeper, champion, subject matter expert—but his or her job responsibility remains the same. This individual maintains an effective, efficient, and streamlined process that either meets or exceeds customers' expectations consistently, i.e., collecting process metrics, analyzing process variation, and confirming the alignment between the business process with customer needs and expectations.

The process owner is usually a senior-level manager who should:
- Support team objectives.
- Confirm that the project manager has the necessary skills to be successful.
- Determine roadblocks or political land mines that might hinder the project.
- Be a member of the steering committee.
- Participate in project reviews.
- Assist the project team with process details and historical data.

The process owner generally is responsible for validating all project team measurements and analysis associated with the process. His or her opinions concerning process improvement or replacement are important. Even if the project proves successful, in the final analysis it's the process owner who must live with any outcome or changes to process capability.

THE PROJECT TEAM MEMBER'S ROLE

One of the most important aspects of a project is how it will be organized to deliver the project work. The project manager uses a team charter to define the required project roles and responsibilities, clear accountability, and unambiguous channels of communication. Having a well-defined project scope ensures that the project will run smoothly and have the best chance of succeeding.

Definition: A *project team charter* is a document that defines the roles and responsibilities for each project team member.

How do you get team members to collaborate and communicate effectively throughout the organization? Here are some suggestions:

- Reduce waste and improve productivity through smooth communication and workflow.
    - ☐ Abide by a standard method for accessing and manipulating common information, templates, and pertinent documents.
    - ☐ Use a document control program to easily author, modify, attach, store, and retrieve documents related to a project or task.
    - ☐ Receive alerts or notices for all relevant occurrences (for example, task assignments, overdue issues, or issue assignment).
    - ☐ Provide access to a list of team members and contact information.
    - ☐ Provide access to discussion threads of project team communications.

- Systematically report all pertinent events through a single point of entry.
    - ☐ Access customized views according to access privileges, role description, and status.
    - ☐ Read only relevant parts of the project database.
    - ☐ Enter work hours, costs, and comments against assigned projects, milestones, and tasks.
    - ☐ Update individual resource profiles, customize the project calendar to reflect pre-existing events, such as vacation or training, and review work packages and responsibilities.

THE RESOURCE MANAGER'S ROLE

Another important role of the group manager is to provide the human capital needed to staff the project teams. These managers are responsible for providing trained, skilled staff when projects need them. This presents resource managers with a big challenge: Too few people limit the number of projects the organization can undertake, but too many underutilized people increase overhead costs.

Not only must the organization have the optimum number of people available at a given notice; these pinch hitters also must have the right skills. The trick is to keep human resource use high without negatively affecting medium- and high-priority projects.

After the 60-percent break-even point, every percentage increase in utilization goes straight to the bottom line. The average utilization rate is 60 percent to 68 percent, and optimal utilization rate is 75 percent. To achieve this, resource managers must align the right resources with the right project initiatives at the right time, all the time. They also must eliminate time on the bench, develop strategies to secure and retain scarce resources, and capture and leverage valuable intellectual capital.

How can resource managers ensure that their strategies will drive utilization up to improve bottom-line profits? Here are some suggestions:

- Maintain an efficient and informative resource database.
    - ☐ Approve and complete employee updates of resource information.
    - ☐ Assign cost and selling rates of skill sets, which will allow for budget estimating prior to procurement.
    - ☐ Manage access privileges to views, reports, documents, and all other system data.
    - ☐ Track employees' time at the project and task level by requesting, accepting, modifying, or rejecting time sheets.
    - ☐ Provide individual resource performance evaluation reports.
    - ☐ List outsourcing and hiring options for tasks and activities requiring skills that aren't available internally.
    - ☐ Calculate resource loading, and forecast resource needs based on proposed and in-progress work.
    - ☐ Using generic and resource profiles, determine current total internal and external resource pool capacity, demand, availability, and utilization.

Once you've developed your database, strategically manage your resource pool to achieve optimal utilization. To do this, you must:

- Assign resources across multiple programs, locations, and functional work areas.
- Make assignment decisions in light of all relevant resource profile data, including:
    - ☐ Basic identification data such as name, location, job title, etc.

- ☐ Availability for a given period and scheduled assignments across multiple projects
- ☐ Qualified, exhaustive list of competencies and skills, level of proficiency level, documented experience, as well as cost and selling rate per competency and/or skill
- ☐ Background information (e.g., experience, area of expertise, personal preferences and interests, industry, work and project history, location preferences)
- ☐ Location information: geographic, organizational, or workflow group
- ☐ Project performance ratings by project manager for past completed tasks
- ☐ All related attachments (e.g., résumé, references, publications)
- ☐ Calendar and status—including assignments and exceptions
- ☐ Billable utilization by resource

■ Effectively balance supply and demand by:
- ☐ Identifying the type, quantity, and location where additional capacity is needed to undertake a new initiative
- ☐ Ensuring that proposed resources faithfully match profiles in the project manager's needs list
- ☐ Capturing changing staff requirements brought about by real-time events on the project

■ Secure and retain resources:
- ☐ Determine estimated effort, location, type of competency, skill, and proficiency required to perform a particular task.
- ☐ Identify the optimum quantity and types of resources needed.
- ☐ Pinpoint available knowledge and skills within the organization.
- ☐ Evaluate and improve the resource effort for optimum scheduling impact.
- ☐ Identify opportunities for reducing duration through effort splitting.
- ☐ Locate and leverage knowledge acquired by a resource from previous work-product assignments to improve current task performance.
- ☐ Align most skilled resources with highest priority initiatives and projects.

THE PROJECT OFFICE'S ROLE

Most midsize and large-size organizations should have a project management office. Depending upon the number and complexity of projects in an organization's portfolio, this office might be as simple as one-person who serves as a competency clearinghouse or complex enough to span

> "The recent success of many project offices that addressed the year 2000 problem has proven the project office to be a 'best practice' for delivering successful projects."
> —**Gartner Research**

several departments. Whatever their size, project offices focus on the three project management Cs:

- Communication
- Contractors
- Costs

Developing and implementing an effective communication plan is becoming increasingly difficult as projects grow more complex, and we rely on a distributed workforce and outsourcing for many aspects of them. It's important, then, that a communication plan addresses not only specific project team's and executives' needs but also the needs of all other project teams. Due to inherent problems related to oral communications, project teams should develop explicit communication plans that effectively use modern communication technology, supplemented by frequent human communication exchanges such as meetings, progress reports, and daily briefings.

> "Information systems [IS] and application development organizations that fail to qualify contractors' business understanding and administer contracts will receive deliverables that don't address at least 15 percent of critical requirements in three of four contracts."
> —Gartner Research

Using contractors and consultants to outsource project activities and even manage an organization's projects is becoming commonplace. Organizations can't afford to maintain processes that aren't part of their core competencies. Activities such as personnel management, information systems, application development, project management, and call centers are routinely outsourced. Thus, for many projects, success or failure rests in the hands of contractors and consultants. Unless an organization sets up an effective contracting system that ensures only the best contractors are selected, projects are vulnerable to mismanagement and failure.

Accurate cost and schedule estimating and tracking is critical to successful projects. All estimates should be accompanied with an accuracy estimate (for example, "$2.8 million ± 30 percent, project to be completed by July 30, 2007 ± two months"). Estimating skills are honed over time. Project office personnel should develop approaches that improve the accuracy of project estimating methodology, using data collected from past projects and their experience with managing different projects.

> "Sixty-two percent of companies with active project management officers report 'healthy' or 'very healthy' profitability."
> —Robbins-Gioia Project management firm survey

PROJECT OFFICE DUTIES AND RESPONSIBILITIES

The project office's mission is to deliver projects—on schedule and on budget—that meet promised functionality at a satisfactory quality level. The project office performs five roles to aid the organization and fulfill this mission:

- Develop a standard project management methodology.
- Evaluate resource estimates.
- Ensure that all projects have a comprehensive and accurate project plan.
- Conduct project phase reviews and ongoing project status analysis.
- Keep management advised of portfolio status.

Developing Standard Project Management Methodology

This is a critical project office responsibility. A number of approaches and tools are available to manage projects. The project office should evaluate them all to determine those best suited to the organization. The office should then document the organization's project management standards and train project managers and team members on how to use these tools. A consistent, common set of tools and procedures along with trained people are essential to managing the project portfolio.

Evaluating Resource Estimates

The project office should validate business assumptions related to project and lifecycle costs. Based on its experience with other projects, the office can provide insight into a project's likely effect on people and the resistance it might provoke when it's finally implemented. If too many projects are underway in a specific area, people there will be incapable of coping with all the changes, and the area will become dysfunctional. Project office feedback to the executive team will influence their decisions about project priority and how resources are committed.

Ensuring That All Projects Have Comprehensive and Accurate Plans

Developing a project plan requires a cooperative effort between the project team and project office. Based on collected data from past projects, the office can advise the team about the risks involved in proceeding with the project and how to apply best practices. Serving as a competency center, the project office can help improve a project plan's accuracy and the potential for success of the project itself.

Conducting Project Phase Reviews and Ongoing Status Analysis

Establishing appropriate action plans to keep projects on schedule and budget is a very important role the project office plays. Office staff must remain objective about the projects they're assigned. It's easy to become so involved in a project that real risks are overlooked.

The project office must provide an independent, objective evaluation at each phase. As each of the various project phases occur, it's equally important that the project office recognizes ongoing progress, or the lack thereof. This will ensure that aggressive, effective corrective action is taken to keep quality, costs, and schedules from being compromised.

Keeping Management Advised About Portfolio Status

This communication is critical to ensure that resources are used most effectively. The executive team should know about projects with unacceptable risks so it can take appropriate action. The *Wall Street Journal* reports that, on average, a project is cancelled after fourteen weeks with 52 percent of its total budget spent. Moreover, many project teams know their projects are likely to fail six weeks before they're cancelled. This means that if the executive teams had been aware of these projects' true status early on, they could have saved 50 percent of the initial investment.

> "IS organizations that establish enterprise standards for project management, including a project office, cut their major project cost overruns, delays, and cancellations by 50 percent."
> —**Gartner Research**

It's also imperative that project managers are told about the status of projects critical to the success of their own, and the project office is in an ideal position to do this. Slippage in a supporting project can be disastrous to another project, but with proper notification, work-around approaches often can be implemented to minimize the effect of delays.

PROJECT OFFICE TYPES AND STYLES

We've seen one-person project offices that function as information repositories and disseminate project management best practices and methodologies. At the other extreme, we've seen project offices that serve as comprehensive centers of excellence, providing project expertise and oversight to entire organizations. Often these offices act as matrix managers for the total organization, managing a project across functional silos.

There are three types of project office structures:

- Project management information center model
- Project management center of excellence model
- Project management function model

Project Management Information Center Model

This model provides a central knowledge warehouse where standards, best practices related to project methodology, and copies of project reports are stored and available to the organization. Project managers still report to, and are funded by, the individual business unit. This model lets project teams select their own approaches to project management but doesn't ensure that a common, project management tool set is used throughout the organization. Therefore, it falls short of fulfilling a project office's mission because it doesn't ensure standardization or oversight of ongoing projects.

The information center model is often the first step in evolving toward a full-blown project office. Implementing a project office often meets with considerable resistance from the staff in the various business units because they think it will reduce their control over projects that affect them.

Project Management Center of Excellence Model

This model has a full-time staff and is responsible for all projects in the organization's portfolio. This project office functions as a consultant, mentor, and trainer for the organization on project management methodologies. Top management authorizes the project office to establish, with cooperation from the business unit, the project management practices and methodologies that will be used throughout the organization. The office is responsible for documenting, updating, and communicating these operating procedures, and all project managers have a dotted-line reporting responsibility to the project office. It also establishes training classes and documents that are used by project managers and team members. The project office conducts project-closeout reviews on active projects to define best practices that can be reused. With this model, the project office is an overhead-support administrative activity.

Project Management Function Model

The project management function model is the most comprehensive of the three models. This project office has direct control over all projects: It either directly manages projects by supplying the project manager or has oversight responsibility for the project. The approach used to manage the projects will vary within the organization, based upon the project's strategic importance, scope, and duration. The project office is responsible for ensuring the integrity of the following documents or estimates before a project is approved:

- Scope
- Cost
- Risk
- Resources
- Requirements
- Return on investment
- Effect assumptions

The project office will either assign one of its staff to manage the project for a small, less-critical project, or it will approve or appoint a capable project manager. Throughout

> "60 percent of the enterprises will use external source workers to fulfill more than half of their IT activities."
> —Gartner Research

the project, the project office is responsible for coordinating the project and ensuring that action is taken when projects stray from their objectives. The project office also plays a major role in evaluating and selecting project suppliers and consultants. In this model the chief project manager serves on the executive project review team.

PROJECT OFFICE STAFFING

The size of the project office will depend upon the model that's used, the number of active projects, and their complexity. To support a project information center, one subject matter expert is adequate for most organizations. The other two models require a manager and support staff. Typical project offices are staffed with six to twenty-five employees. In large organizations, individual business units will have their own project offices, which report by dotted line to the corporate project office. In these cases there may be hundreds of project managers connected, directly or indirectly, to the corporate project office.

The project office staff typically falls into six categories:
- Best practices and/or process experts
- Relationship managers
- Project managers
- Administrative support staff
- Librarian
- Change agents

The project office should be an evolving organization. It should start out conservatively, addressing the organization's business needs, and then evolve through the various project office models, adding layers of capabilities to its staff and profile. Don't hesitate to use a combination of the three models presented to meet your organization's best interests.

MYTHS VERSUS TRUTHS

The following will provide you with valuable guidance about project sponsors, managers, and charters.
- Myths:
    - ☐ A project sponsor's role ends when the project starts.
    - ☐ The project charter is a rigid contract that should never be changed.

Project Operating Structure

- Truths:
  - ☐ If a project manager does the technical work, then no one is managing the project.
  - ☐ Project managers must be proactive in all they do.
  - ☐ The project sponsor must be willing to understand all the project details.
  - ☐ The project charter is a living document.

> *Lots of this chapter doesn't apply well to small companies. Especially the stuff on Project Management Center.*

CHAPTER III

PROJECT MANAGEMENT KNOWLEDGE AREAS

"You must understand the rules to win the game."
—HJH

Combining the Project Management Institute's nine knowledge areas with the four new areas we believe are essential for success makes a total of thirteen project management knowledge areas. They are:

- Integration management
- Scope management
- Planning and estimating management
- Document and configuration management
- Time management
- Financial and cost management
- Quality management
- Human resource management
- Communications management
- Risk management
- Procurement management
- Organizational change management
- Portfolio management

Everyone who manages a project should have a detailed understanding of each of the thirteen areas. It's also advisable that all members of the project team have a working knowledge of them.

PROJECT INTEGRATION MANAGEMENT

For the past decade organizations have reorganized, downsized, outsourced, consolidated, and changed their processes to the point where they now launch changes through numerous short-term projects that provide shorter time to market at reduced costs.

Project Management Excellence

There are two levels of project integration management, micro and macro. Micro-level project integration management occurs when a project manager assembles the many inputs from various project leaders and team members into one consolidated and coherent project deliverable. Think of this integration effort as the glue that combines the many sub-characteristics of work (i.e., the output of individual tasks) into a single, seamless organizational benefit.

Take, for example, a software integration project. With one platform, integrating software components is a fairly straightforward undertaking. However, for a project with multiple platforms, in multiple-software environments, within organizations with multiple processes, integration becomes a much greater challenge. Add to that the sub-characteristics of integrating software modules, data-conversion scripts, security elements, Web interfaces, and the project integration management process becomes an extremely important component of project success.

Successful integration management requires attention to many different micro levels. A few of the more prominent are listed below.

- Process integration deals with the domino effect, where any adjustment made to one process will affect others as well. Preprocesses must realign with the redesigned process, and post-processes can expect to receive output sooner from the redesigned process. Although processes usually are viewed as separate entities, no single process can operate independently. In most modern organizations a full transactional cycle usually begins with suppliers and continues through inputs, processes, outputs, and the customer experience.
- Data integration ensures that the right data are available to those who need them. The analysis also assures management that stored data are optimized for customer profiling, aren't redundant, and aren't misused in any way that would jeopardize a relationship with a customer.
- Operational integration ensures that any operational system infrastructure and support assistance (e.g., a help desk) can recover from operational failures. The analysis also assures operational management that systems don't consume excessive resources and appropriately respond to environmental requirements.
- Performance integration ensures that any system or project modifications meet predefined standards with respect to speed, cycle time, and resource use.
- Software integration testing ensures that business processes have been implemented as required. In addition, the same techniques can be used to test the viability of user requirements.
- Requirements integration ensures that customer requirements are complete and integrated across functional organizations.

Project Management Knowledge Areas

With macro-level integration, the project team members report directly to the project manager for project-related work and have dotted-line responsibilities to the functional manager. This approach greatly simplifies project integration management activities.

Project integration management is a subset of project management that includes the processes required to ensure that project elements are properly coordinated. It consists of:

- *Project plan development.* Taking the results of other planning processes and putting them into a consistent, coherent document.
- *Project plan execution.* Carrying out the project plan by performing the activities included therein.
- *Overall change control.* Coordinating changes across the entire project.

PROJECT SCOPE MANAGEMENT

This important process ensures that a project includes all the work required—and only the work required—to be successfully completed. One of the most common reasons for project failure is the inability to properly define or effectively manage scope. Properly implementing the process requires support from all project team members, especially the project manager and sponsor.

If a project's scope changes during the initial phase, the effects of that change will affect elements such as schedule, cost, and performance less than if the scope changes during the final phases.

Purpose of Project Scope Management

Project scope management ensures that a project focuses only on the work required for successfully completing a project. The process identifies and averts work that falls outside

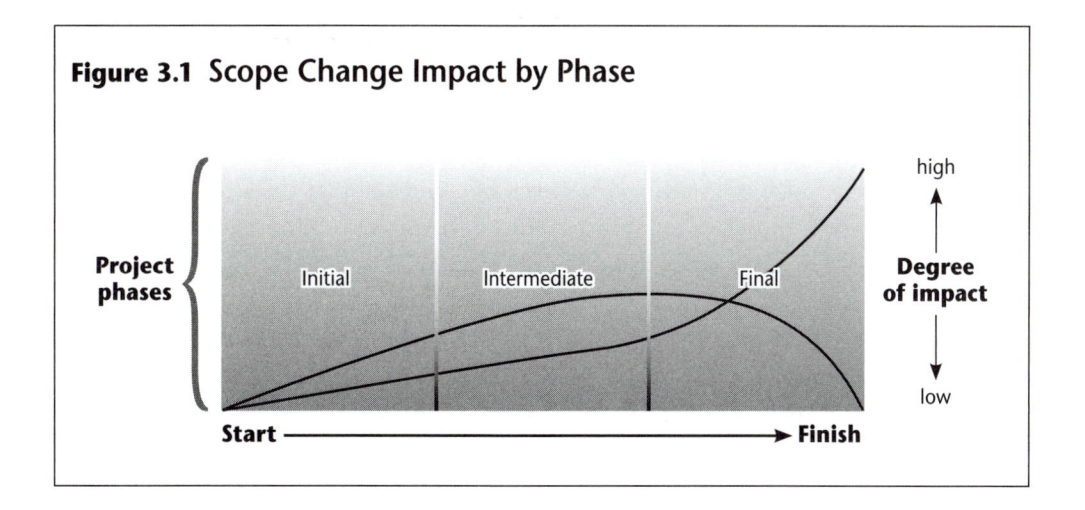

Figure 3.1 Scope Change Impact by Phase

Project phases: Initial | Intermediate | Final

Start → Finish

Degree of impact: high ↕ low

the scope and that contributes to delays and overruns. It includes processes for defining and approving initial scope, and identifying, authorizing, and managing changes to scope. The project scope management process was developed to standardize how project scope is defined and controlled. Using this management technique will ensure rigorous control of project scope while facilitating change in a controlled manner to a project's cost, schedule, and performance baselines.

Although scope changes usually are expected over the life of a project, they must be documented and reviewed by the project sponsor and stakeholders for effects. Approved changes affect almost every part of a project plan. Approved changes must be incorporated into the schedule, budget, return-on-investment calculation, scope document, team charter, communications plan, deliverable list, and quality plan. All changes should be documented and analyzed for frequency modes, affected areas, organizations or departments that push change, and lessons learned. The changes should be allowed only if there's total agreement among the sponsor and stakeholders. Once the change is approved, timelines and budgets should be updated to reflect the change.

Project Scope Management and Change Requests

All members of the project team who are affected by the project (e.g., customers, internal team, external partners, sponsor, organizations) should be included in the process of reviewing the scope and then approving any changes to the scope baseline. Participation is critical to the success of this process, and particular support is required from the project manager and sponsor. The project manager should manage this process to ensure that the scope is properly defined during the planning phase of the project life cycle. The individuals requesting scope changes should document their reasons on a change request (CR) form. The CR should be reviewed during regularly held project meetings and maintained in a central tracking database or log and particular attention given to how change affects the dimensions of cost, schedule, and performance.

Components of Project Scope Management

Usually there are two major components of a project's scope: product and/or service scope and project scope. Product and/or service scope include all the functions and features of the delivered product and/or service. Project scope includes all the work necessary to design, build, deliver, and test a new process, enhancement, or new function as defined in the project's scope and task details section of the work breakdown structure.

Definition: Work breakdown structure (WBS) is a deliverable-oriented grouping of project elements, which organizes and defines a project's total scope. Each descending level represents an increasingly detailed definition of a project component.

Project Management Knowledge Areas

Project components can include products or services. The word "scope" usually refers to both components of project scope unless specifically noted otherwise. Scope is initially defined during a project's planning phase. At the end of this phase, the product and/or service scope as well as the project scope are fully defined as part of the project plan. Scope review and approval by all stakeholders, including the project team and sponsor, are critical at this point. This is when the scope is frozen and a final review is made of the budget, schedule, resources, dependencies, assumptions, constraints, and WBS. The project approach is defined and committed to by all stakeholders.

Scope is one of the most important elements of a project. All changes to project scope statements should be rigidly documented, reviewed, and then evaluated by project stakeholders for potential benefit to and inclusion in the project.

Product and/or service scope give definition to the features and functions of either a new or enhanced product or service. Changes to scope should be driven directly by customer needs and requirements. Detailed design components, descriptions, and work plans give the project scope substance. Once identified, project scope is documented in a project plans' high-level requirements section.

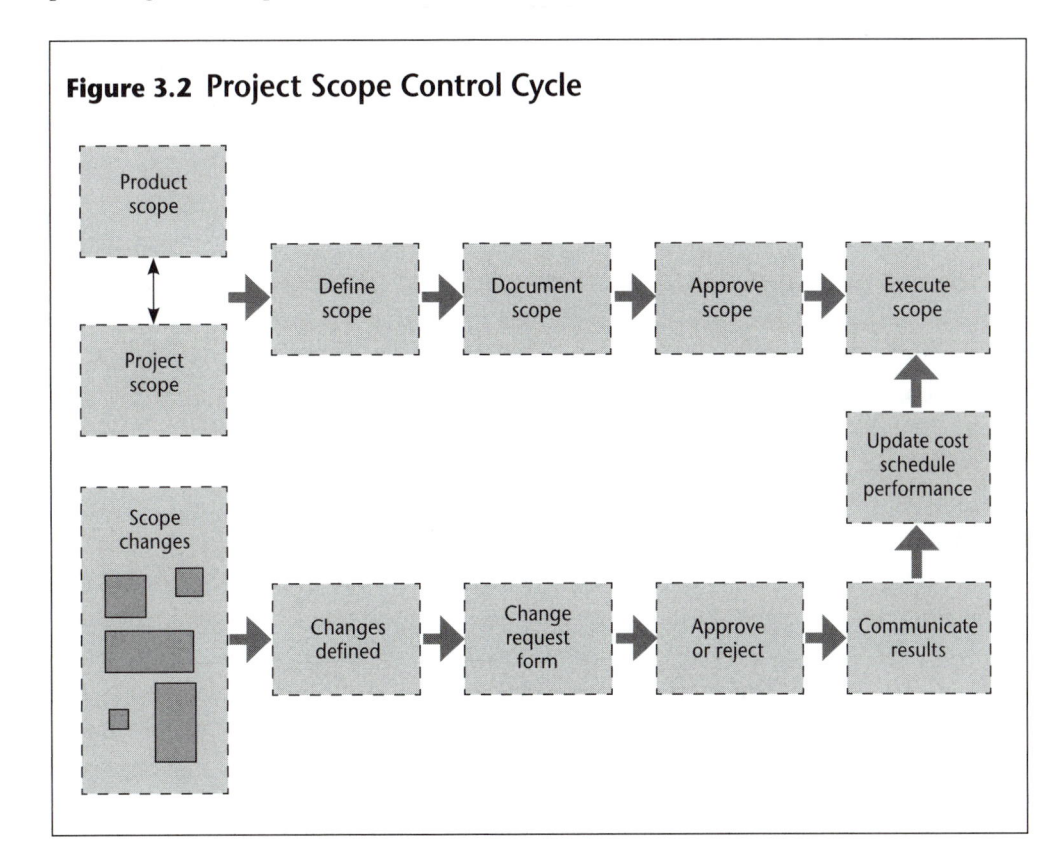

Figure 3.2 Project Scope Control Cycle

Project scope is similarly defined during the project's planning phase; however, the project manager is the primary person responsible for interfacing with project stakeholders, including the customer, to define and develop requirements specifications. The project manager usually provides verification for the business reasons of a project by substantiating the problem and opportunity for improving customer satisfaction. During this period, a detailed project scope statement (what's in or out of scope) is issued, and stakeholders agree to the project's specific focus. Questions such as the following seven are useful for determining if a project is of high priority:

- Why this project?
- Who's the customer?
- What data have been collected to understand customer requirements?
- What are the business reasons for completing the project?
- How will we verify that the project provides value to the business and its customers?
- What are this project's boundaries?
- How will we know if the team succeeds?

These inputs, coupled with the project manager's experience, will permit the project team to complete the components of the project plan: customer and business requirements, conceptual and detailed design, project management reporting relationships, procurement plan, resource plan, work breakdown structure, schedule, scope document, constraints and assumptions, performance objectives, risk analysis, cost-benefit analysis, team charter (signed), budget, and change strategy.

Reviewing and Approving the Project Scope Statement

At the end of a project's planning phase, the sponsor and/or executive steering committee must review and formally approve the scope statement and project plan. Approving the project plan elements completes the initial definition of scope for the project. In subsequent project phases, the project manager, team, and sponsor can use the items as the basis for reviewing requested changes to scope.

Changes to the Project Scope

Once the project plan is signed, the baseline is set for cost, schedule, and performance. Throughout the project's life cycle, scope change requests will occur. Changes might begin from within or outside the project. Business personnel, customers, suppliers, end users, team members, or management personnel might request changes to project scope. The changes may be in product or service scope, project scope, or the project work breakdown structure. For the project scope management process to work, it's imperative that all project members are aware of change requests and participate in deciding how the change might affect project schedule, cost, and performance. All changes to scope should be identified and documented in a controlled manner for review and approval.

Unnecessary changes to project scope should be resisted. Often, in the course of reviewing project scope changes, a project team's lack of experience and knowledge about business processes or products and services can encourage "scope creep" that will jeopardize an important aspect of the project. By enlisting the entire team's help in controlling scope, the project manager has a much better chance of success. Through team meetings, sponsor meetings, peer reviews, and other communication channels, the project manager can foster an environment of scope management while still meeting the project's business objectives.

Change within most projects is inevitable, but defining a rigorous project scope management process permits the team to understand and evaluate how change might affect the project's schedule, cost, and performance. This control will encourage full stakeholder commitment.

Documentation of Project Scope Change Requests

Persons requesting a project scope change should document any new requirement by filling out a change request form. Impact assessments are usually included with the request so all affected team members can identify additional cost, schedule, performance, and other effects resulting from the change. The project manager and sponsor will use the information in their review for either approving or rejecting the change request. Project stakeholders can reject any request they determine is unacceptable for the project, but they should give due consideration to all requests, especially those coming from customer or business personnel.

Updating Cost, Schedule, and Performance Information

If a change request is approved, the project team must update schedules, budgets, and performance commitments to reflect the change. Monthly reports should indicate the revised baselines, and any cost-benefit analysis should also be updated.

Summary

One of the most common reasons for project failure is the inability to properly define or effectively manage scope. Implementing the process described in this chapter provides an effective approach to build scope management into projects. Properly implementing the process requires support from all members of the project team, special attention from the project manager, and the added support of the project sponsor and steering committee.

PROJECT PLANNING AND ESTIMATING MANAGEMENT

"If you fail to plan, you're planning to fail."
—HJH

Here are three words and their definitions to consider:
- *Estimate:*
  - ☐ To make a judgment as to the likely or appropriate cost, quality, or duration
  - ☐ To evaluate
  - ☐ A rough calculation
  - ☐ A preliminary calculation of cost of work to be undertaken
  - ☐ An opinion

- *Predict:*
  - ☐ To state, tell about, or make known in advance; foretell

- *Guess:*
  - ☐ To predict or assume (an event or fact) without enough information to be sure
  - ☐ To suppose; judge

You'll note that an estimate is a rough calculation and as such should always be accompanied by an accuracy estimate (for example, $2.5 million ±10 percent). When it comes to cost estimates, the following are good guidelines:
- Order of magnitude (e.g., -25% to +75%)
- Budget estimate (e.g., -10% to +25%)
- Definitive estimate (e.g., -5% to +10%)

In this chapter, there's a good deal of overlap between project planning and estimating management, and project integration schedule and time management. We've added project planning and estimating to the Project Management Body of Knowledge's (PMBOK) nine knowledge areas because there's so much interaction between scope, time, schedule, and cost during planning and estimating activities. To develop a project plan and estimate, you must define:
- Outputs to deliver at each phase, based on the project scope
- Activities and tasks to create the deliverables or outputs
- Effort required to perform activities and tasks
- Skills required to perform each activity or task

Figure 3.3 Project Planning and Estimating Management Activities

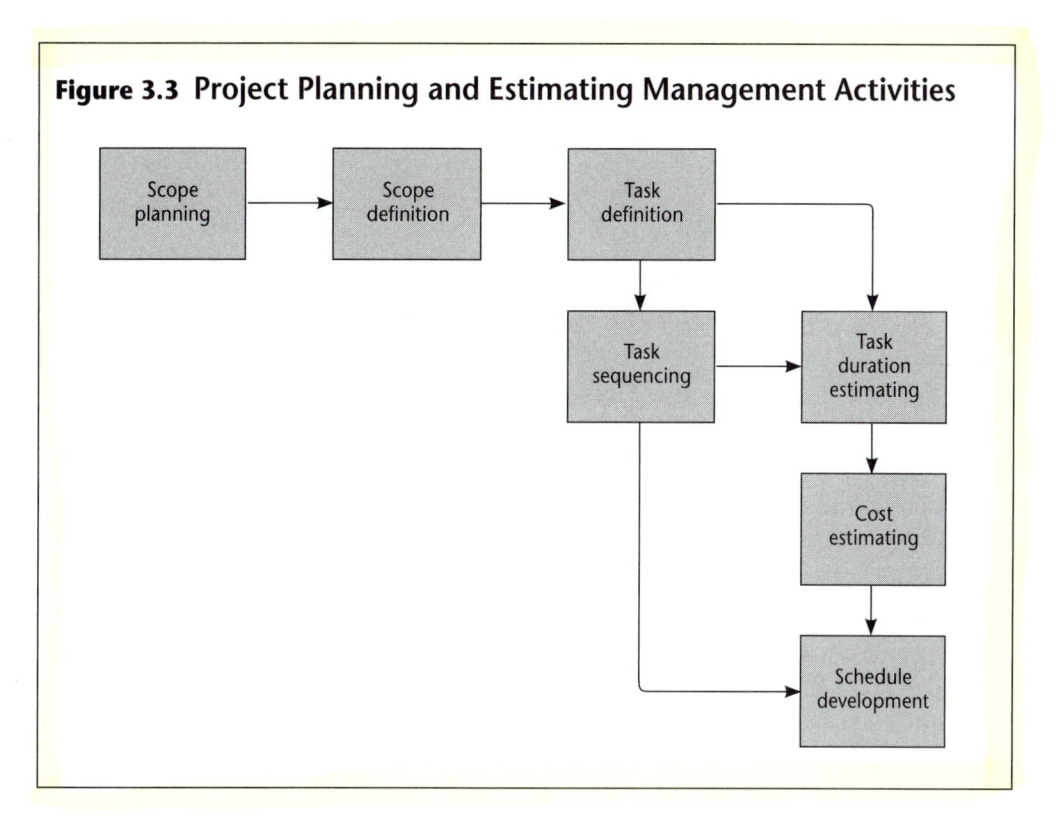

- Sequence each task must follow
- Cost related to each activity and task

The outcome from this cycle is the project schedule, cost, and resource requirement. They all have an effect on each other. For example, if an activity requires a Six Sigma Black Belt and none is available, the project might be delayed four months and $20,000 might be spent to train one. (*Note:* we've duplicated planning and estimating activities in project cost, schedule, and human resource management to comply with PMBOK.)

Project planning and estimating isn't a one-time activity. It's a cycle that must be repeated each time a change occurs to a project. There are many important components to a project's success. Of them, project management involves properly planning and estimating tasks. The project planning and estimating process was developed to define the standard approach for planning and estimating projects. Keeping a project progressing steadily is a crucial element of project control.

Without proper planning and estimating, the most well-defined requirements and deliverables might end up unrealized or uncompleted. Even the best project team members require knowledge of project tasks so they can integrate their deliverables with previous or ensuing activities.

Project Management Excellence

Project planning and estimating management means developing and continually refining project work plans, or work breakdown structures, throughout a project's life cycle. At a minimum, refining (i.e., replanning) coincides with the end of a phase. For example, at the end of the planning phase a project plan is delivered as part of the project binder.) By the end of the planning phase, business and technical requirements are detailed and validated.

Research shows that the project planning and estimating process is the most critical phase and where much of the project time is spent. Planning's many benefits include:

- Reduced uncertainty and team anxiety
- A guide for project execution for team members
- Consideration of all factors that might affect the project, such as constraints, assumptions, and decisions
- A detailed understanding of project deliverables
- A basis for monitoring and controlling work
- Enhanced communication

→ *Better budgetary estimates & ROI estimates*

The planning effort begins with the initial project definition and ends with continually refining project work plans or the work breakdown structure. The WBS is rigorously maintained throughout the project's life. A work plan that consists of detailed tasks, resource estimates, and project deliverables is a component of the project plan. The remaining phases are in the work plan and include a high-level projection of tasks, effort, and deliverables, as well as detailed and validated business and technical requirements.

At this juncture a project team will prepare detailed plans containing design tasks, resource estimates, and deliverables. Additionally, the project manager should update the high-level plan for the entire project. Similarly, as new information and past project performance become available at the end of each phase—selection, initiation, planning, execution, control, and closeout—the process is repeated to prepare accurate plans for the next phase and an improved projection for the project.

The amount of detail in a project plan and how far ahead one can see depends on where the project is in its life cycle. Early project planning focuses on defining the steps needed to develop a project's scope. Once the scope is documented and requirements and deliverables defined, a more thorough estimate of the project can begin. Ensuring the project team understands the level of confidence indicated by the estimate is important to project success. Sometimes it's better to provide a range estimate rather than a single date. An estimate for a whole project during the initial business case most likely will carry a very low confidence level, whereas an estimate for implementing and testing a system, given after completing the detailed design, should have a very high confidence level.

Constraints and Assumptions

At a minimum, the project plan is modified based upon project constraints and assumptions. A project constraint is any factor that limits the project team's options for delivering the project. For example, if a project manager is told that he or she must deliver the project for under $100,000, that budget constraint will limit solution options. A project assumption is a factor that's considered true, real, or certain for planning purposes. For example, when launching a project during the summer months, a project manager might determine that every member on the team will take at least one week of vacation.

Project Plan

"Plans are worthless, but planning is everything."
—**Dwight D. Eisenhower**

Documenting the project plan is critical in moving customer requirements from a defined state toward one of discrete and measurable deliverables. The project manager carries this effort forward. Team members should participate in the planning and estimating effort to increase their motivation for a successful project. Sponsor buy-in is also critical across the project life cycle, so both the sponsor and project team should sign the project plan and approve any changes made to it that might affect their expectations for success.

Most project managers are requested to give project estimates before requirements are completely documented. Based on the Project Management Institute's best practices, the first estimate is sometimes referred to as an "order of magnitude" and is an approximation that carries a -25 percent to 75 percent confidence level with it. Other names for this estimate are "preliminary" and "feasibility."

A budget estimate carries a confidence level of -10 percent to 25 percent. This is the project estimate that's provided after the planning phase is over but before a detailed level of design has been examined.

A definitive estimate has a confidence level of -5 percent to 10 percent. This estimate usually is provided after the project plan is completed and examined.

Project Milestone Plan

A milestone is a significant event in a project, such as completing a major deliverable. It's a clearly identifiable point in a project or set of activities that commonly denotes a reporting requirement or completion of a large or important set of activities. It's a task with a duration of zero used to measure a project's progress or signify completion of a major deliverable.

A milestone plan such as the one shown in figure 3.4 is a communication tool that provides the project manager, project team, sponsor, steering committee, and other project stakeholders with a high-level view of the project.

Figure 3.4 Project Milestone Plan

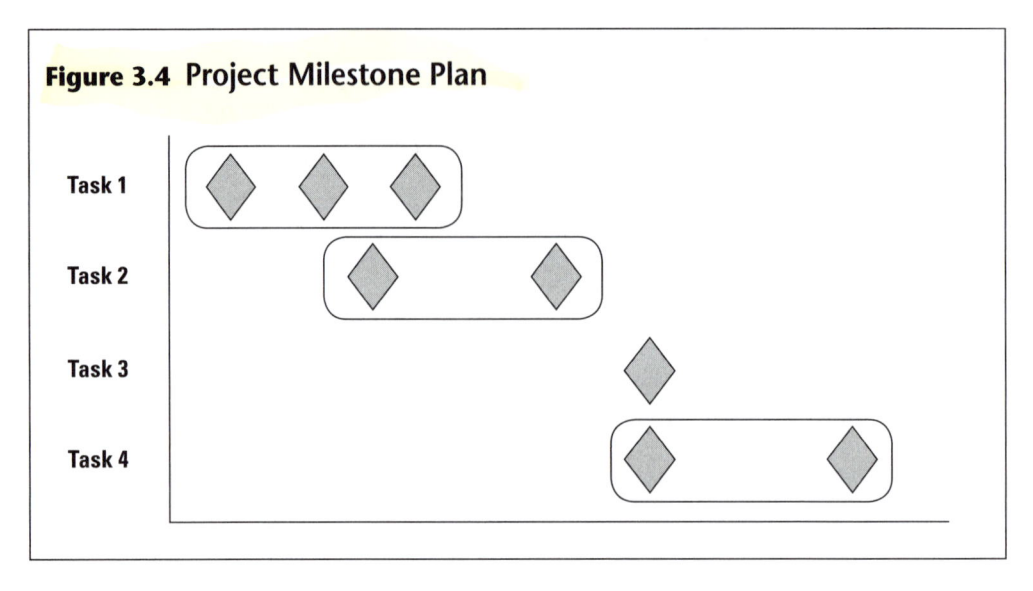

Task 1

Task 2

Task 3

Task 4

A project milestone plan depicts major project deliverables organized according to logical highlights. The primary activities that drive the work from one milestone to the next are identified. The plan also should illustrate any project-specific checkpoints or off-ramps, and existing deliverable dependencies. Most important, the high-level milestone plan shows the connection between each major deliverable and the stakeholder(s) to whom it is important, clearly demonstrating how stakeholder needs drive the project while facilitating better communication during project execution.

This plan is usually built through a series of iterations during the project's planning initiative and then updated throughout the project's life cycle. Typically the plan covers the entire cycle and is detailed enough to explain interdependencies, upcoming milestones, and project status to the project team, sponsor, and steering committee. The plan must also provide enough information so stakeholders can understand variance effect that's traceable to each team's project work plan across the project life cycle.

Project Work Breakdown Structure

A work breakdown structure or work plan is fundamental to planning project activities and estimating project timelines. The WBS is a critical project management tool for planning, estimating, and (later) controlling a project. Figure 3.5 shows a high-level WBS for a new jet design.

The WBS should contain summary tasks, detailed executable tasks, and milestones that mark the completion of a key deliverable. The summary tasks and subtasks usually are sequenced. The detailed executable tasks are estimated and rolled up to both summary and project level (a process known as bottom-up estimating). As the project progresses, the WBS is updated with actual hours worked, tasks completed, additions made, and items

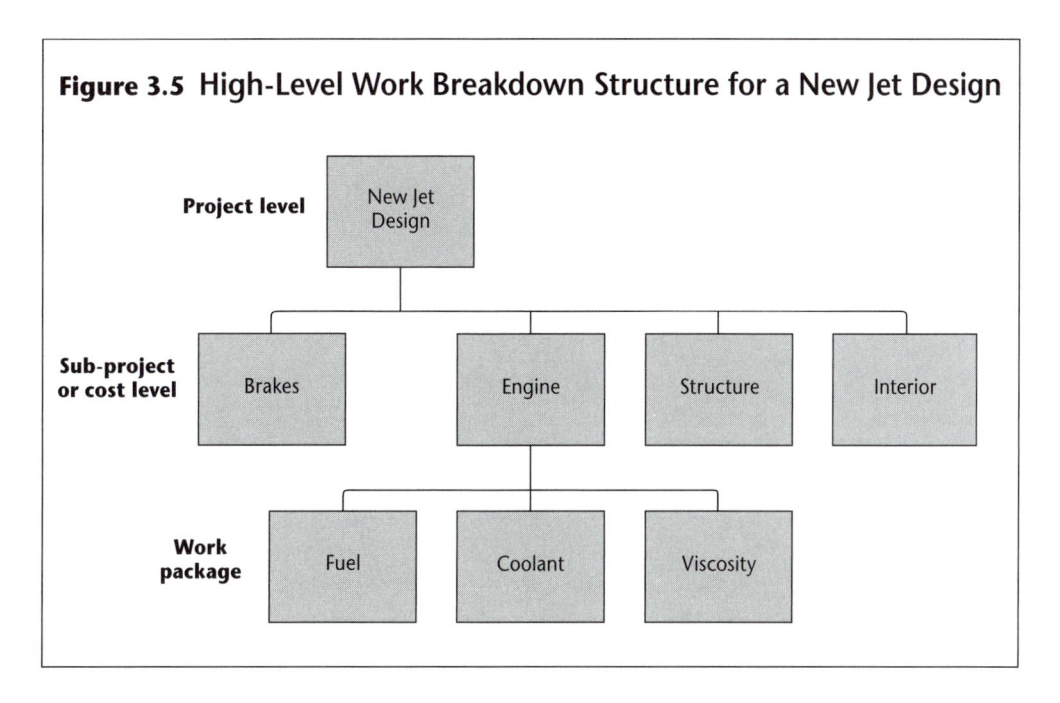

Figure 3.5 High-Level Work Breakdown Structure for a New Jet Design

Project level: New Jet Design

Sub-project or cost level: Brakes, Engine, Structure, Interior

Work package: Fuel, Coolant, Viscosity

removed as the project scope changes. The WBS is the fundamental tool for managing all the tasks necessary to complete a project, and the schedule is developed from the WBS's work-package level.

There are three different levels associated with the WBS:

- *Project*—all costs roll up to this level
- *Cost*—level where costs are managed
- *Work package*—lowest working level that project can be defined

Creating a high-level milestone plan is the first step in the planning process. The plan is then expanded into the more detailed work plan or work breakdown structure. Once the WBS is broken down into discrete executable tasks, the lowest level is called the "work package." This level should provide a high level of confidence and in fact establish scope definition for each scheduled deliverable throughout the project.

Tollgates and Stage Gates

Tollgates, also called phase gates or stage gates (this last term was developed by Robert G. Cooper), are templates or road maps for driving projects from idea to launch and beyond. They're decision points that allow for sponsor review.

Just as a cost-benefit analysis is presented to senior management for project approval, additional validations of project performance are reviewed and approved during a tollgate exercise. To prepare for this review, the project manager and team usually verify key

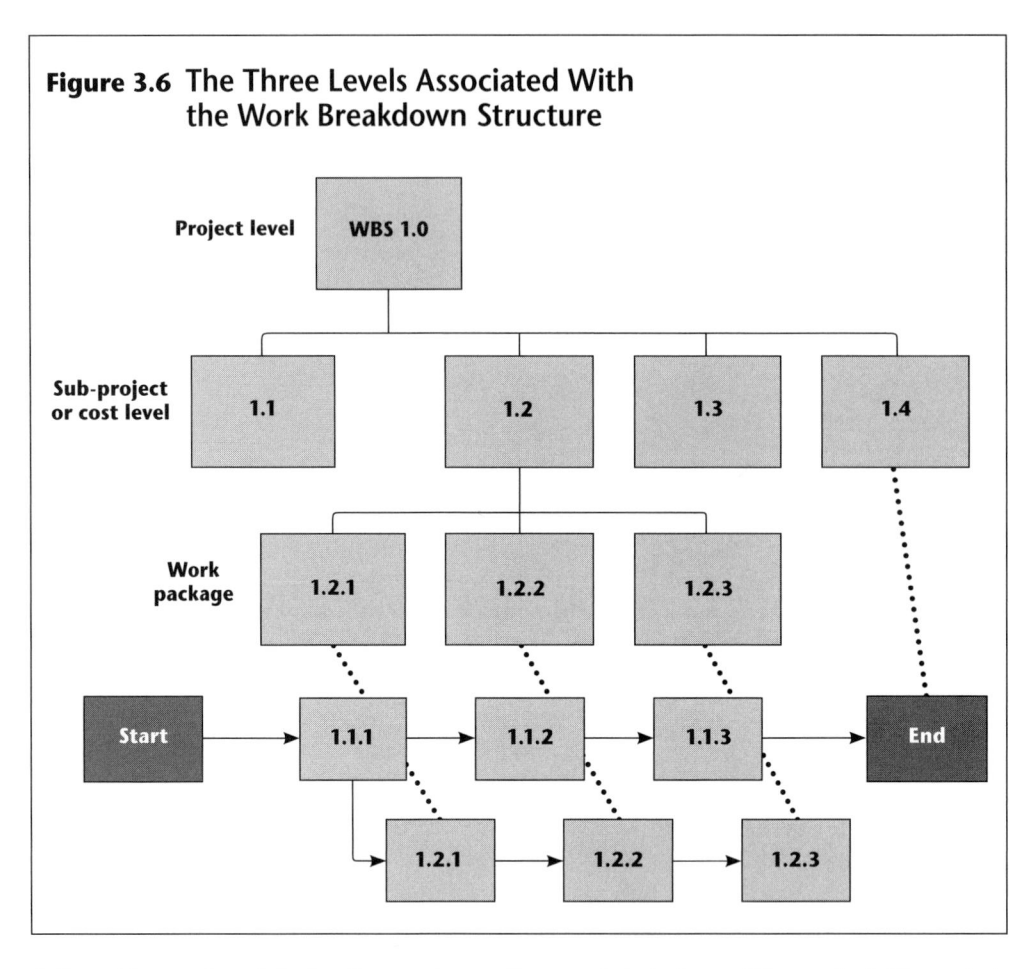

Project Management Excellence

Figure 3.6 The Three Levels Associated With the Work Breakdown Structure

```
Project level                      WBS 1.0

Sub-project
or cost level      1.1      1.2       1.3       1.4

Work
package         1.2.1    1.2.2    1.2.3

Start  →  1.1.1  →  1.1.2  →  1.1.3  →  End

              1.2.1  →  1.2.2  →  1.2.3
```

deliverables produced during the most recently completed phase of the project. These decision points enable all stakeholders to ensure that every deliverable is aligned with project objectives. The decision involves deliverable approval, rejection, or rework. If the work is rejected, the funding might be revoked for the project's remaining phases.

"Through 2003, organizations using rigorous gating criteria to move projects from the requirements phase to the development phase will save more than 25% in organizational cost for canceled projects."
—**Gartner Research**

Definition: *Stages* or *phases* are a set of prescribed and concurrent activities that should incorporate best practices.

In most cases activities and tasks are performed in parallel, not in sequence. Each stage or phase is preceded by a gate, which is used to verify that all activities and tasks are satisfactorily completed. Gatekeepers can choose to go ahead, kill, hold, prioritize, or recycle the project. The following are typical questions that are asked during a gate:

- How good a job was done by the project team?
- Was the stage or phase executed in a quality fashion?
- Does the project make good economic and business sense?
- Is the next phase's project plan sound?
- Is the action plan sound?
- How important is this project to the organization?

The outcome of the gate is that the project is prioritized in relationship with the other projects and resource allocation decisions are made.

Figure 3.7 is a typical new product development stage and stage-gate cycle.

Developing the Task Structure

The task definition activity organizes the entire project into executable tasks that are completed throughout the project life cycle. During this process the scope, risk, assumptions, constraints, and deliverables are documented and approved.

The project manager, along with the project sponsor and team, defines the major deliverables for each project phase and with that information develops the high-level milestone plan. The project leaders and team members render the high-level plan into discrete, executable tasks. As the project is broken down into simpler sets of tasks, the confidence of project delivery becomes greater.

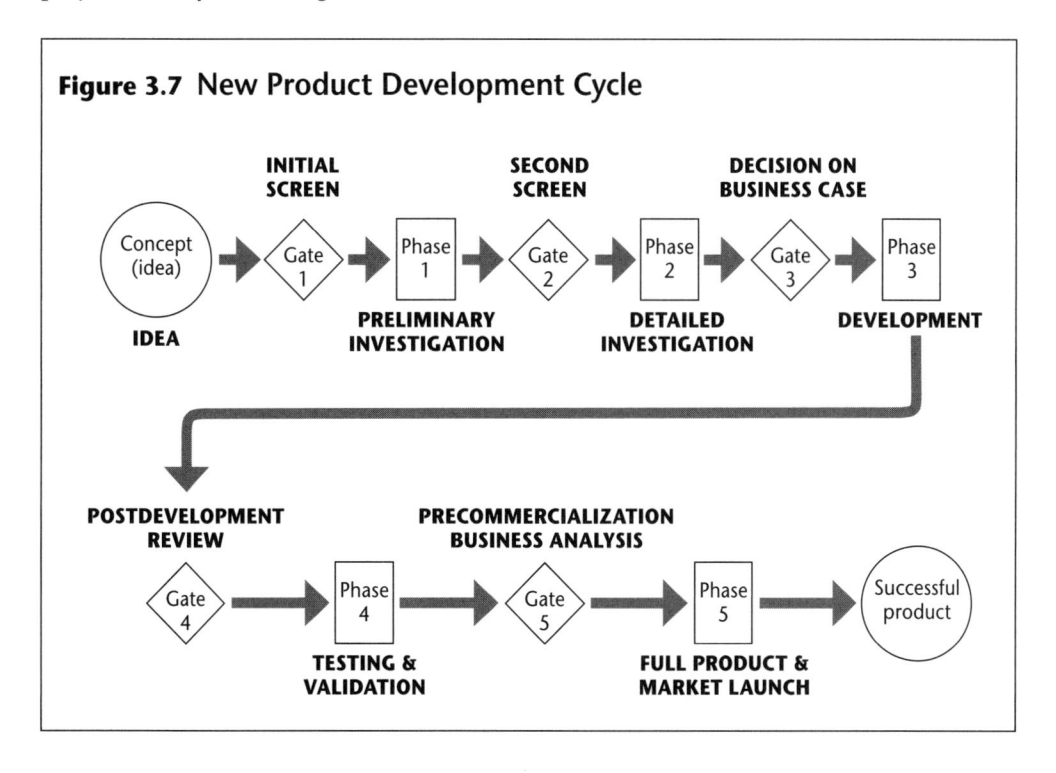

Figure 3.7 New Product Development Cycle

Task Sequencing

Task sequencing involves identifying and documenting the proper sequence and interaction between tasks. Certain tasks naturally follow in a prescribed sequence known as a mandatory dependency. For example, you must access the right software module before you actually write the code, and then you must write the code before the code is tested.

There may be times when a discretionary dependency is invoked even though it's not inherent to the prescribed process, but this dependency usually doesn't affect project scheduling. An example would be testing-strategy documentation that's normally created during the planning phase but can be completed as late as the early execution phase.

A third type of dependency is an external dependency, when something must be accomplished outside of the project's realm and if it isn't delivered, it would hamper an activity or task necessary for the project's success. An example would be unique hardware necessary for project testing that should be delivered prior to the start of testing. If the project subphase in question isn't tested completely, it could cause the project to fall behind schedule.

A project can also be dependent on output from another project to meet its own cost and schedule commitments. An example would be an alternate project that must upgrade software on a server prior to running new software on it. If the upgrade isn't completed, the current project delivery might not be tested in the right environment.

There are several relationships involved with sequencing tasks:

- *Finish to start*—successor starting depends on predecessor completing
- *Finish to finish*—one successor's completion depends on another successor's completion
- *Start to start*—one predecessor starting depends on another predecessor starting
- *Start to finish*—predecessor starting depends on successor completing

Estimate Task Effort and Duration

Generally, the more experience someone has in performing a task, the more accurate the estimate he or she gives the project manager will be. Many variables are used to estimate how much effort (or duration) is needed to complete a particular task and how much duration (or elapsed time) will be required. These variables include known constraints, assumptions, risks, historical information, and resource capabilities. The quality of estimates is dependent on the quality of information and the project life cycle phase the project is in.

For example, if a senior programmer leaves the organization and a less experienced programmer takes his place, the actual amount of time for a programming task might be 25 percent to 50 percent higher than originally estimated. In that case, unless a contingency was placed aside, the project would run over estimate by the amount indicated. When a person assigned to perform a task is known, it's best to let that person estimate the task with the team leader and project manager who review the estimate. There are two well-known reasons for this procedure:

Project Management Knowledge Areas

- The person performing the task should have the expertise and past experience with that type of estimated task and should be able to give an educated guess
- If the person performing the task provides the estimate, he or she will have a sense of "owning" it and will work hard to achieve it.

> "Estimating is experience-based, not technology-based."
> —HJH

If you don't know who will perform the task but people with more expertise are working close to the task that needs estimating, it's wise to let these experts prepare the estimate and then add a 25-percent contingency to cover a less experienced person carrying out the task.

Certain tasks are effort-driven with no constraints around the duration. Others are only duration-driven. For example, the walls of a house that can't be painted until the sheetrock is taped and textured is an effort-driven task. A duration-driven task would be more like painting the walls twice: The second coat can't be completed until the first is dried, no matter how many painters the project manager has assigned to the job.

An accepted practice with task duration is the "eighty-hour rule," which establishes that each individual should have some task due approximately every two weeks, representing a low-level milestone for him or her to reach. The project manager must take all estimates provided by the team members and leaders, roll them up, and review the project plan as a whole. The intention here is to spot an issue with the overall project schedule by examining the proportion of phases within stage(s) or iteration(s).

Develop the Schedule

Once you've estimated the time it takes to perform each activity, defined each activity's inputs and outputs, where each of these inputs come from, and where each output goes, you can start to develop a project schedule. This defines the start and finish date for each activity. Many things must be considered when developing a schedule. Some of them are:

- Activity duration estimates
- Resource requirements
- Resource availability
- Constraints (imposed dates or milestones)
- Assumptions
- Input from other projects
- Transportation delays
- Risk management plans
- Lead and lag times

Project Management Excellence

Although a number of software tools are available that can help you develop and optimize a schedule, we'll discuss a very simple approach we've found to be effective. We like to start with the output delivery date and work backward. From that point, we place the activity that will deliver that output to the customer on the right-hand side of a sheet of paper.

As an example, suppose your consulting firm has just conducted an employee-opinion survey for a customer. You've returned to your office with the survey sheets in hand. The next key delivery to your customer is on May 30, when you'll present the customer-survey results. Note in figure 3.8 that May 30 has a boxed-in point representing the deadline for presenting the report. Before that can happen, however, the consultant must travel to the client's office six hours away, so we include May 29 to complete that step.

Note also that that Saturday and Sunday aren't listed on the timeline axis of the graph in figure 3.8 because we don't want to schedule work on weekends. This builds in a little safety margin in case things go wrong.

The inputs the consultant needs to present the report are the PowerPoint slides he'll be using and copies of the report and travel arrangements. These three inputs are required for the consultant to travel to the client. Note that scheduling travel plans occurs on May 4.

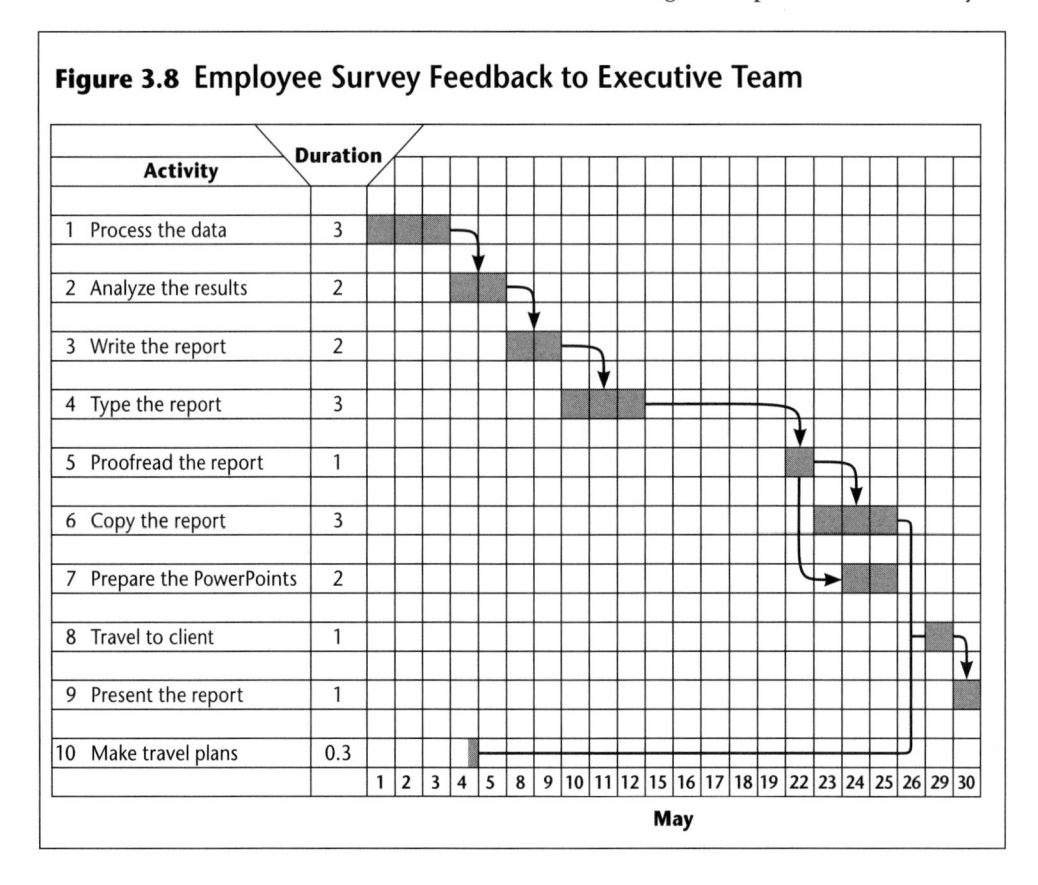

Figure 3.8 Employee Survey Feedback to Executive Team

Activity	Duration
1 Process the data	3
2 Analyze the results	2
3 Write the report	2
4 Type the report	3
5 Proofread the report	1
6 Copy the report	3
7 Prepare the PowerPoints	2
8 Travel to client	1
9 Present the report	1
10 Make travel plans	0.3

May

This is necessary because company policy requires consultants to make travel plans at least two weeks early to ensure minimum fares and best possible connections.

Input necessary to preparing the PowerPoint slides and duplicating the report includes having the final report proofread and approved. The latest date this can happen is Monday, May 22, because the report masters must be taken to the printer on May 23.

The input needed to proofread the report is a completed, typed report. Note that the report's schedule requires that it be completed five days before it's proofread. The reason for this delay is because the consultant, who's written the report, will be on assignment and won't be available for this project during the week of May 15.

Basically, when you create a schedule you determine when something must be delivered and then consider the activities required to deliver that output as well as the inputs required to provide the deliverable. Then you schedule the inputs and define what's required to generate them. This process is repeated until the schedule is complete.

Put another way, to develop a schedule you define a deliverable and then back up to define what actions are required to produce it, including the actions' duration, the inputs required to provide the output, and any additional transportation time that's involved.

The problem with this approach is that often the total cycle time is unacceptably long; often the start points have already passed. As an alternative, one of the following two techniques are used:

- *Crushing*. This is an approach in which cost and schedule are analyzed to determine how to obtain a greater amount of compression for the least increase in cost.
- *Fast tracking*. This is a means of determining if activities that would normally be done sequentially can be done in parallel. It also evaluates the possibility of assigning two individuals to an activity to reduce its duration. Fast tracking often results in rework and increased risk.

Five mathematical analysis techniques can help define duration limitations and reduce the total cycle time. They are:

- *Critical path method (CPM)*. This creates a path through the schedule that defines the total project cycle. Understanding the path allows the project team to focus on a smaller group of activities to determine how to reduce the project cycle time. Each time a critical path is eliminated, a new one is created for the project team to work on.
- *Critical chain method (CCM)*. This looks at the schedule to determine what resource restrictions have been imposed on the total cycle time. This allows you to assign additional or more skillful resources to reduce cycle time.
- *Graphical evaluation and review technique (GERT)*. This allows for a probable treatment of both work networks and activity duration estimates.

Project Management Excellence

- *Program evaluation and review technique (PERT)*. This uses a weighted-average duration estimate to calculate activity durations. It ends up with a PERT chart view of the project.
- *Simulation modeling*. Some people use this method to help reduce cycle time and cost, but we haven't found it particularly useful.

The most frequently used method to document a schedule is with a bar chart called a Gantt chart (see figure 3.9), which lists each activity that must be performed and visually indicates an activity's duration as well as the interrelationship between activities.

Other types of graphic presentations used to show schedules are project network diagrams and milestones charts.

Managing the Schedule

Once the initial schedule has been developed and approved, many factors can cause it to change. Some of them are:
- Changes in scope
- Issues that come up
- Risk mitigation plans that must be implemented
- Misunderstood requirements
- Slippage of other projects
- Changes in priorities
- Key staff leaving the project
- Late input from suppliers
- New requirements
- Poor time estimating
- Rework of outputs

Although many things can cause a project schedule to change, it's very important that management maintains control over the schedule. Any time a schedule change is necessary, a change request should be processed for approval by the appropriate management team. It's critical that effective configuration control be exercised over the schedule and other affected documents, such as the project cost estimate.

Often whenever a schedule is in danger of slipping, the project team develops a schedule recovery plan. This plan defines why the schedule is in jeopardy and outlines a corrective action plan to ensure the external customer receives a quality output on schedule.

Project Management Knowledge Areas

Figure 3.9 Combined Three-Year Improvement Plan

Typical Gantt chart

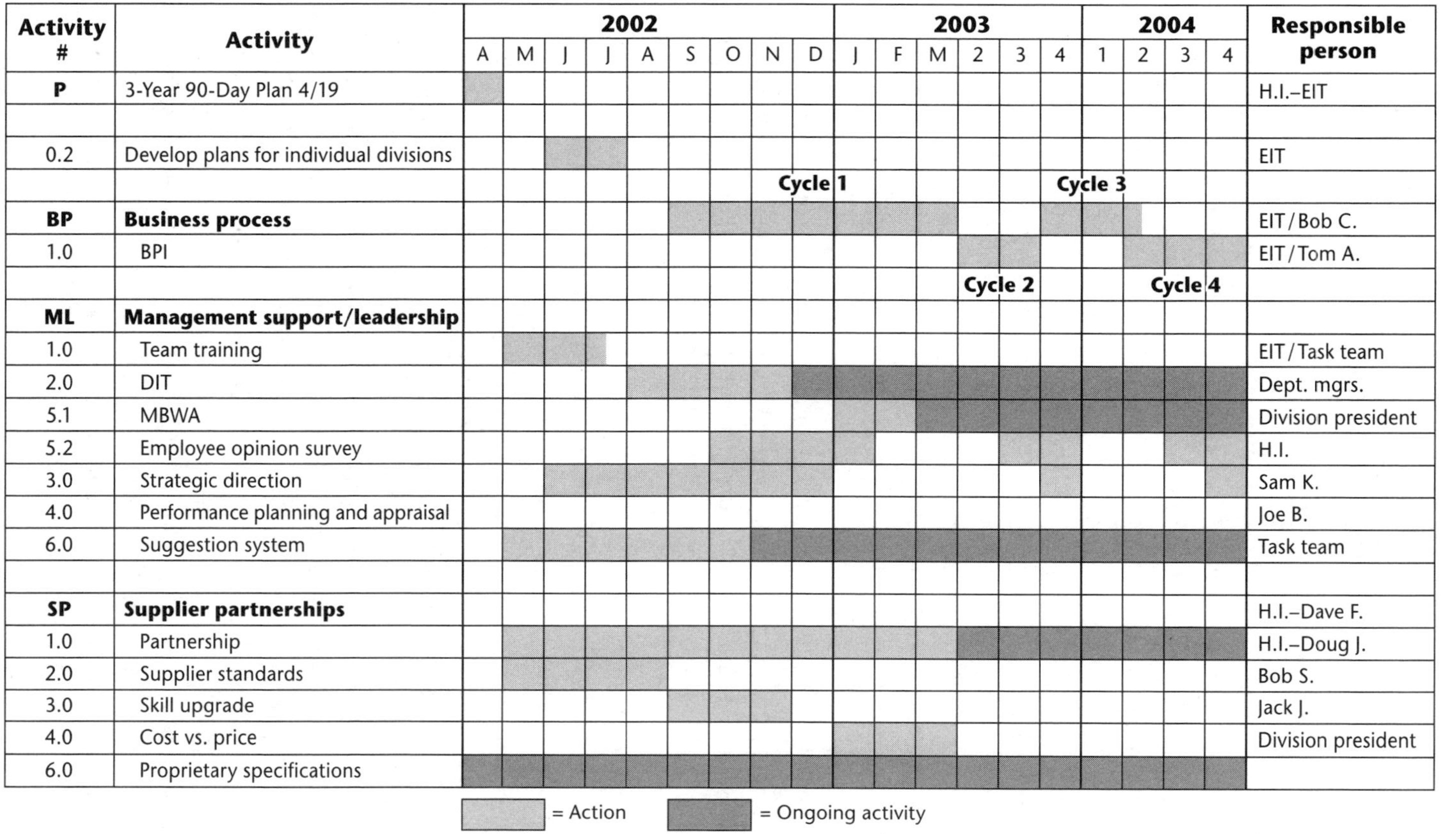

Activity #	Activity	2002 A M J J A S O N D	2003 J F M 2 3 4	2004 1 2 3 4	Responsible person
P	3-Year 90-Day Plan 4/19				H.I.–EIT
0.2	Develop plans for individual divisions				EIT
BP	**Business process**				
1.0	BPI	Cycle 1	Cycle 2	Cycle 3 ... Cycle 4	EIT/Bob C. / EIT/Tom A.
ML	**Management support/leadership**				
1.0	Team training				EIT/Task team
2.0	DIT				Dept. mgrs.
5.1	MBWA				Division president
5.2	Employee opinion survey				H.I.
3.0	Strategic direction				Sam K.
4.0	Performance planning and appraisal				Joe B.
6.0	Suggestion system				Task team
SP	**Supplier partnerships**				
1.0	Partnership				H.I.–Dave F.
2.0	Supplier standards				H.I.–Doug J.
3.0	Skill upgrade				Bob S.
4.0	Cost vs. price				Jack J.
6.0	Proprietary specifications				Division president

= Action   = Ongoing activity

63

PROJECT TIME MANAGEMENT

"Good estimators aren't modest: If it's huge, they say so."
—HJH

Project time management is a subset of project planning and estimating management that includes the processes required to ensure timely completion of a project. This subset consists of:

- *Activity definition*—identifying specific activities that must be performed to produce the various project deliverables
- *Activity sequencing*—identifying and documenting interactivity dependencies
- *Activity duration estimating*—forecasting the number of work periods that will be needed to complete individual activities
- *Schedule development*—analyzing activity sequences, activity durations, and resource requirements to create the project schedule
- *Schedule control*—monitoring changes to the project schedule

"There's never enough time to do it right the first time, but there's always enough time to go back and do it again."
—Anonymous

Project time management's primary purpose is estimating the effort (or time) required to do a project, measuring the time expended on the project, and taking action so individual tasks don't exceed their time estimates.

PROJECT FINANCIAL (COST) MANAGEMENT

Project financial (cost) management is a step-by-step process of resource planning and cost estimating, budgeting, and control. A project's early phases might have a lower cost estimate accuracy than later phases. Cost estimates improve in accuracy as details surrounding the project and work plan increase.

Cost management first ensures that funds are available to successfully complete the project and then tracks and controls the funds to prevent an overrun. It includes preparing periodic updates of actual versus planned project costs and a schedule based on accomplishments to date. It's a subset of project management that includes the processes required to ensure a project is completed within the approved budget. Cost management consists of:

- *Resource planning*—determining which resources (e.g., people, equipment, materials) and what quantities of each should be used to perform project activities
- *Cost estimating*—developing an approximation (or estimate) of the costs of the resources needed to complete project activities

- *Cost budgeting*—allocating the overall cost estimate to individual work items
- *Cost control*—controlling changes to the project budget

Cost management's primary purpose is estimating the cost related to performing a project, measuring the amount of money expended on the project, and taking action to ensure that each task doesn't exceed its allotted budget.

PROJECT QUALITY MANAGEMENT

Project quality management improves the probability of project and solution success by identifying and then correcting or preventing process or solution quality issues that cause delays, overruns, and inferior solutions. Project quality management includes embedding quality checkpoints into project work plans, e.g., peer or quality assurance reviews to evaluate project quality at the end of a phase. This means identifying quality management plan(s) and standards, developing quality management communications, executing a project's quality plan, analyzing results of implementing the project's quality process, and repeating and refining the project's quality management plan when necessary.

Project quality management is a subset of project management that includes the processes required to ensure the project will satisfy the needs for which it was undertaken. It consists of:

- *Quality planning*—identifying quality standards relevant to the project and determining how to meet them
- *Quality assurance*—evaluating overall project performance regularly to ensure projects will satisfy relevant quality standards
- *Quality control*—monitoring specific project results to determine if they comply with relevant quality standards, and identifying ways to eliminate causes of unsatisfactory performance

Project quality management's primary purpose is to ensure that deliverables meet the documented requirements and needs of the intended user(s).

It's very important to ensure that the quality plan includes the following two parts:

- *Prevention.* What's done during the project to ensure quality (e.g., training, reviews, gates, requirement statements, audits, change management, team synergy, surface issues)
- *Inspection.* What's done at the last step of each deliverable to ensure quality

PROJECT HUMAN RESOURCE MANAGEMENT

> "Few enterprises are committed to strategic resource planning (i.e., to a process for systematically aligning strategic business plans with human resource acquisition, training, reskilling and retention)."
> —Gartner Research

Project human resource management's purpose is to match the right skills, experience, interests, and availability with project staffing requirements to ensure quality work is produced efficiently. This subset of project management includes organizational planning, staff acquisition, and team development and training.

Project human resource management includes the processes required to make the most effective use of the people involved within the project team. That requires:

- *Organizational planning*—identifying, documenting, and assigning project roles, responsibilities, and reporting relationships
- *Staff acquisition*—getting the human resources needed assigned to and working on a project
- *Team development*—developing individual and group skills to enhance project performance

PROJECT COMMUNICATIONS MANAGEMENT

Project communications management helps sustain strong project sponsor, stakeholder, and team support and involvement by providing the right information, at the right time, in the right format, delivered by the right person to the appropriate stakeholder. Project communications management can be both internal and external to the organization. It might be periodic, as in performance reporting (e.g., weekly project status reports), or a one-time event, as in publicly announcing a new product.

This subset of project management includes the processes required to ensure timely and appropriate generation, collection, dissemination, storage, and ultimate disposition of project information. That requires:

- *Communications planning*—determining stakeholders' information and communication needs: who needs what information, when they'll need it, and how it will be given to them
- *Information distribution*—making needed information available to project stakeholders in a timely manner
- *Performance reporting*—collecting and disseminating performance information. This includes status reporting, progress measurement, and forecasting
- *Administrative closure*—generating, gathering, and disseminating information to formalize phase or project completion

PROJECT RISK MANAGEMENT

> "Information systems organizations that lack stringent risk assessment procedures will continue to cancel more than 20 percent of application development projects in the execution phase."
> —Gartner Research

An issue is a situation, action, problem, decision, or question that, if not resolved, might affect the project scope, schedule, cost, or quality. Issues surface from all project levels and sources. Issue management's purpose is to proactively identify issues that, if not resolved, will impede the project. The issue management process must establish an effective channel for obtaining decisions and approvals prior to when a project will be impeded.

Issues can become scope change requests, depending on the alternative chosen or decision to be made. If the preferred decision requires a scope change, then the issue enters the scope management process.

Project risk management is a subset of project management that includes the processes concerned with identifying, analyzing, and responding to project risk. That requires:

- *Risk identification*—determining which risks are likely to affect the project and documenting the characteristics of each
- *Risk quantification*—evaluating risks and risk interactions to assess the range of possible project outcomes
- *Risk response development*—defining enhancement steps for opportunities and responses to threats
- *Risk response control*—responding to changes in risk during the course of the project

PROJECT PROCUREMENT MANAGEMENT

Project procurement management includes the processes necessary to acquire goods and services from external organizations. That involves documenting a procurement plan, planning the solicitation of goods and services, soliciting suppliers for goods and services, selecting the source and/or supplier, administering the contract, and closing the contract out when complete.

Project procurement management is a subset of project management that includes the processes necessary to acquire goods and services from outside the performing organization. That requires:

- *Procurement planning*—determining what to procure and when
- *Solicitation planning*—documenting product requirements and identifying potential sources
- *Solicitation*—obtaining quotes, bids, offers, or proposals as appropriate
- *Source selection*—choosing from among potential sellers

- *Contract administration*—managing the relationship with the seller
- *Contract closeout*—completing and settling the contract, including resolving any open items

ORGANIZATIONAL CHANGE MANAGEMENT

> "Those who prosper in our unconstant world accept change as a positive force and can persuade others to do the same. Those fearful of change or unable to rally others in new directions will be steamrollered with the volatility of modern organizations. You can get others to go along with useful change with a minimum of resistance."
>
> —Alvin Toffler
> Author and futurist

This part of project management isn't part of the PMBOK concept covered in *A Guide to the Project Management Body of Knowledge*. Occupational change management (OCM) focuses on the people side of a project. It helps prepare those affected by the project to accept and, when required, commit to the change, even to look forward to it. The OCM subset of project management consists of:

- *OCM planning*—defining the level of resistance to change and preparing a plan to offset the resistance
- *Define roles and develop competencies*—identify who will serve as sponsors, change agents, change targets, and change advocates, and then train each individual on how to perform the specific role
- *Establish burning platform*—define the situation in a way that status-quo costs become prohibitively expensive. In such circumstances, major change isn't just a good idea; it's a business imperative.
- *Transformation management*—implement the OCM plan. Test for black holes and lack of acceptance. Train affected personnel in new skills required by the change.

PROJECT PORTFOLIO MANAGEMENT

> "Those businesses that implement a systematic process for managing their projects' portfolios clearly outperform the rest."
>
> —Robert G. Cooper
> Professor of marketing,
> McMaster University
> School of Business

Most of our discussion to this point has been on how to do projects right, but equally important is doing the right projects. Most organizations must consider many projects to improve their performance, far more than the resources available to support them. In addition, proposed projects usually cost more and take longer to complete than the sponsor estimates. Project portfolio management concerns how an organization spends its discretionary capital and people resources to ensure it reaps the most benefit from the projects it undertakes. It's the means by which an organization can turn strategy into operational activity.

Project Management Knowledge Areas

As we've seen, it's difficult enough to manage one project, but with a portfolio of projects, the complexity and difficulty increases a hundredfold. A study on project portfolio management conducted by Northwestern University's Kellogg School of Management found that 80 percent of senior executives reported that a lack of financial skills in their information technology departments made it difficult to track IT investments' value.

Organizations are plagued with problems like:
- Too many approved projects for available resources
- Poor project mix
- Poor view of the total project portfolio
- Effects created on one or more projects when another slips
- Projects failing to provide the projected performance improvement
- Project knowledge and best practices not transferred to proposed and ongoing projects

It's not enough to perform and control an individual project well. In addition, an organization must select winning projects and manage their portfolios of approved projects. This requires an effective online reporting system that summarizes project status at least once a week, if not daily. Such a system allows management to identify problem projects and instigate corrective action to keep projects on track. In most organizations today, close adherence to schedule is more important than cost. The executive team also needs a "history warehouse" to compare proposed projects to actual costs and cycle-time data from completed projects. This allows the team to determine if the estimates are accurate. Management wouldn't approve one-third of proposed projects if it knew how long they're going to take and how much they'll cost.

Too Many Approved Projects

This problem occurs when management approves too many projects for the available capital and skilled human resources, or when it approves projects that require more resources than originally projected. The solution is easy to state but hard to implement: The organization must kill the projects that are lowest on its priority list until a balance is established between program requirements and available resources.

> "A rigorous and formalized project-portfolio management strategy was considered fundamental to success."
> —**Norbert Turek**
> *Information Week*

Usually projects are approved one project at a time with little or no consideration about the total workload. It's easy to identify the types of people required for projects, and in many cases, even name individuals who should be assigned without considering their total workload. In this way individuals end up committing 160 percent of their time, which results in less-than-satisfactory job performance and failed projects.

Project Management Excellence

Figure 3.10 Human Resource Availability Versus Time

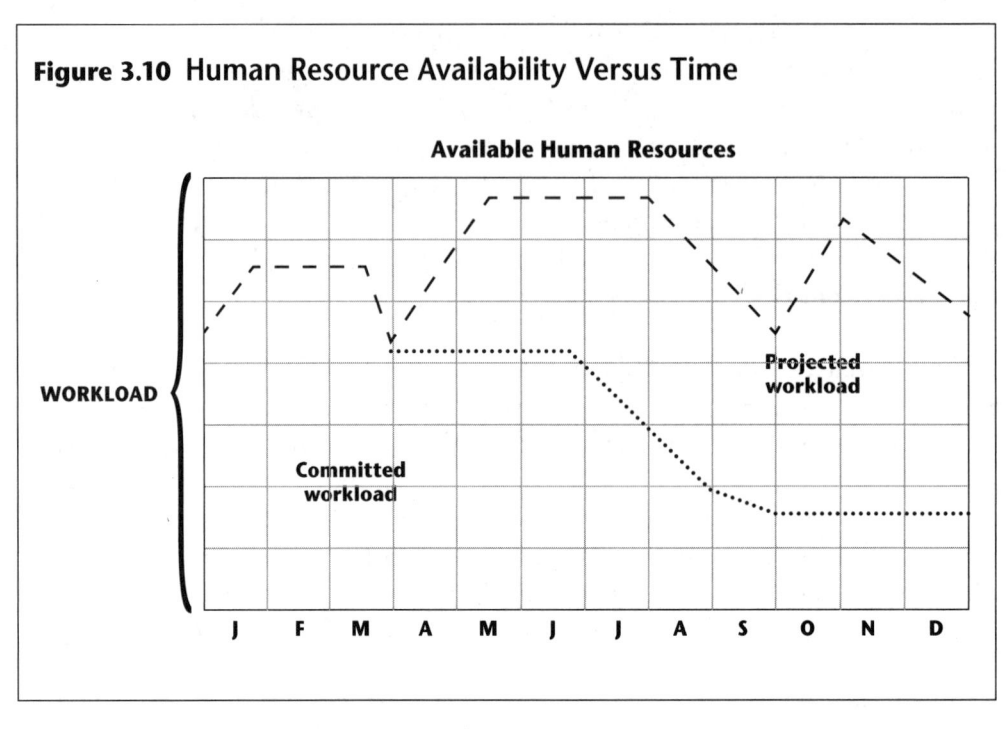

Figure 3.11 Skills Requirements Versus Resources

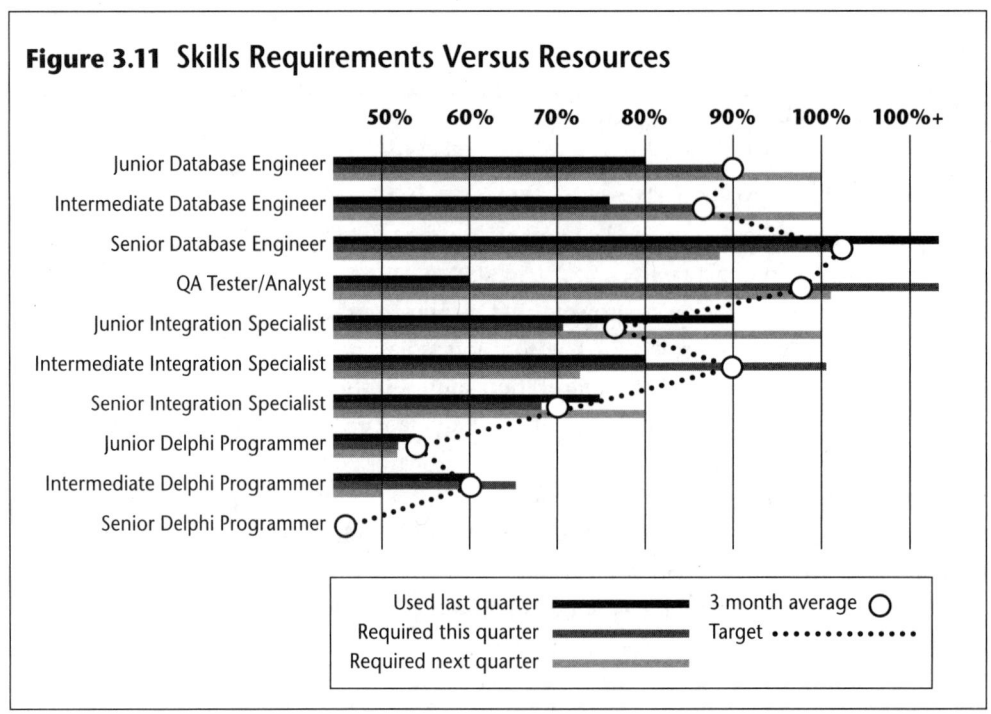

Another consideration is the skills required to perform project activities and tasks. All too frequently an adequate amount of human resources are available (see figure 3.10), but these people don't have the skills required to perform the tasks in the project portfolio (see figure 3.11).

When a skill mismatch occurs, management has only four options:
- Kill the project.
- Train someone to do the job.
- Hire people with the proper skills.
- Subcontract the work.

The first option reduces the organization's total performance. The last three options increase the project's cost.

Having unskilled or too few people performing project activities causes major problems. Unskilled people make errors that result in schedule slippage and increased cost. Overworked people cut corners and, as a result, project output doesn't meet committed requirements.

The long-range fix is to prepare a skills forecast and then train people who have surplus skills, or hire people to fill the void. Another approach is to hold off on low-priority projects that require critical-skills people. This requires forced ranking of projects, and that's always a difficult task. Too often we use tools such as net present value (NPV), which was developed for single projects, not a portfolio of projects. To add to the problem, NPV calculations are less accurate during a project's early stages when the first go/no-go decision must be made. We've seen data indicating that NPV estimates could be off by an average of as much as 300 percent.

The best time to stop a project you don't know is going to succeed is *before* you start it. One approach to prioritizing projects is to use scoring models that include considerations such as:
- Strategic fit and importance
- Market effect
- Competitive advantage
- Profit opportunity
- Resources required to implement

> "The best time to stop a project that you don't know is going to be successful is when you start it."
> —John Carrow
> CEO, Unisys Corp.

With this scoring model you select the considerations that must be evaluated when making a decision about a project's importance to the organization. Then for each project, the selection team rates each consideration on a scale of one to ten. The sum of the individual consideration ratings is the weighting factor for the project. This allows an organization to compare the importance of all its projects and assign priorities accordingly. Sometimes the individual considerations will be assigned different weighting factors. For example, the

Figure 3.12 Evaluating a Project's Importance

Project A			
Consideration	**Rating**	**Weighting**	**Rating**
Impact on customer	1 2 3 4 5 ⑥ 7 8 9 10	3	18
Impact on morale	1 2 3 4 5 6 7 ⑧ 9 10	1	8

critical considerations might be given a weighting factor of three while minor considerations would be assigned a weighting factor of one. (See figure 3.12.) If the consideration would have a major effect on output to the external customer, it would usually be rated a three. Normally, considerations that would affect only morale would be rated a one unless morale was a major problem within the organization.

Our analysis indicates that one-third of all projects undertaken wouldn't be approved if the executive team knew how long they were going to take and how much they'd cost. For this very reason it's important that a knowledge management system, which collects historical data about actual project-cycle time and cost, is a component of the project portfolio management database. This allows the executive team to compare project cost and cycle time estimates to past actual performance for similar type projects to gain a realistic view of a proposed project's true cost, cycle time, and effect.

Poor Project Mix

If the executive team doesn't manage the project portfolio, too many small projects tend to be approved. Many executives will approve small, low-cost projects with less scrutiny than they give to complex ones. Because they have an immediate affect on profit, quick-payback, short-range projects are very attractive to executive teams. Certainly these projects are important, but the organization also must invest in its future. Pools of money and human resources should be set aside to ensure the proper balance of projects, such as:

- Long-term versus short-term projects
- Technical development projects versus extension projects
- High-risk versus low-risk projects
- Modifying versus firefighting projects

The key to proper prioritization is the quality of input data, not the decision model.

"The sophistication of the model exceeds the quality of the data in most cases."

—HJH

Ongoing Project Portfolio Management

Project portfolio management goes far beyond project selection. It's used at each phase gate to determine if the project is still viable. Depending on the data collected at each gate, the project can be dropped, put on hold, reprioritized, or approved to move on to the next phase. As questionable projects are defined and dropped, remaining projects are compared individually against the total project portfolio and ranked according to priority.

Project portfolio management isn't simply a go/no-go activity; it's also a corrective action system. It can provide the executive team and project office with exception notices that alert them to problematic projects. The team can then either salvage or cancel the projects before additional resources are expended waiting for a scheduled phase gate. Figures 3.13 and 3.14 are typical examples of project portfolio exception reports that highlight problem projects.

Project Portfolio Review

Horizon Blue Cross Blue Shield's CEO holds quarterly project reviews of his direct reports to analyze the organization's thirty-nine largest projects—all budgeted for more than $1 million and representing only 15 percent of the organization's project portfolio. Each CEO of Horizon's eighteen divisions conduct similar reviews. As a result, Horizon is ahead of schedule on its legacy-reduction effort.

At least twice a year, the project portfolio review team (comprised of executives) should conduct a comprehensive review of all projects. The review team checks on the phase gates to confirm the organization's needs and strategies are being supported. The reviews are based upon an analysis of how strategic imperatives have changed as well as changes in the marketplace since the last project portfolio review. The process identifies overall bottlenecks that have occurred across projects and their affect on the portfolio. During the meeting all project data are discussed and project prioritization is adjusted as needed. In addition, the portfolio balance is reviewed, and action plans are generated to ensure proper balance. Each project competes against the others for resources and ranking. Typical factors that are reviewed during the meeting are:

- Availability of technical resources
- Two-year return on investment
- Confidence in the project team
- Confidence in resources and scheduled excellence
- Alignment with the organization's business plan

> "There's a visibility and accountability now that wasn't there before. Some people don't like it; they feel it cramps their style. But the results have been great."
> —**Pamela Miller**
> **Vice president of Enterprise Solutions,**
> **Horizon Blue Cross Blue Shield**

During the meeting the portfolio review team will identify mandatory projects that can't be touched. They'll also identify projects that should be dropped. Projects that fall in the middle of these extremes are then force-ranked, based upon selection criteria established by the team.

Project Management Excellence

Figure 3.13 Sample Project Performance Chart

Projects	Dates 2000											2001		Forecasted finish date
	Feb	Mar	Apr	May	Jun	July	Aug	Sep	Oct	Nov	Dec	Jan	Feb	
Litton														3/1/01
Bosch														1/15/01
BofA-S.F.														3/1/01
BofA-S.J.														3/1/01
BofA-L.A.														3/1/01
FAC														5/1/01
Ord. entry														4/1/01
Proj. mgt.														7/15/01
Six Sigma														6/1/01
Opport. mgt.														4/10/01
Supplier load														4/1/01
H.R. control														4/1/01
Customer inv.														6/1/01
														3/7/01

February 2001

= On time and on budget
= On time and over budget
= Late and on budget
= Late and over budget

74

Figure 3.14 Sample Executive Exception Report

January 31, 2001						
Project name	Project manager	Priority	Days late	Forecasted Over budgeted $	%	% Complete	Issue #
Litton	Tom PM1	900	20	–	–	80%	P01-113
Customer inv.	June PM5	900	37	0.8M	23%	78%	P13-68
Bosch	Ruth PM3	700	28	–	–	100%	P02-21
FAC	Hue PM8	600	28	0.8M	26%	42%	P06-12
Supplier load	Tom PM1	600	–	0.5M	28%	73%	P11-81
Project mgt.	Pierre PM4	500	–	0.8M	26%	50%	P08-69
H.R. controls	Chan PM7	300	32	1.4M	23%	22%	P12-38

Rules:
More than twenty days late
More than $0.49M over budget
More than 30 percent over budget

Project Portfolio Management Software

Many organizations' portfolios include large projects that involve hundreds of skilled employees working concurrently. Consequently, executive teams require constantly updated views of all projects so they can make intelligent business decisions.

As indicated in figure 3.15, projects, resources, and knowledge must all be managed to gain real business intelligence and effectively maintain a project portfolio. Here's why:

- *Project management*—because executives need to know the status of projects and what resources are required for them
- *Resource management*—because executives need to know which resources are used and which are available
- *Knowledge management*—because executives need to capture best practices, potential problems, and actual-performance data from previously implemented or current projects

To adequately manage a project portfolio, you must look at trends in the total calculation of projects in many different ways. (See figure 3.16.)

Figures 3.17 and 3.18 represent long-term analyses of a standard accounting program software project run by a theoretical organization. Figure 3.17 provides an analysis of the variation in costs and duration in a histogram format. Figure

> "Project portfolio management software is helping Horizon Blue Cross Blue Shield of New Jersey, a $6 billion-plus health insurance provider, make its move from a not-for-profit to a for-profit health insurer."
> —Norbert Turek
> *Information Week*

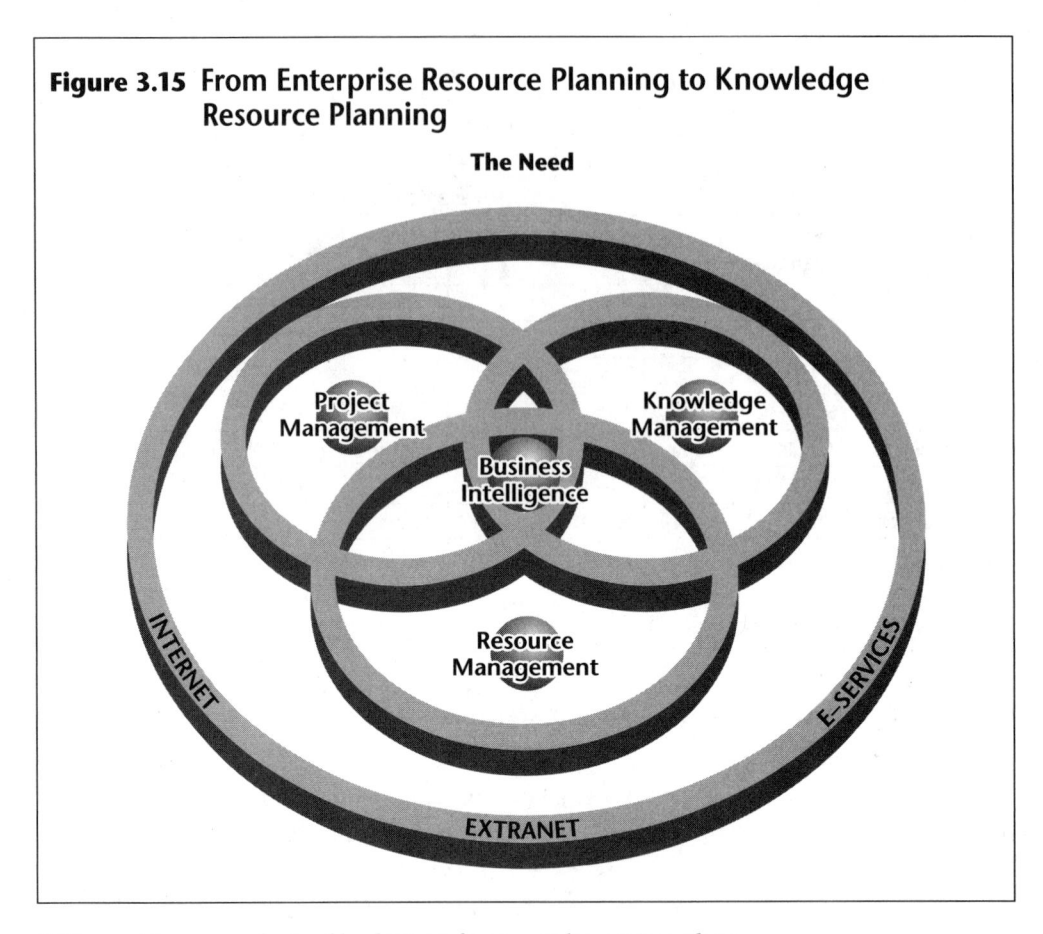

Figure 3.15 From Enterprise Resource Planning to Knowledge Resource Planning

3.18 provides an analysis of budget performance by project phase.

Figure 3.19 is an analysis of why changes in scope occurred and their effect on the project portfolio.

It's imperative that organizations include a project resource management database in their project portfolio management software. This database should include not only committed and actual time expended by projects but also a skills inventory for each employee. Management can then analyze human resource needs by skill level, as indicated in figure 3.18, and use such data to define future hiring requirements and employee training programs.

A resource database also allows people to be notified when a task in an individual project slips and consequently increases their available free time. Additional assignments can fill in these voids. An individual is automatically put on the availability list if his or her workload drops below a preset value, usually seven days of unscheduled work, but some organizations set it at as little as one. In consulting firms like IBM and Cap Gemini Ernst & Young, where the break-even point is about 53 percent utilization, a 5 percent improvement in uti-

Figure 3.16 Business Intelligence

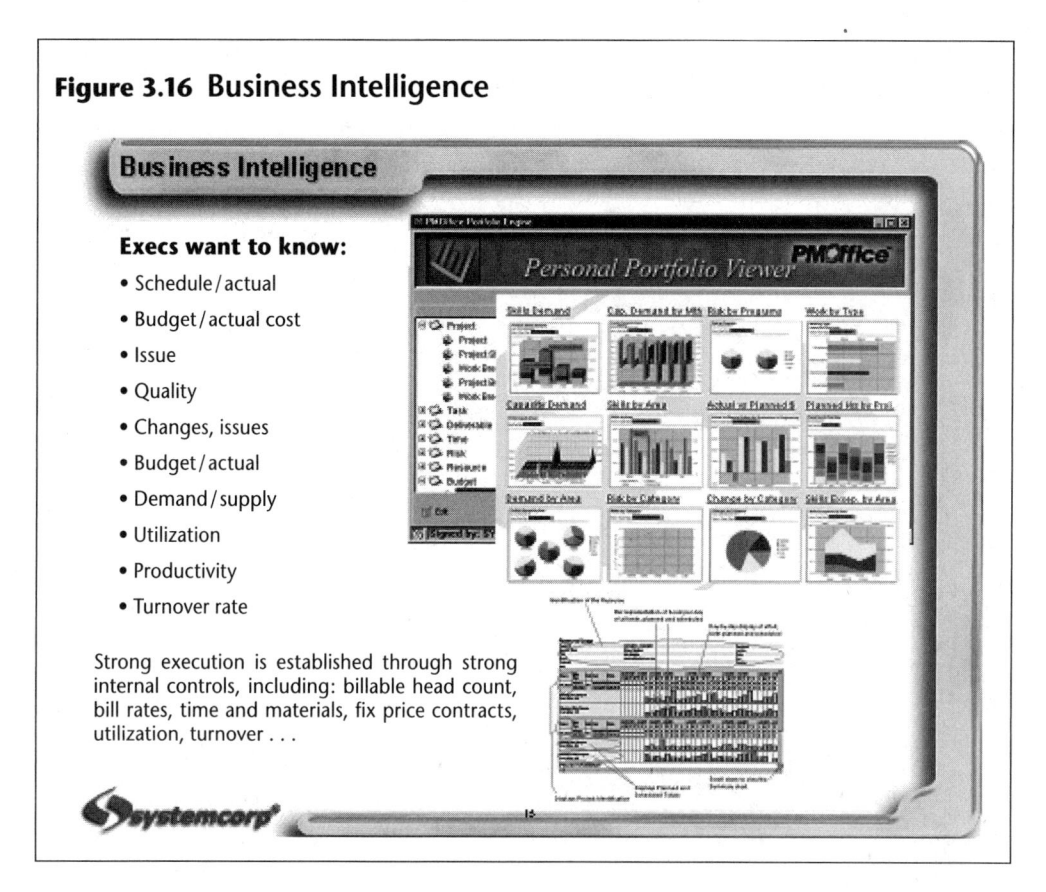

Business Intelligence

Execs want to know:
- Schedule/actual
- Budget/actual cost
- Issue
- Quality
- Changes, issues
- Budget/actual
- Demand/supply
- Utilization
- Productivity
- Turnover rate

Strong execution is established through strong internal controls, including: billable head count, bill rates, time and materials, fix price contracts, utilization, turnover . . .

lization, from 58 percent to 63 percent, doubles the organization's profit. However, when the required input doesn't arrive on time and isn't reported to the management team, the individual makes work or slows down to compensate, a poor use of this valuable additional resource.

Among other things, project portfolio management software should provide templates of typical projects that include actual performance data and related materials as well as output data. This allows the project team to take a proven work breakdown structure (WBS) and quickly modify it to meet the specifications of their present project. This greatly reduces the time required to prepare a WBS while drastically improving the quality of the estimates and process flow.

A number of companies sell project management software packages. Some of them are:
- Artemis International Solutions
- Microsoft Project
- Primavera Systems
- ABT/NIKU
- PlanView

Figure 3.17 SAP Cost and Duration Variance

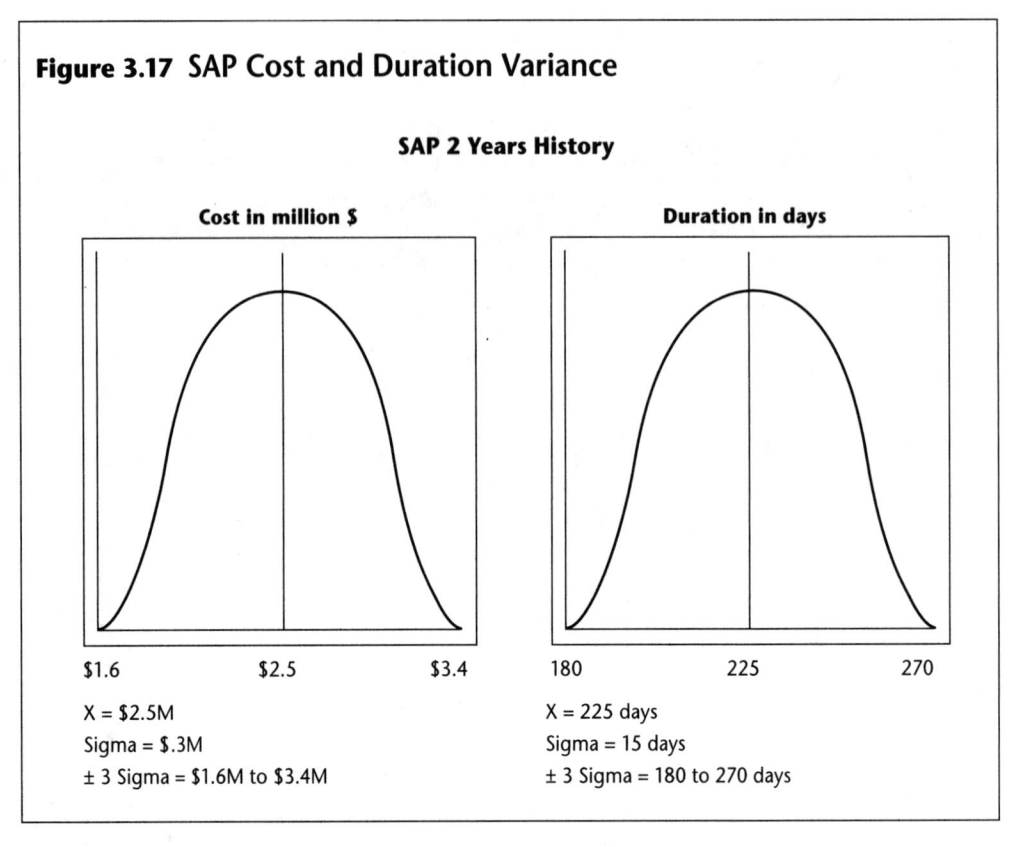

SAP 2 Years History

Cost in million $

$1.6 $2.5 $3.4
X = $2.5M
Sigma = $.3M
± 3 Sigma = $1.6M to $3.4M

Duration in days

180   225   270
X = 225 days
Sigma = 15 days
± 3 Sigma = 180 to 270 days

- Changepoint
- Lawson Software
- Pacific Edge
- Business Engine
- Systemcorp

Gartner Group rates Systemcorp's PMOffice as the most advanced of all the project management software solutions, but Microsoft Project is the most used. Microsoft Corp. owns at least 80 percent of the application, and because it's simple to use and has very few special requirements, it's somewhat limited in what it can do. Usually an organization starts with Microsoft Project and then migrates to more advanced packages. Most advanced software packages are completely compatible with Microsoft Project and allow for easy migration. One strong advantage of Microsoft Project is its resource-leveling package that's extremely effective.

> **"We're always looking for the 90-percent [market] solution."**
> —**Zena Girdler**
> **Product manager, Microsoft Project**

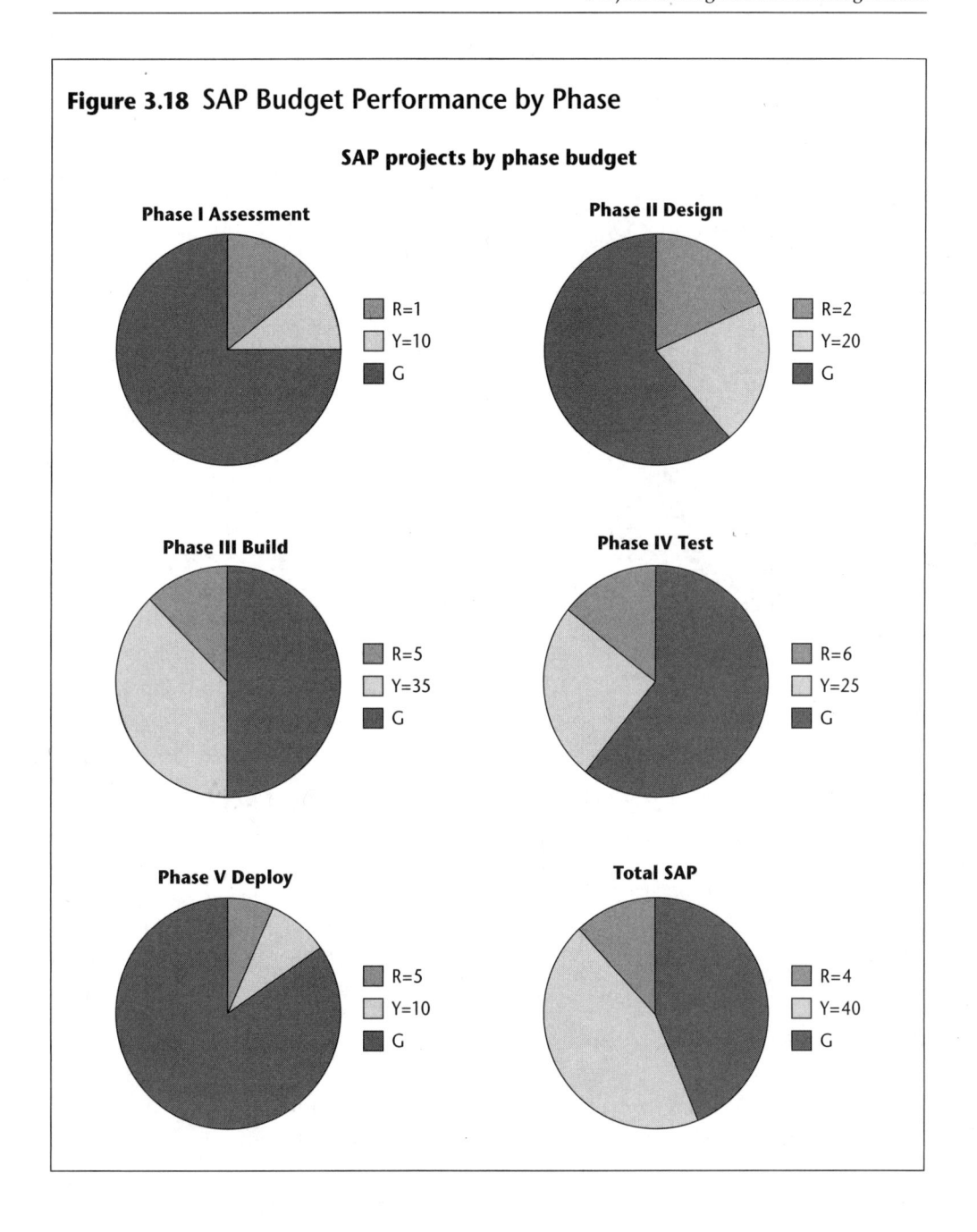

Project Management Knowledge Areas

Figure 3.18 SAP Budget Performance by Phase

SAP projects by phase budget

Phase I Assessment
- R=1
- Y=10
- G

Phase II Design
- R=2
- Y=20
- G

Phase III Build
- R=5
- Y=35
- G

Phase IV Test
- R=6
- Y=25
- G

Phase V Deploy
- R=5
- Y=10
- G

Total SAP
- R=4
- Y=40
- G

Figure 3.19 Scope Analysis

Scope change driver

Why
- New requirement 18%
- Change requirement 41%

Effect
- Budget increase 10%
- Budget and/or schedule decrease 8%
- Schedule increase 12%
- Budget and schedule increase 70%

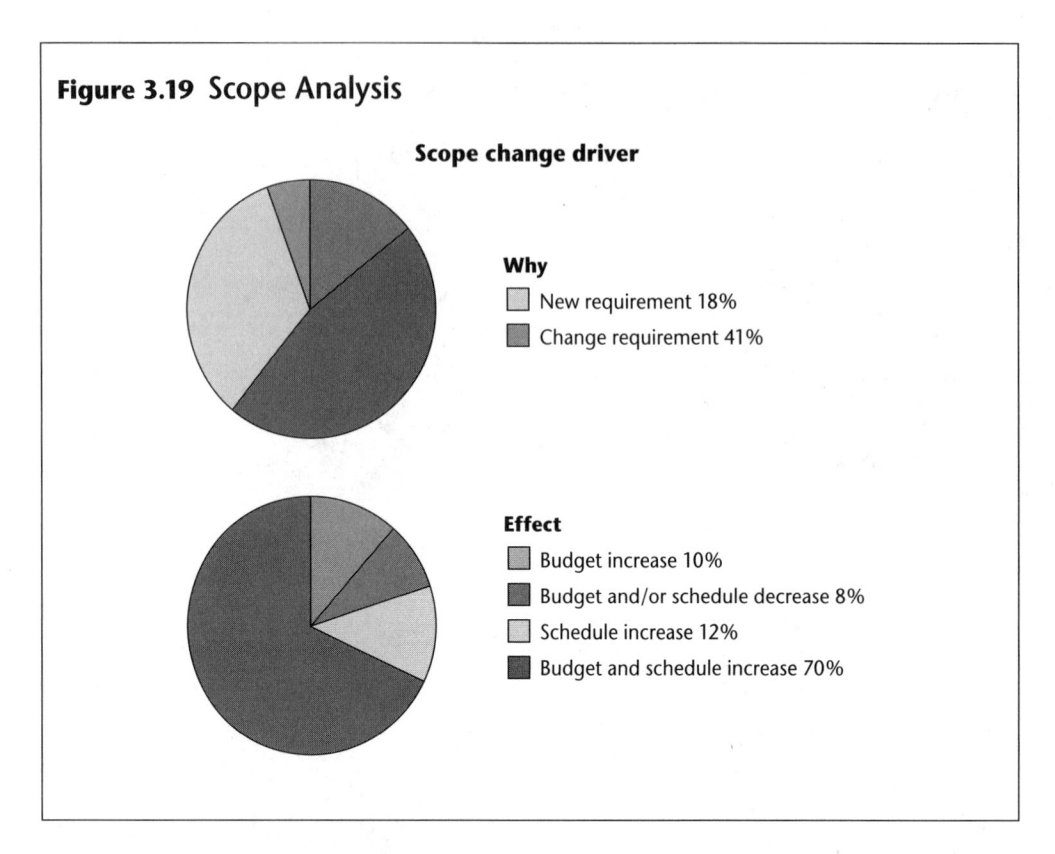

PROJECT DOCUMENT/CONFIGURATION MANAGEMENT

Project document/configuration management is a documented procedure designed to accomplish the following:
- Identify and document the functional and physical characteristics of an item.
- Control changes to deliverables and documents.
- Document changes and their status.
- Audit items to verify conformance to requirements.

In many cases, document management is a systematic effort to manage a project's changes. In other cases, it's used to ensure that a project's product description is correct and complete.

Each time a change occurs to a project's documents or potential project's outputs, a control number or letter in the document management program changes. All changes must be approved by a predefined set of individuals. These change requests are accompanied with an explanation of why the change is being made and how the change will affect the project (e.g., a change in cost or schedule). One of the most overlooked tasks of project documentation/configuration management is removing out-of-date documents and drawings from the process.

> "Managing a project is a lot like driving a car at night. You can see only as far as your headlights illuminate, but that's enough to get you home safely."
>
> —HJH

CHAPTER IV

PROJECT SELECTION

"Most projects start on a high note in the black and end up on a low note in the red."

—HJH

The project management life cycle is neither complicated nor hard to understand. We break it down into the six phases shown in figure 4.1. Projects, especially large-scale ones, are easier to control if they're reviewed at the tollgates set up at the end of each phase.

Project management is a methodology that involves cycles. Remember that a project is a temporary endeavor with a specific beginning and end. The cycle for project selection, initiation, planning, execution, control, and closeout will vary depending on the goals the team is pursuing (i.e., information technology, process improvement, or new products or services.)

A phased approach provides not only a consistent and repeatable project-delivery framework, but also allows for project evaluation by means of gates or decision points. The phase and subphase life cycle applies to all types of projects and ensures that the project team maintains momentum from phase to phase, and that proper decisions are made to avoid resource commitments where inappropriate. For example, it's critical for the project sponsor to give clear directions during the project initiation phase to ensure the team focuses on requirements as it enters the planning phase.

The components that constitute team direction are included in the project planning phase. However, gathering requirements can begin before formally signing off on the project plan if the project manager and sponsor feel confident in the project's direction. However, there's a risk that if scope and objectives aren't clearly defined prior to defining requirements, the project team could spend time and money pursuing the wrong activities.

The same can be said for phase-level decision points or gates. For example, while completing the planning phase—which includes updating the business case and cost-benefit analysis (CBA), and securing management approval to proceed—the project team could proceed with execution-phase tasks, as long as the project manager and sponsor are confident the CBA will support continuing the project. This would make optimum use of resources and keep team momentum going.

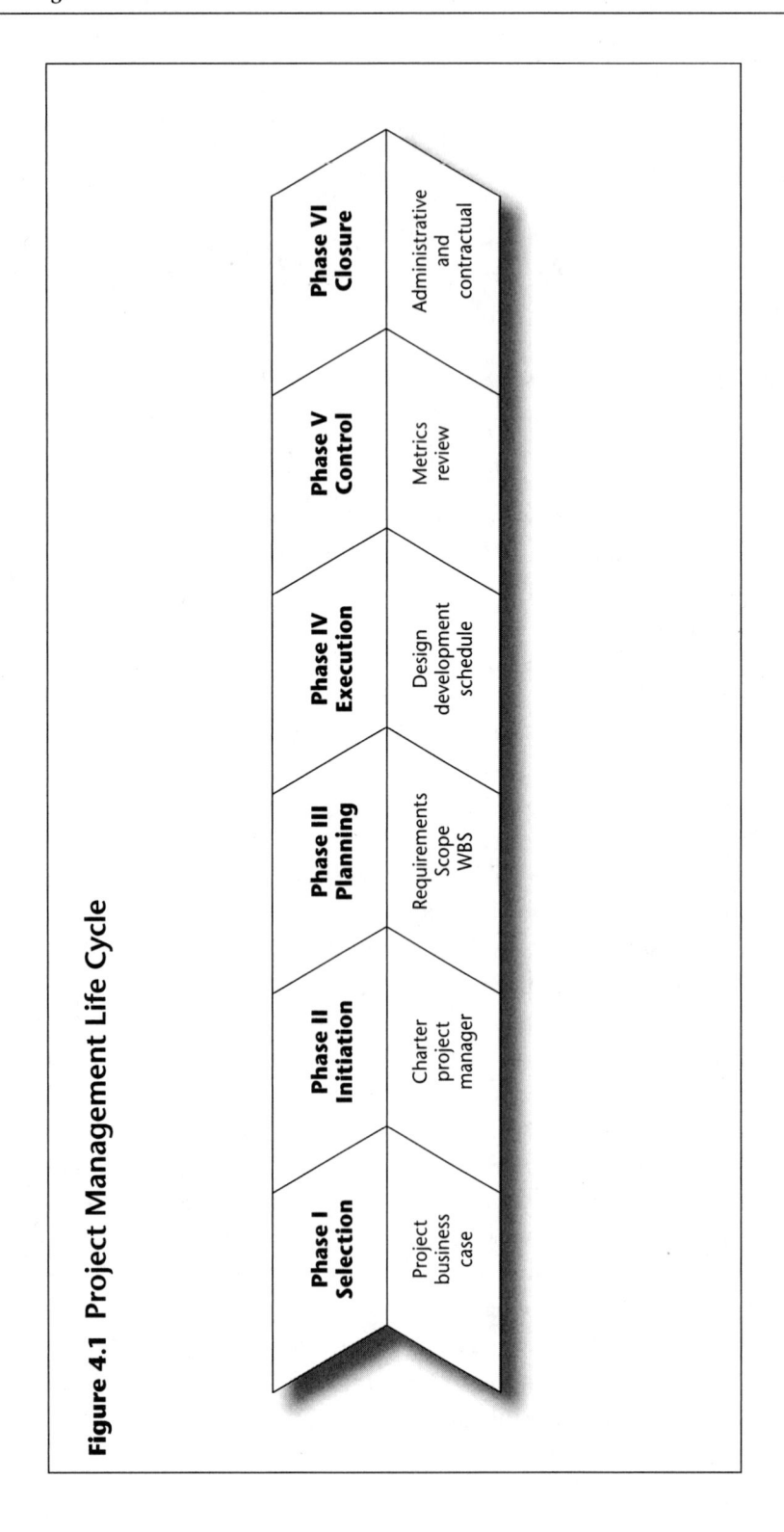

Figure 4.1 Project Management Life Cycle

Phase	Deliverable
Phase I Selection	Project business case
Phase II Initiation	Charter project manager
Phase III Planning	Requirements Scope WBS
Phase IV Execution	Design development schedule
Phase V Control	Metrics review
Phase VI Closure	Administrative and contractual

Decision points or tollgates should be required at the end of each phase. These points enable project sponsor and managers to evaluate the business case, CBA, project progress, and plans for the remaining activities. Moreover, tollgates provide an opportunity for refining the project work plan and realigning it with business objectives. In this way, the plan's accuracy will improve as each phase is completed.

SUBPHASES

Project subphases are used to analyze, launch, and monitor subcomponents of the work effort required to achieve targeted business objectives. By breaking down phases into subphases, the project manager and team leaders can monitor the teams' progress more effectively. The subphases within each phase are further divided into tasks assigned to specific team members. All subcomponents in a phase must be completed before the project can move forward to the next phase in its life cycle. Project phases usually answer the question, "What must be accomplished for the project to succeed?" Subphases answer the question, "How will the project will be achieved?"

PROJECT SELECTION ACTIVITIES

Figure 4.2 shows the activities that must be addressed in selecting projects that will provide the most value to the organization.

Once an idea is identified, a project can be conceived. The idea can come from anyone within or outside the organization and through any process (e.g., someone calling the service center with a complaint). With the exception of extreme cases, most project requests are

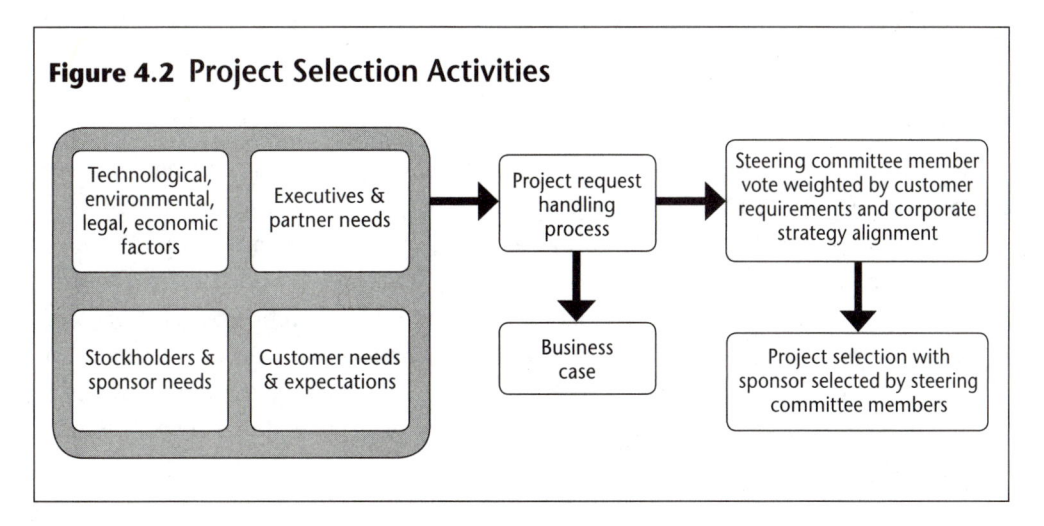

Figure 4.2 Project Selection Activities

handled through a special voting process. Although a firm's steering committee members usually don't overlook recommendations for projects, not every project is, or should be, selected. As international revenue opportunities shrink from the effects of a weak global economy and customers demand better products at cheaper prices, executives are increasingly pressured to find creative ways of maximizing project returns. No longer is a flexible pricing strategy the only customer consideration for conducting business; customers now insist on customized products and services to meet the needs of their specific markets. This has caused companies not only to rethink their product and service design but also to redesign the tools they use from day-to-day.

One of the most critical tools for an organization today is project management, because it's the only proven method of reducing time to market, streamlining costs, and creating avenues of opportunities through a logical, structured, and team-driven process. In conjunction with establishing a project-management focus on corporate initiatives, nimble companies are also cutting costs through process-improvement initiatives, which create additional need for project managers skilled in process improvement.

In addition to those strategies, companies are attempting to slash costs by outsourcing noncustomer-focused business efforts (e.g., information technology, help desks, billing, and service areas) that represent large-scale projects themselves. For instance, although all service calls might go through the same toll-free number, the calls might be rerouted to an outsourced destination that's geographically closest to the person requesting service. The outsourced agents are trained in the same service skills as employees who work in the main office. These partners are also called "virtual companies" because they're considered part of an organization even though they're located in far away places like Mexico, India, and China.

Combined, all the initiatives mentioned here create the need for a variety of project managers and new project management skills. Therefore, any successful project must begin with a robust project prioritization process. As the world becomes more competitive, the necessity for "getting the right project delivered correctly the first time around" takes on an entirely new meaning.

Environment

An organization can experience a tidal wave of change at any given moment in time, and how it deals with that can make the difference between project success and business failure. Two major categories of environmental change are external and internal.

External influences can affect projects significantly, and therefore must be factored into project selection criteria. External factors can take the form of technological, legal, economic, social, and/or political changes. Some of these influences are easier to predict than others; however, it's impossible to ignore any of them because external environmental factors greatly affect both projects and companies. Some of the firefighting crises that result from ignoring external factors are:

- Misalignment between strategic and tactical goals
- Changes in business culture
- Changes in how an organization does business
- Changes in how an organization enters new markets
- Communication changes
- Changes in risk factors
- Changes in the way companies prepare for the future

Internal influences can also affect projects and must therefore be taken seriously. These can take the form of changes to products, services, core competencies, financial conditions, and workforce constraints. Projects must be ideally suited to an organization's flexibility, innovation, and speed to market. Project selection should always be weighted by internal characteristics that are important to remaining competitive. Conducting a CBA and determining payback period, operational cost savings, and the expected value of risk usually help frame internal business considerations. Although some projects are undertaken to build an infrastructure for the future, an organization can't survive long without meeting mission-critical objectives of today.

Stakeholders

A critical component of selecting a project is to align it with stakeholders' and stockholders' needs and expectations. When projects aren't aligned with business-owner expectations, a project's value is usually undermined through stakeholders' complaints and stockholders' noticeable dissatisfaction.

The project sponsor typically takes the lead in advocating the greatest benefits of each project opportunity by answering the following questions:

- What do stakeholders expect from any project initiative?
- How will stockholders view project results?
- Where does the organization want to be one year from now?
- What projects will get us where we want to be?
- Which projects will solidify customer loyalty?
- How do we optimize our organization's resources?

The answers to these questions provide insight into the business owner's expectations. When the answers are considered as project criteria, project communications are established at the highest levels first. Interactive planning is critical for business success.

Needs

Every project must be evaluated on its own merit, and most of the time that merit is based on how closely project deliverables satisfy internal requirements. Although requirements are important, customer needs are even more critical to project success because customer needs are different than requirements. Requirements are fixed and mostly internal, but customer needs change continuously over time. A requirement that satisfies a customer today might generate new customer needs tomorrow and/or fail to meet all customer needs that are critical to product or service quality. The Quality Council of Indiana illustrates this point perfectly in its overview of customer needs: "Maslow's hierarchy of needs would be a good illustration of the advancement of needs (physical, safety, love, esteem, and self-awareness). As an individual's needs are fulfilled, he/she advances up the hierarchy. As the customer obtains a suitable product or service (the basic needs are fulfilled), they will look for new attributes." (CSSBB 2001, page III-33.)

Organizations have known for a long time that customer needs constantly change. Microeconomics show, using "utility curves," that a customer who buys a vanilla ice cream cone will be less likely to immediately buy another because the desire for vanilla flavor has been satiated. Until recently, organizations chose to ignore customer needs when evaluating project deliverables. Now project focus has turned from internal product and/or service design to customer-driven product and/or service-related "critical to quality" deliverables. The best way to stay aware of changing customer needs is to profile the customer population and then integrate the premier-customer base into internal-organization processes.

Tools that assist in profiling the customer population and solidifying loyalty include:

- Face-to-face interviews
- Focus groups
- Customer surveys
- Product and/or service steering committees, which include five of the organization's largest customers

Customer Expectations

The way businesses approach and deal with their customers is crucial to customer loyalty and stability. Now businesses not only define their purposes in accordance with customer drivers, they also use customer issues as a means of increasing customer-focused processes in their day-to-day activities. This new approach has improved loyalty and commitment of both the business and its customers, as evidenced in better quality, shorter cycle times, and more effective communications between everyone involved.

The critical tasks of a customer-focused organization take the following form:

- Analyze customer issues.
- Look for root causes of issues and eliminate customer dissatisfaction.

- Translate customer needs into new processes to improve effectiveness.
- Eliminate nonvalue-added process steps to improve cycle time and satisfaction.
- Survey customers frequently to determine how to reduce turnover.

No longer do companies emphasize products and services from an "inside-out approach" (i.e., where executives pore over business reports and determine which products and services should be marketed based on profit potential). A successful organization takes the "outside-in approach" and listens to the voice of the customer. In this environment, the business aligns itself to be more customer-focused and -oriented. The way to maintain the customer base and increase satisfaction is to constantly monitor where customer expectations are heading.

Project Handling Process

Most companies have numerous project opportunities, downsized operations, limited capital, overworked resources, increased competition, and demanding customers. Decisions concerning which projects to move forward and which to reject are more important than ever. During project selection meetings, every executive has his or her own agenda that will promote the likelihood of success in specific domains of influence. For that reason, the project handling process must be clear, based on tangible evaluation criteria, and unbiased in terms of selection.

The first priority in initiating an effective project handling process is to make sure all work requests go through the project selection committee. Sometimes project team members are approached directly by department managers, directors, and/or organizational decision makers, and requested to perform "quick hit" tasks. (Supposedly, these tasks take only a few minutes to complete.) This approach is called "interrupt-driven work strategy" because these requests—usually wish-list items—interrupt more meaningful work assignments. As interrupt driven tasks stretch from minutes into hours, even days, of extra work, the "interrupt driven" team loses focus on approved and assigned project deliverables.

The second priority is to require the department vice president, who is usually on the project selection committee, to sign all work requests so that important project work flows to project team members. Team members, incidentally, should be in a position to tell someone requesting interrupt-driven work that they're authorized to work only on project deliverables approved by the project selection committee.

The third priority is to require that all projects be assessed on tangible evaluation criteria, including:

- Competitive benchmarking
- Cost-benefit analysis (CBA)
- Return on investment (ROI)

- Net present value method (NPV)
- Internal rate of return (IRR)
- Payback period method (PPM)
- Percent return over cost of capital
- Risk factors
- Implementation schedule

Regardless of the methods used, projects should be selected, prioritized, and implemented on the basis of:
- Greatest financial benefit (over cost of capital)
- Shortest payback period
- Fewest overall risk factors
- Shortest implementation schedule

Select Projects That Eliminate Waste

A good rule of thumb when selecting projects is to look for and approve projects that eliminate waste. Focus on changing or eliminating activities that add no real value in the following areas:
- Process waste
  - ☐ Inspecting incoming products
  - ☐ Duplicated activities
  - ☐ Just-in-case activities
  - ☐ Activities with no internal or external customer
  - ☐ Tasks with no successor
  - ☐ Unused reports, data, or decisions
  - ☐ Bureaucracy
  - ☐ Anything the external customer wouldn't pay for
  - ☐ Activities that add more cost than the product's value

- Transportation waste
  - ☐ Movement between departments
  - ☐ Movement between stock locations
  - ☐ Transportation to meetings
  - ☐ Transportation from suppliers
  - ☐ Travel to work

- Wasted motion
  - ☐ Official layout
  - ☐ Mailing letters and packages

Project Selection

- Error waste
  - ☐ Retyping letters
  - ☐ Scrap and rework
  - ☐ Call backs
  - ☐ Misunderstood directions
  - ☐ Customer complaints
  - ☐ Personal problems

- Production waste
  - ☐ Making too little product, which results in:
    - Lost sales
    - Upset customers
    - Unused resources

  - ☐ Making too much product, which results in:
    - High level of inventory
    - Obsolete products
    - Expensive handling

- Inventory waste
  - ☐ Too much inventory
  - ☐ Wrong inventory in stock
  - ☐ Wasted space
  - ☐ Money tied-up

- Waiting waste
  - ☐ Delivery delays
  - ☐ Not meeting commitments
  - ☐ Poor priorities
  - ☐ Work overloads
  - ☐ Poor decision making
  - ☐ Poor understanding of requirements
  - ☐ Missed opportunities

The Business Case

Every project should have a business case. This should be completed at a high level by the potential project sponsor and manager prior to the selection process. A business case usually displays the high-level costs and benefits of launching a project and includes a level of detail that enables the steering committee to adequately determine whether a project should be considered, approved, and funded. Once the project is approved by the senior steering committee, the project sponsor is assigned.

Some components of a good business case are listed below.

- Business case owner's name
- Affected organizations
- Affected business processes
- New products or services
- Business purpose
- High-level objectives or deliverables
- Metrics for measuring success
- High-level timeline
- High-level cost-benefit analysis
- Approximate size of the project in cost, people, and elapsed time
- Clearly identified project stakeholders
- List of assumptions, constraints, dependencies, and risks

Project selection includes identifying and notifying business leaders (i.e., the steering committee) that a project might affect their domains of influence. Notification and early involvement helps prevent business surprises that might cause delays later in the project's life cycle. Involving senior staff early in the process also helps to identify areas of concern where executive buy-in might be missing.

Once the steering committee approves the business case, the project is approved. At that time, a project manager is assigned and initial funding is approved.

Steering Committee

The steering committee is generally responsible for establishing the process and criteria for project selection, prioritization, and funding within their business operating components. The process of analyzing new project opportunities should occur periodically, generally no less than once a quarter. The larger the organization, the more difficult it is to choose a project that moves high-level business strategy. For that reason, some companies break down projects and strategy into big-picture or corporate Xs (i.e., requirements) and Ys (i.e., results) versus branch-specific or business Xs and Ys, which they can render into optimization equations.

Some project constraints such as limited investment capital, time considerations, and opportunity costs (i.e., the return on investment given up by investing cash in one project rather than another) are instrumental in determining which projects are selected. Consider the case of Amazon.com. The online megastore focused on prioritizing those factors that improve convenience for its customers. After a few years of continued progress in this area, Amazon has now set the market trend for bookstores.

Project Review

Members of the steering committee conduct the project approval review. The committee meets, usually once a month, to discuss the most important topics of project methodology. These usually consist of the following elements:
- Status of currently approved projects
- Capacity planning
- Funding changes
- New project opportunities
- Prioritization
- New projects that should be selected and launched

The review is a formal critique conducted by the executive staff and driven by organizational policy, customer needs, and/or emergency organizational requirements. The steering committee attempts to minimize the frequency of emergency requirements—which require a firefighting operational mode—and focus project methodology on proactive and beneficial planning.

Senior Management's Role in Project Selection

Senior management is responsible for aligning business strategy with project tactics. Consideration should be given to balancing the workload within the organization and ensuring that all functions are participating. This concentrates attention on critical issues, sets priorities for resources, and ensures that the effort is manageable. Although this approach is relatively simple, management must ensure that:
- Pet projects aren't chosen over more critical projects.
- Objectives and hard facts support requirements.
- Decisions are supported by a CBA.
- Customer complaints are included in the selection process.
- High-cost processes are streamlined.

Most customer-focused companies use the weighted-selection method to achieve these ends. With this approach, top management gives each of the six project factors a rating from one to ten for the ten categories considered critical to the organization. A rating of one indicates that a project is difficult to do anything with, or that it offers little advantage to the organization. A rating of ten indicates that a project is very easy to change, or that it adds optimum value to the business. The ratings of the ten categories are totaled for each project, and the totals are used to set project priorities. Top management then decides which project should be addressed immediately and those that can be scheduled for later in the year or ignored entirely.

Once projects are selected and approved, the project management office along with the project sponsor and senior management are responsible for assigning a project manager whose level, skills, and experience are consistent with the project's requirements.

Project-Benefit Monitoring

Because projects are investments and expected to generate a return, tracking, monitoring, and ensuring that benefits are achieved determines a project's ultimate success. Therefore, the business case and especially the CBA should be updated continuously throughout a project's life cycle. Many business cases deteriorate over time because the CBA isn't properly maintained when changes to scope, resources, and funding occur. The project sponsor is responsible for ensuring that individual responsibilities are assigned and controls put into place to periodically monitor and report on project performance.

Project-benefit monitoring compares the benefits achieved against the original business case and project objectives. Projects should implement processes for tracking anticipated benefits against actual benefits by:

- Establishing which business processes are affected
- Establishing technical performance indicators
- Establishing benefit expectations
- Determining and monitoring the link between project timeline and financial measures
- Implementing an ongoing reporting process

Only through project-benefit monitoring can the true value of project deliverables be determined for business and customers alike.

CHAPTER V

PROJECT INITIATION

Once the right project is selected by the steering committee and the sponsor is assigned, then project initiation, the first significant phase of the project life cycle, begins. (See figure 5.1.) This phase brings together the steering committee, project sponsor, and, once he or she is chosen, the project manager, thereby solidifying the shared vision of success. The output of the project initiation phase is the project charter and an assigned project manager.

PROJECT SELECTION

Selecting the right project can mean the difference between a successful venture and a waste of time and money. The executive committee must consider many things before it approves a project, including:
- Is the project a critical-success factor?
- Will it be a best practice?
- How accurate are the cost and cycle-time estimates?
- What's the sponsor's past history?
- What are the risks?
  - ☐ Effect on culture
  - ☐ Effect on resources

- Will the project give a competitive advantage and if so, for how long?

Figure 5.2 is a simple guide to project selection.

Any project selected by the steering committee represents an organization's commitment that the requirements provide a business advantage and will be delivered within a specific time frame. In other words, the executive staff will arrange funding, resources, and time, and a sponsor will be assigned as a steering committee spokesperson for the project. This doesn't always mean the project will succeed. Adapting an organization's future vision to today's global economy means constantly aligning with the changing parameters of customers, economy, market, executive staff turnover, new leadership, the project manager's

Figure 5.1 Introduction Activities

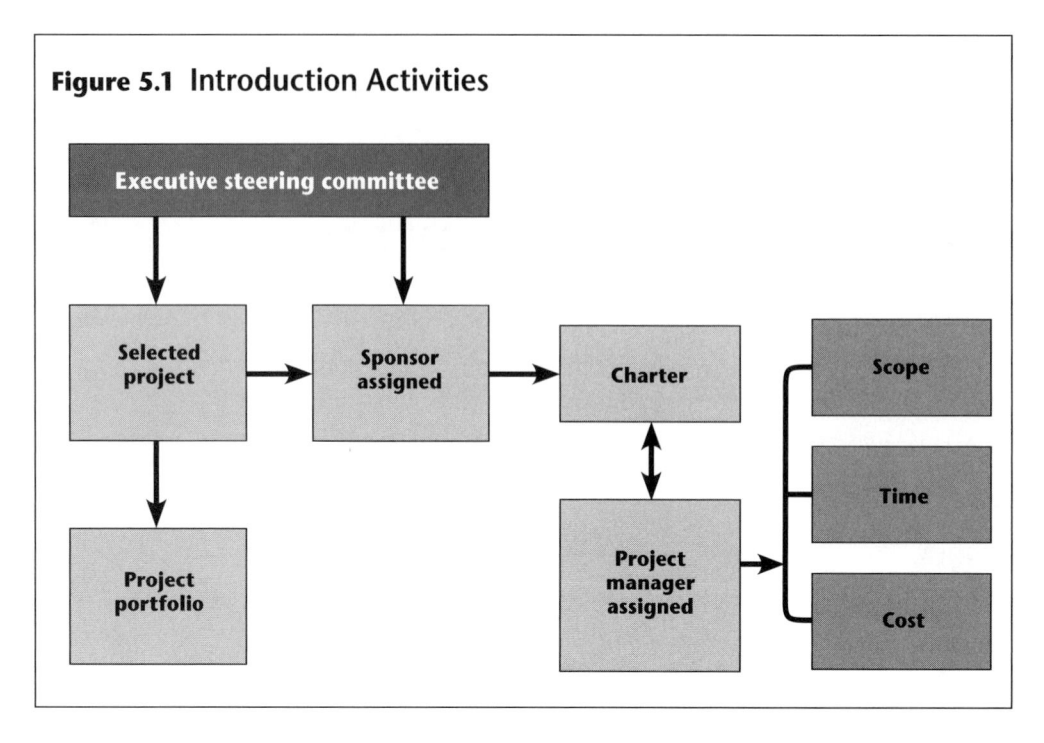

experience, and team dynamics. There are many things that can hamper a project's progress; however, project selection is a sincere effort to launch the best projects for the good of the entire organization—stakeholders, stockholders, and employees. Some of the principles underlying a successful project philosophy are listed below.

- The chosen project represents a commitment by the executive staff.
- The project will be the driving force for organizational change and excellence.
- Project deliverables will drive the scope of work for assigned team members.
- Once empowered, the project manager will be accountable for success.
- Skilled employees will be freed from existing duties to focus on project success.
- The project has a business case that demonstrates an acceptable return on investment.
- Funding will be provided to the project manager for project completion.
- Deliverables will be broken down into specific objectives and assigned.
- Team dynamics that encourage success will be practiced.
- The voice of the customer has been infused into project requirements.

Selecting a project means the organization has also committed to a series of activities and tasks that are critical to its success. The executive staff arranges for dedicated resources, time, funding, support, and equipment. The project will move forward into the planning and implementation phases of the project life cycle.

PROJECT PORTFOLIO

Approved projects are placed in a project portfolio usually located on the internal local area network so that project commitments, funding, resources, and status information is available for review around the clock. Because an organization will be involved with various types of projects simultaneously, each category should be listed along with other relevant factors discussed in this chapter. The ten major project categories are:

- *Process improvement projects.* This is where the current performance of an important process is derived, the future performance requirement established, a project alternative chosen to effectively improve process performance, and the process realigned with customer needs and expectations.
- *Process reengineering projects.* This is redesigning a current process to achieve maximum alignment with customers and realize a seamless optimization model.
- *Seamless organizational projects.* This is integrating systems to substantially reduce total business cycle time across all organizational parameters.
- *Supply-chain management project.* This is dramatically improving supplier effectiveness and reducing the costs of conducting business (e.g., e-requirements, e-bidding, e-procurement, e-status, and e-closure), establishing a superior supplier communication model, and increasing receivables turnover through the use of electronic data interface and electronic funds transfer.
- *Transactional process/Web-integration projects.* This is fully enabling transactional processes (e.g., order entry, accounts receivables) over the Internet and improving opportunities for customer business in a twenty-four/seven model.

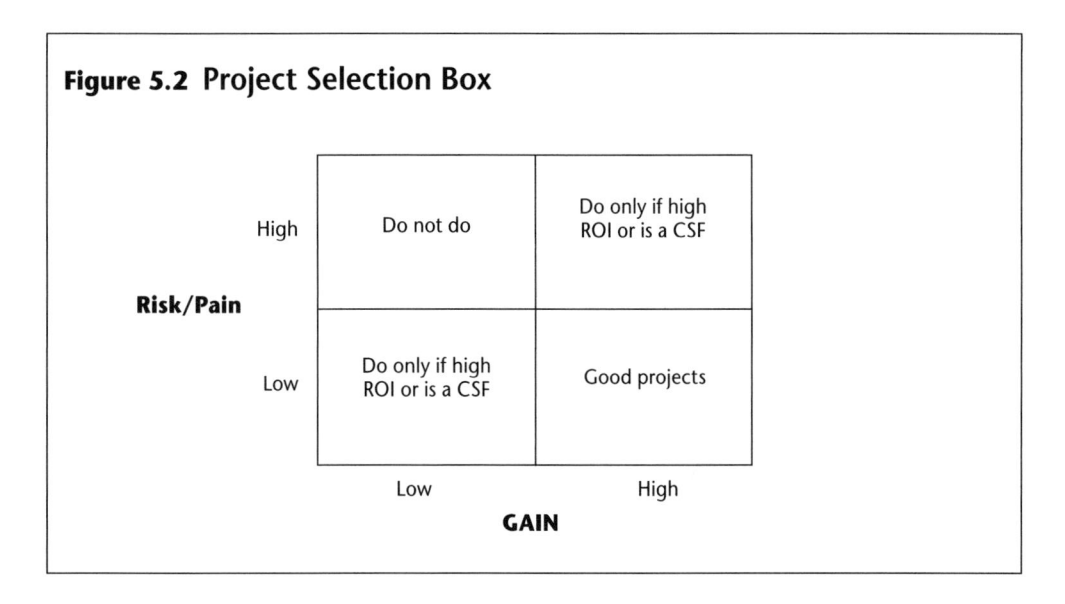

Figure 5.2 Project Selection Box

		Low GAIN	High GAIN
Risk/Pain	High	Do not do	Do only if high ROI or is a CSF
	Low	Do only if high ROI or is a CSF	Good projects

- *Data warehousing projects.* This is using data to segment and profile customer revenue, satisfaction, and spending trends, and using software algorithms to search for useful patterns in historical data for conducting business.
- *Customer relationship management projects.* This is establishing connections to increase customer retention, enhancing customer experiences with the business, reducing customer turnover, and improving projections about the lifetime worth of customer business.
- *Technology projects.* This is implementing evolutionary and revolutionary technology to provide the architecture and infrastructure necessary to improve products and services, and remain competitive in today's globally competitive market.
- *Outsourcing projects.* This is significantly changing boundaries by partnering with resource companies throughout the world that specialize in cutting-edge technology, knowledge, manufacturing, and skills-management areas that complement the organization's production products or services while decreasing operating costs.
- *Functional management projects.* This is improving the operating efficiency of one functional area within an organization. Although this type of project is a complete waste of time, some companies remain stovepipe-oriented and suffer the inefficiencies and high operational costs associated with this organizational structure.

No matter which type of project is selected, once it's placed in the portfolio, project status is tracked against the factors for success. Tangible and intangible factors come into play when success is considered. Tangible factors can include scope, timelines, costs, deliverables, and control. Intangible factors can be based on the sponsor's effectiveness, project manager's efficiency, and the project team's ability to make the necessary sacrifices to realize success.

SPONSORSHIP

For a team to succeed, upper management support is crucial. This means a project must align with its sponsor's personal performance objectives. If it isn't, that sponsor will spend time achieving the objectives upon which his or her performance will be based. Upper, middle, and line management must have an enthusiastic attitude about project success and team empowerment. This means everyone, from the project team up to the executive staff, must be aligned and willing to share responsibility and accountability.

CHARTER

A project charter is a formal document that defines a project's mission, scope, objectives, time frame, and constraints.

Besides defining mission objectives, the project charter identifies the project sponsor and manager, authorizes the sponsor to free up funding and approve resources, and authorizes the project manager to select a project team and begin the planning phase of the project life cycle.

The steering committee usually creates the project charter, which is one of the most effective ways of giving a project team formal acceptance, direction, and support. The charter also outlines and models what's in and out of scope, and identifies the project's prioritization and size. An effective charter normally includes:

- Constraints—specific timelines, funding limits, and preassigned resources
- Project name—provides a name by which the project can be identified
- Project number—every project should be assigned a unique number
- High-level scope—aspects of the project that are in or out of scope
- Affected areas—which areas in the organization will be affected by the project
- Expected deliverables—identifies deliverable products and/or services
- Project sponsor—identifies the project sponsor
- Project manager—identifies the project manager
- Timelines—gives high-level timelines for the project
- Resource approval—provides authorization for the necessary resources
- Cooperation—identifies which managers must cooperate with team (by providing data and other resources)
- Funding—a "rough order of magnitude" amount of project funding
- Prioritization—rates this project's priority against other approved projects

Once the project manager is assigned, the project charter can be renegotiated based on output from the project's planning phase. Although the executive staff can accurately identify those processes within the business most in need of change, the project manager and team will be more aware of the actual facts after the project is planned, customer needs considered, data measured, facts analyzed, and multiple options considered.

PROJECT TEAM ACTIVITIES

One of the most important aspects of project preparation is forming the team that will realize either the success or failure of project deliverables. The project manager uses a team charter to define the required project roles and responsibilities for each team member. The charter also provides clear accountability, deliverable timelines, team ground rules for interaction, and unambiguous communication channels for success. All team members sign the charter to acknowledge their understanding of what's expected of them. Team responsibilities include, but aren't limited to:

- Support the team leader.
- Attend team meetings.
- Contribute ideas and status information at meetings.
- Complete assignments.
- Strive to meet deliverable timelines.
- Address issues and/or barriers to performance.

A well-defined project scope is important for ensuring that team members understand the project's priorities. Sometimes common courtesy and respect are more important than pushing members to perform. Every team member is responsible for making sure that respect is equally distributed.

STAGES OF TEAM DEVELOPMENT

Bruce W. Tuckman first introduced the concept of phases in team performance in his article, "Development Sequence in Small Groups" (*Psychological Bulletin*, June,1965). Most groups of people go through four phases of development, he noted, which represent different levels of team performance. The phases are:

1. Forming
2. Storming
3. Norming
4. Performing

This sequence has been substantiated many times since 1965, either through direct observation by project managers or by psychologists who research and study areas of team performance.

Forming

Team formation is the first phase of development. A team's performance is usually at the lowest level of maturity during this phase. Team members, meeting for the first time, act as individuals and aren't convinced that other members will cooperate on deliverables. Usually they don't fully understand the extent of their individual roles and responsibilities. Members look to the project leader or manager for direction, guidance, and support at this point. If the leader or manager is weak, this phase will continue for some time; with a strong manager, the team will move quickly toward a higher level of overall performance.

Storming

Team storming is the second phase of development. During the storming phase, individual performance slowly matures to the point where people begin to work as a team. However, many members test the boundaries of authority to determine the extent of their own authority and assess how serious the team and/or leadership is about deliverables and performance. Conflict is frequent during this phase. Once the team is mature enough, members themselves will deal with unacceptable member behavior (e.g., working around the member or insisting on improved performance). At this point, though, it's the leader who sets the standards of team behavior, usually by referencing rules of conduct in the team charter. If they're dealt with immediately and politely, members will understand the project's seriousness and convert their resistance into buy-in and loyalty. Because the team has only recently started the project effort, members might feel overloaded, anxious, and unfocused, so leadership is a critical component of moving performance forward and increasing morale.

Norming

Norming is the third phase of team development. During this phase, a sense of team togetherness, purpose, and effectiveness forms. The team makes tanbgible progress, and members can visualize success. Membership becomes special as the team works together to develop norms of behavior, commitment toward deliverables, loyalty toward the leader, and routine standards for everyone to follow. The frequency of conflict diminishes, but a team must experience norming before it can move on to performing. That's because a group of individuals can't optimally interact until it normalizes (i.e., reaches an acceptable routine) as a team. Instances of individualism still surface during the norming phase because some people take longer to socialize than others, but the team usually looks for consensus among team members.

Performing

Performing is the last and most productive phase of team development. During this phase, the level of team maturity is high because the team has developed relationships, boundaries, commitment, and purpose. The team is structured and conducts very successful team meetings where members provide ideas, broach issues, suggest best practices, and offer support to other members. Team members are willing to make the necessary personal sacrifices for the good of the project. Consequently, goals are achieved and members become concerned if they don't meet deliverable timelines. This phase is also known as optimization and promotes ideal working conditions for a team. During the performing phase, the team leader might want to introduce team lunches or get-togethers that offer an added dimension of socialization to team dynamics.

PROJECT TEAM PERFORMANCE

Because a project is highly dependent upon each team member's sense of project accountability, the project manager should ensure that all team members include the project's success as part of their annual performance objectives. The manager should work with team members' functional management as well as other team members to define and document performance objectives. This simple effort ensures success because team responsibilities are aligned with annual performance objectives.

Project Team Training

Many projects result in new technology or cutting-edge operating processes, and training courses are essential to keep team members abreast of changes within their areas of work. One method of achieving this is through just-in-time learning supported by actual project deliverables. This approach promotes team collaboration, develops a common

Figure 5.3 Advantages and Disadvantages of Virtual Teams

ADVANTAGES	DISADVANTAGES
■ Access to resources with the right skill	■ Direct control
■ Reduced office space costs	■ Communications
■ Round-the-clock shifts	■ Problem turn-around time
■ Greater use of employees	■ Time zone changes
■ Lower costs	■ Culture

understanding of new project opportunities, and offers real-time training to improve work plans and deliverables. Preferably, training needs should be completed prior to starting the project. At a minimum, team members should receive training in team dynamics and basic project management before beginning a project.

Managing Virtual Teams

Project teams are becoming more "virtual," meaning that the members aren't physically on site. Virtual teams offer many advantages:

- Broader access to resources with the right skills
- Reduced office space costs
- Around-the-clock shifts
- Lower operating costs

Virtual teams also enable the project manager to increase resource oversight through more frequent status meetings, more detailed designs, and more hands-on testing cases.

But there are also some disadvantages associated with virtual project teams:

- Direct control is limited.
- Communications take more effort due to time zone variances.
- Problem turnaround time might take longer.
- Cultural changes might drive team-member relationship training.

Figure 5.4 Project Target Board

Problem Statement	**Project Duration/Resources**
42% of all claimants call in to check their claim prior to its resolution. 62% of claimants felt that the process was taking too long.	90 days Team of five people 15 total team hours per week
Scope	**Deliverable**
The project will look at how customers are informed of payment procedures and how interim contact is handled from when a customer sends in a claim form to the point at which they receive a check.	1. Reduce incoming claimant calls by 50%. 2. Reduce average check cycle time by nine days. 3. Streamline claim-handling process.
Risks	**ROI = 5 to 1**
The project will result in a cultural change to the organization. There must be a communication plan that will allow the employees to transition to the new process.	Estimated high-level savings will be $10,000 per week. Estimated costs will be $2,000 per week.

PROJECT TARGET BOARD

The project target board is a one-page overview that defines:
- Problem statement
- Project scope
- Risks
- Project duration/resources
- Deliverables
- Return on investment

The project target board provides management and the project team with a one-page view of the project and the project team's commitment. Figure 5.4 shows a typical target board.

PROJECT INITIATION SUMMARY

According to the Project Management Institute's role-delineation study, ten tasks make up the project initiation phase. They are:
- Working with the project's stakeholders to define the project's goals and requirements
- Using the scope of work and stakeholders' requirements to develop a list of product and/or service deliverables
- Defining the processes required to produce the deliverables
- Developing a list of project constraints. Be sure the project is in compliance with the appropriate policies, procedures, and laws.
- Documenting assumptions
- Examining alternative approaches to project strategy to define the best value-added approach
- Defining performance criteria required to meet the stakeholders' and organization's quality requirements
- Reviewing the deliverables and processes that will produce them to define resource and skill requirements
- Developing and refining the project budget and schedule
- Preparing a formal document summarizing the task outcomes for the project initiation phase and getting it approved by appropriate stakeholders

CHAPTER VI

PROJECT PLANNING

Once assigned to a project, and having gained an understanding of the initial objectives, the project manager develops a project plan that will adhere to those objectives as closely as possible. (See figure 6.1.) The output of the planning phase is a project plan. During the detailed planning process, the manager might recommend modifying one or more of the original objectives based on new and/or more detailed information. The project sponsor, manager, team leaders, and all team members should approve the project plan. Once approved, the plan provides a practical approach for accomplishing project objectives that everyone can use as a reference for tasks and major milestones.

The project manager should identify those departments or divisions of the organization that will most likely be involved in the project and, where possible, ask representatives from those units to assist in the planning. Ideally, those representatives will become team leaders within their own organizations later in the project. The project manager seeks to gain commitment and experience by involving representatives early in the planning process.

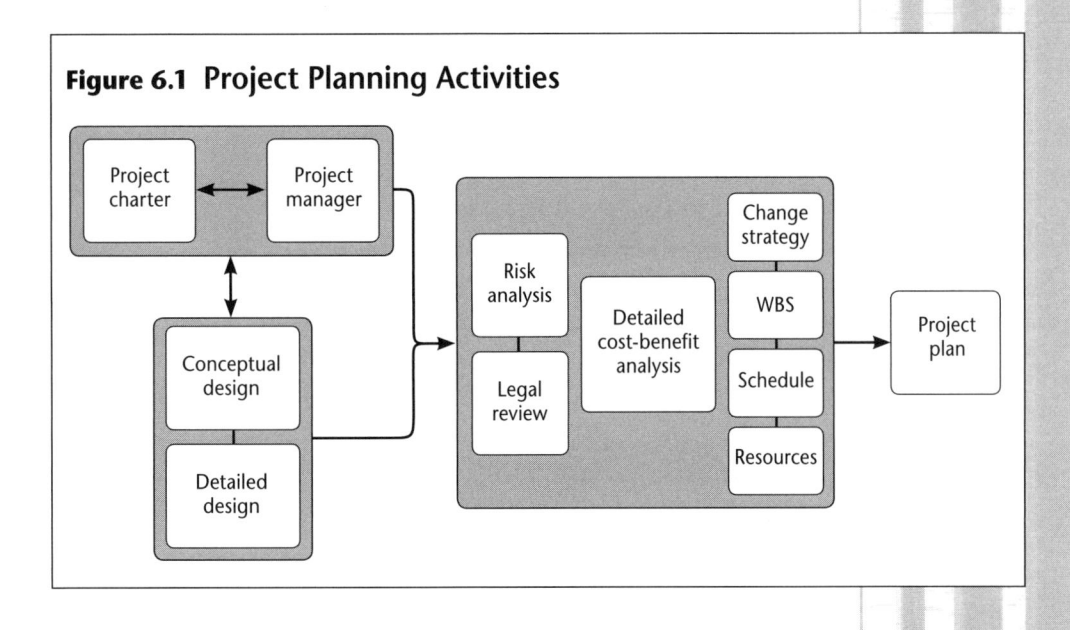

Figure 6.1 Project Planning Activities

The plan can be developed by following a five-step process:
1. Develop scope definition.
2. Develop work breakdown structure.
3. Develop project schedule.
4. Develop project budget.
5. Complete the total plan.

This process will take the team through a series of major planning steps that integrate the plan with project objectives as defined in the project charter and work breakdown structure. By the end of the process, the schedule, budget, and product must be integrated (for example, each piece of the schedule should have a budget and product). These important elements provide the basis for project control.

During the planning phase, the project manager should ensure an open line of communication among the planning team and departments and divisions affected. The planning team will produce a plan that consists of the following templates:

- Scope statement—what's in and out of full project activity
- Work breakdown structure—work package tasks necessary to complete the job
- Requirements—can be both internal and external
- Process analysis—business steps affected by project requirements
- Schedule—start and end dates for every task in the project
- Budget—money required to cover entire project effort
- Conceptual design—high-level explanation of new or enhanced products
- Detailed design—component analysis of changes to processes
- Quality—plans for quality management, assurance, and control
- Procurement plan—deliverables that suppliers must provide for project success
- Time constraints—project start and end dates
- Cost constraints—dollar limitations imposed on the project
- Performance constraints—discrete "must have" deliverables
- Communications plan—how status and progress will be discussed
- Risk analysis—the probability that something might go wrong
- Cost-benefit analysis—total benefits minus total costs
- Team charter—team member roles, responsibilities, and deliverables
- Resource plan—time-phased plans for how workers will be utilized
- Test strategy—scripts the test team will execute
- Change strategy—how the project manager will handle scope changes

Once the initial plan is produced, the project manager reconciles any differences between it and the project objectives. This will probably involve a series of negotiations between the project manager and senior management to resolve any differences. The result must be a marriage between project objectives and project plan.

REQUIREMENTS

Simply stated, a requirement is a unique deliverable statement that will affect a project's scope. Requirements generally provide the "what, when, and under which circumstances" an organization must meet to satisfy a customer.

There are many types of requirements, and collecting and then verifying that all of them have been received has always been a challenge for project managers. Once combined, requirements represent a solution strategy that must be realized to meet executive objectives. Some examples of typical requirements include:

- The order-entry process shall be available to customers over the Internet.
- Accounts receivable software shall include an average payment date.
- LAN-interface channels shall handle one-megabyte load of data.
- The average delivery cycle to ABC Co. will not exceed thirty days.

Each of the requirements above is specific enough that, after project delivery, the project sponsor can state definitively whether the team realized the objective. The successful delivery of any project depends on the clarity of its requirements. Requirements should be:

- Clear
- Concise
- Specific
- Measurable
- Traceable
- Verifiable
- Complete
- Prioritized

Requirements traceability means that each requirement has an audit trail leading back to a business function and specific product, service, technology, and/or customer expectation. The project manager, sponsor, and steering committee use requirements to confirm a project's size. Requirements are also used to prepare tests, training, and procedure modifications.

CONCEPTUAL DESIGN

A conceptual design document provides a high-level overview of business processes, products, or services that will change as a result of project activity. This is where project requirements are initially evaluated, with an emphasis on process, product, service, or technological effects on organizations. The document organizes requirements into specific categories or work groups that are part of the project effort and usually captures the following information:

- Conceptual design number
- Project name
- Project manager and team members assigned
- Narrative of (re)design
- Overview of process, product, service, and/or technology to be modified
- Affected organizations
- Scope of (re)design (i.e., what's in or out of scope for this effort)
- Timelines of (re)design
- Name of person completing the conceptual design document
- Necessary integration between systems and affected organizations
- Associated risks
- Possible organizational effects
- Verification of time, cost, and performance
- Overview of process, product, service, or technology to be modified
- Current process map
- Vision of how process, product, service, or technology will be modified

The conceptual design document also represents the business needs for a specific project domain, so each team leader and member can understand more easily how requirements affect his or her area of responsibility.

Project teams often take many inconsistent approaches for requirements analysis, and the conceptual design document brings some consistency and a standard practice to that effort. The document creates categories of requirements that can assist with verifying both the high-level design and specific factors for success.

If project requirements will affect the domain of technology, then the conceptual design document must include additional areas of requirement clarification, such as:

- Technological (e.g., Internet, database, application, new software)
- Recommended vendors
- Cost constraints
- Infrastructure recommended by vendor

Project Planning

- Knowledge management requirements
- Who needs the data
- Report format
- Functionality

The conceptual design document should be signed by management from all affected operations to encourage buy-in and reduce the frequency of finger-pointing as the project progresses. Team leaders and members will also become more motivated to realize project objectives.

DETAILED DESIGN DOCUMENT

The detailed design document subdivides the conceptual design document into discrete components that team members will use as a project work plan. Those responsible for performing the work usually compile it. The detailed design usually includes the following categories:

- Affected product, service, and/or technology
- Requirements categorized by affected area
- Affected processes
- Suppliers, inputs, processes, outputs, and customers (SIPOC)
- Confirmation of business opportunities
- Data collection strategy
- Recommended modifications

Affected Product, Service, and/or Technology

Current product, service, and/or technology design should be shown in this category, along with an impact matrix or modification chart so designers can understand which areas of product, service, and/or technology require modifying.

Requirements Categorized by Affected Area

Another way of subdividing the conceptual design is categorizing by affected application area. For example, if six requirements necessitate changes to a software product, and that product consists of three applications, the requirements could be categorized by where they affect the individual applications. This procedure assists team members to give a proper amount of planning to their tasks, so once they do begin the work effort, their actions are well thought-out and can be preapproved by team leaders.

Affected Processes

An extensive number of processes occur within any organization. An average of 35,000 business processes, for example, support a medium-size manufacturing organization. The affected process review documented in a detailed design obliges a project team to consider the entire process map as they work. That vantage point not only prompts a better understanding of the requirements' purpose but also a more detailed focus when collecting process data, streamlining the process, removing nonvalue-added steps, and determining how process changes will redesign the way people work. This documentation will serve as the basis of current and future process diagrams.

SIPOC

The person who analyzes the organization's processes must identify only those that affect the product, service, and/or area of technology in question. There is more to analyze than just the input, process, and output that reflect the organization's workings. A SIPOC (supply, input, process, output, customer) diagram looks at the entire spectrum of business parameters, including effects to supplier and customer. These might also require changes to ensure true project success.

Confirmation of Business Opportunities

With this category, team members can determine the true length of time that work efforts will take. They can also verify benefits to the customer and organization. Team members can conduct a comprehensive verification by comparing design details to project requirements, project scope, solution alternatives, organizational opportunities, and project deliverables.

Data Collection Strategy

Design details are best verified through an action plan that includes observing, interviewing affected people (e.g., owner and workers), and measuring business processes. This segment of the detailed design calls for a sampling method to capture data related to the (re)designed process. The best approach is to categorize processes as either discrete or continuous. In addition, the team must define at what point in the process the data (e.g., number of defects) should be collected, who should collect it, and the method by which it should be measured (e.g., trends over time). Someone must also verify the data's accuracy once an appropriate solution is implemented.

Recommended Modifications

The original drawings should be redlined to reflect not only the new project, service, or technology's appearance but also how they'll change in function. Changes to supplier deliverables must also be considered. The customer's reaction to changes should be monitored, and issues addressed as quickly as possible.

"If you don't attack risks, they'll attack you."
—HJH

RISK ANALYSIS

Risk analysis is a subset of project risk management, which makes an overall assessment of future risks that might affect the project. Risk management is something the project manager must pay attention to while managing day-to-day project tasks. He or she should list the risks in weekly project status reports. These risks, and the responses to them, are maintained in a risk log that usually consists of the following categories:

- *Risk number.* Every risk is assigned a unique number.
- *Risk title.* The name assigned to the risk (usually based on its type)
- *Risk description.* A high-level description of the risk
- *Risk date.* The date the risk was documented
- *Severity of impact.* High, medium, or low
- *Person responsible.* Who's responsible for resolving the risk?
- *Action.* What action was taken to control or mitigate the risk?
- *Action Type.* Was the action a short- or long-term fix?
- *Closure date.* The date the risk was closed
- *Required date.* The assigned closing date to correct the risk
- *Management involved.* Who in management was affected and/or involved?
- *Agreement.* Does the affected organization agree the risk was resolved?

Most teams don't deal with risks very effectively. They should be considered a high priority during the project's planning phase and managed on an ongoing basis. If there's a common definition of risk analysis, which is identified in both the project plan and team charter, all members of a project can contribute to identifying, quantifying, and managing risks.

CHANGE STRATEGY

To effectively deal with change, any existing problem that's affected by the change at hand must be compared to a "future state" projection based on detailed requirements. Once the future state model is specified, the project manager can establish milestones, design measures, reporting formats, tollgates, and control mechanisms to assist in achieving the "new paradigm." A traceability matrix is normally used to ensure that all requirements are:

- Incorporated into the future-state model

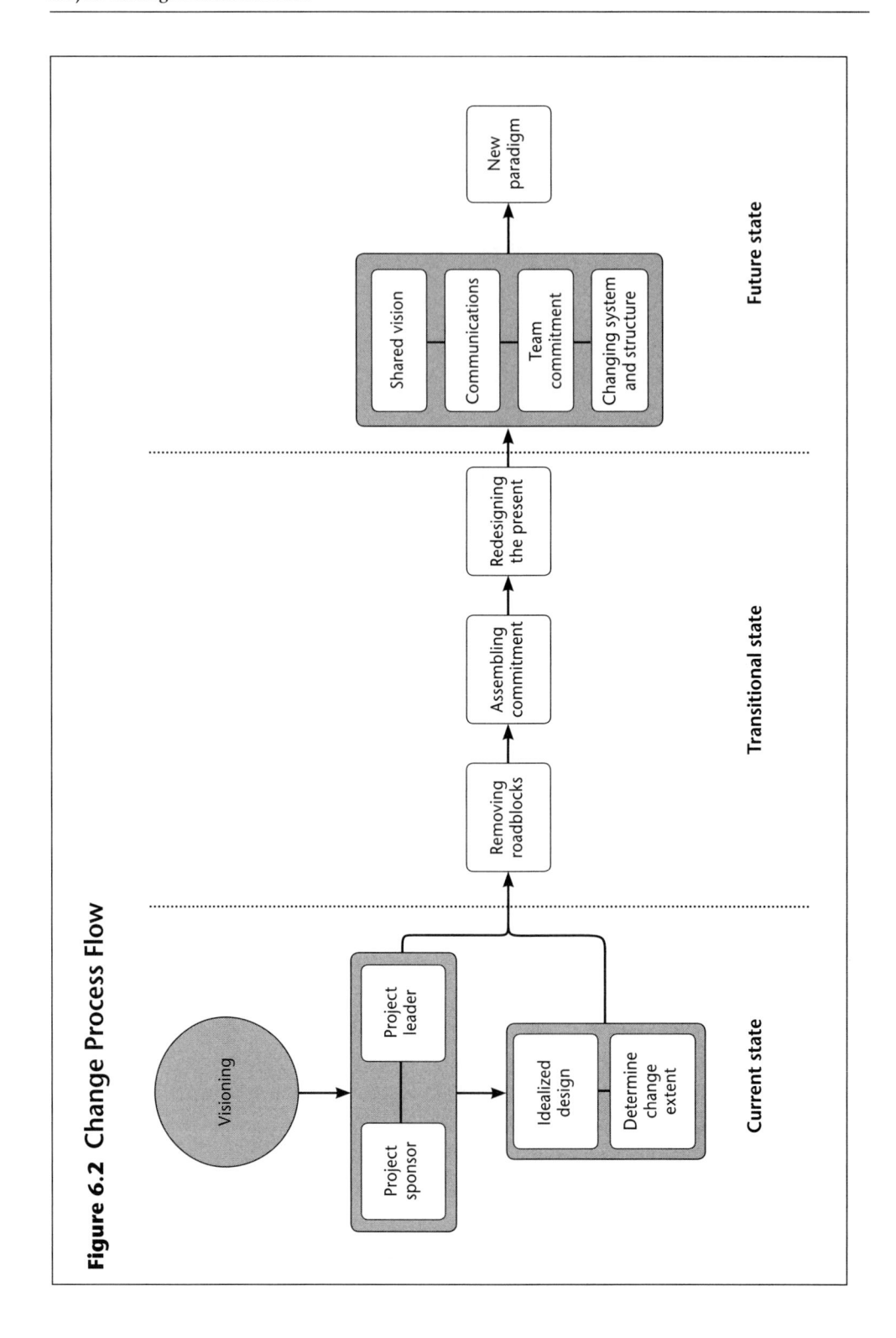

Figure 6.2 Change Process Flow

- Tested and validated
- Reflected in the process changes of the organization

Those affected by the change must be trained on every aspect of it. Figure 6.2 shows the change process flow.

PROJECT ORGANIZATIONAL CHANGE MANAGEMENT

As agents of change, project managers must also help the organization transition to a future state of operation while reducing cultural resistance. To succeed with this requires cross-enterprise cooperation. People aren't born with that leadership skill; they must be properly trained in the areas of resistance, consulting, and overcoming obstacles. In other words, project management isn't just about work plans and milestones; it's also about leadership.

Organizational change management focuses on a project's people side. It helps prepare those affected by the project to accept and, when required, commit to the change and even look forward to it. Many corporate leaders excel in this skill. They not only can motivate team members to accept change but also plan contingency factors that mitigate a change's effect. As part of project management, organizational change management consists of:

- Organizational change management planning. Defining the resistance level to change and preparing a plan to offset it.
- Define roles and develop competencies. Identify those who will serve as sponsors, change agents, change targets, and change advocates, then teach them how to perform their specific roles.
- Establish a burning platform. Define the situation in a way that demonstrates how the cost of the status quo is prohibitively expensive. Under such circumstances, major change isn't just a good idea; it's a business imperative.
- Transformation management. Implement the organizational change management plan, test for black holes and lack of acceptance, and train affected personnel in any new skills the change requires.

Everyone must understand change. As customer expectations of products and services continue to accelerate, organizations will move into a constant state of change, process modification, and struggle. In that environment, only the most respected leaders will succeed.

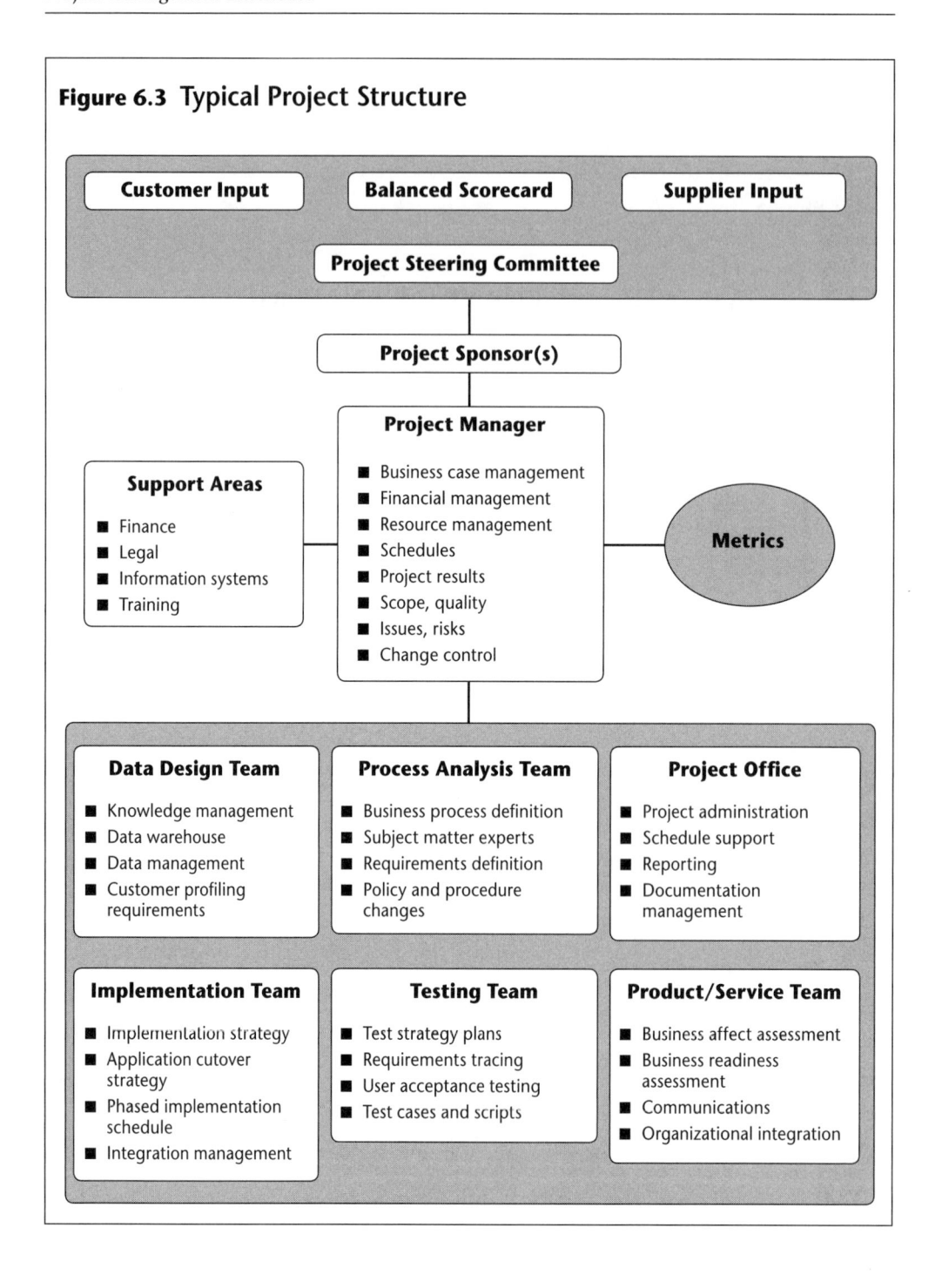

Figure 6.3 Typical Project Structure

Customer Input | **Balanced Scorecard** | **Supplier Input**

Project Steering Committee

Project Sponsor(s)

Project Manager
- Business case management
- Financial management
- Resource management
- Schedules
- Project results
- Scope, quality
- Issues, risks
- Change control

Support Areas
- Finance
- Legal
- Information systems
- Training

Metrics

Data Design Team
- Knowledge management
- Data warehouse
- Data management
- Customer profiling requirements

Process Analysis Team
- Business process definition
- Subject matter experts
- Requirements definition
- Policy and procedure changes

Project Office
- Project administration
- Schedule support
- Reporting
- Documentation management

Implementation Team
- Implementation strategy
- Application cutover strategy
- Phased implementation schedule
- Integration management

Testing Team
- Test strategy plans
- Requirements tracing
- User acceptance testing
- Test cases and scripts

Product/Service Team
- Business affect assessment
- Business readiness assessment
- Communications
- Organizational integration

PROJECT STRUCTURE BASED ON PLANNING PHASE RESULTS

As previously noted, numerous studies show how many times projects are late, canceled, or viewed as failures by customers. When good people get bad results time after time, the root cause often points to the project management operating structure. Therefore, one of the most important aspects of project success is forming a project-operating model early on with well-defined roles and responsibilities, clear accountability, and unambiguous channels of communication. The project operation is the center of all project activity, usually maintaining metrics on project successes and failures while providing the project manager and team with focus, clarity, methodology, and best practice templates.

Figure 6.3 shows how a typical project is structured. In it you can see how an open, cooperative, and flexible operating model can support supplier innovation and external customer needs along with internal project team capabilities. In this example, the steering committee, project sponsor, manager, support organizations, and necessary project team organizations work harmoniously to integrate project deliverables across an entire seamless organization.

The project operational structure changes depending on an organization's type, culture, and the project's complexity, size, and requirements; however, the need for an appropriate structure remains critical to operate a successful project team.

PROJECT OFFICE

The project office is accountable to executive management and provides project administrative support to help produce or update deliverables from the common project management processes. In turn, each project manager generally reports to a vice president of project management so projects can share best practices. When used effectively, the project office can support all the control elements of a large-scale project. Small- to medium-size projects might not have a project office; however, it's highly recommended that a project office monitor every project to make the most effective use of capacity planning, resource allocation, change management, and project quality control.

Process Team

The process team determines how processes within an affected organization will change. This team usually samples process data, measures them for accuracy, analyzes trends, determines root causes, and works with other teams to redesign all the factors associated with a process change, including job changes.

Implementation Team

Process team members could also serve on the implementation team, which is responsible for developing alternative solutions, and then verifying the approaches for implementing each of them.

Data Design Team

The data design team is responsible for designing and implementing interfaces into the database, an aspect of corporate knowledge management. The team also verifies standards, security and data accuracy, and confirm that data are available to those who will use them.

Testing Team

This team is responsible for tracing every requirement through the testing effort. It's usually this team that discovers lost requirements, functional gaps in the deliverable, and project efforts that don't meet requirements.

Product and Service Team

The product and service team advertises the functionality of the new, or modified, product, service, process, or technology. This team is trained to handle the expected types of customer calls about the new deliverable so it can assist anyone who has questions about them.

THE ENGAGEMENT MODEL

Bringing together numerous groups and skills is essential to project efficiency, quality, and success. For projects with information technology elements, the engagement model is designed to involve the right people at the right time with the right accountabilities. It's invoked very early in a project's life cycle, usually during the initiation phase and complements and supports the project's organization by defining the primary points of contact for inter-practice team coordination.

An engagement model's primary objectives are to:
- List whom the business should contact for each type of system request
- Stipulate, within the systems community, whom to contact for what
- Clarify roles, responsibilities, and accountabilities to all team members
- Establish a consistent, repeatable process for engaging system services
- Establish a standard, enterprisewide approach for engaging infrastructure

To meet these objectives, the engagement model relies on five key leadership roles:
- *Project sponsor (or business partner).* Initiates project requests, approves business deliverables, and provides active sponsorship.
- *Project manager.* Provides project status to project sponsor. One project manager is assigned for the project. (Others can perform team leader roles or manage subprojects within the teams.)
- *Process owner.* Serves as primary point of contact into the business, develops service level agreements, and ensures authorizations, funding, and engagement personnel are in place. The process owner is a project team member, and the project manager coordinates with this person when providing status to the project sponsor.
- *Business system analyst.* Serves as the primary point of contact into the information technology organization and is accountable for business integration. The business system analyst is a project team member.
- *Information technology manager.* Serves as primary manager of the information technology organization participants and is accountable for coordinating and overseeing IT effort across the project. This manager provides subproject(s) status to the project manager by rolling up projects' status provided by information technology teams leaders.

For any team to work well, it must be properly staffed. Selecting project team members should be based upon the skills needed and the personal attributes of the individuals.

PROJECT PLANNING SUMMARY

According to the Project Management Institute's role delineation study, seven tasks make up the project planning phase. They are:
- Develop an execution plan by refining project documentation and using the updated documents to baseline the scope of work.
- Develop the work breakdown structure (WBS).
- Prepare a resource management plan and obtain resource commitments for people, materials, and space—internal, external, and procured.
- Refine estimated work efforts and cost. Update project baseline, schedule, and budget.
- Define project controls required to manage project changes, communications, risks, quality, and human resources.
- Develop the formal and comprehensive project plan.
- Obtain project plan approval from appropriate stakeholders to start the project execution phase.

CHAPTER VII

PROJECT EXECUTION

During the execution phase of a project life cycle, the product, service, and/or technology is developed and delivered. This is one of the most important phases of all, where the project's business benefit actually materializes.

Project team members should emphasize robust development, adherence to standards, testing, team dynamics, and quality assurance. With technological projects, the focus should be on rapid application development, reusing objects, and applying standards for testing. The quality of any code development is assessed and evaluated by performing code reviews, measuring performance, and tracking the number of defects that are directly attributable to the code versus the design.

The complexity of today's organizations and their projects requires information technology support to manage and control the portfolio of projects that are underway. It's no longer acceptable to manage individual projects. The interrelationship and effect of the entire portfolio must be considered and managed. The various software products—Systemcorp's PMOffice is a typical example—are designed to manage project portfolios and fill three needs:

- Project management
- Resource management
- Knowledge management

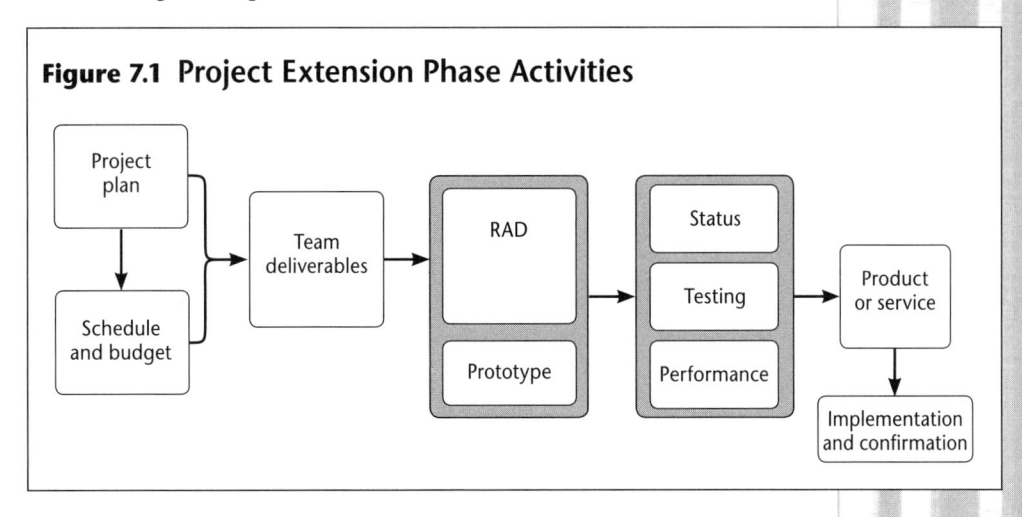

Figure 7.1 Project Extension Phase Activities

Project Management Excellence

In many organizations, projects must be managed not only in the originating organization but also throughout the supply chain. The added challenge of managing projects through three to four tiers of suppliers increases the complexity by ten to twenty times. To aid in this problem, software products such as Virtual Enterprise Solutions' distributed work management software does this job well.

RAPID APPLICATION DEVELOPMENT

Rapid application development (RAD) is a term used to describe parallel efforts associated with developing information systems. The coding process takes project requirements and translates them into specific language constructs. The step prior to coding is usually completing a detailed design document, where requirements are broken down into modules of affected code.

Rapid application development is the best way to speed up the coding process so the customer can realize earlier gains. Traditionally, 100 percent of the code would be required before testing could commence. The testing process would consist of a unit test, followed by integration, system level, and finally regression tests. That sequence took a lot of time, and the deliverable that resulted often required an unacceptable level of rework.

The RAD model minimizes time in coding and maximizing benefits to the customer. Other steps include:
- Plan for the greatest benefits in the shortest period of time
- Apply the 80–20 rule to determine if 80 percent of development functionality is tied to 20 percent of the workload
- Break down a project into multiple prototypes based on customer satisfaction
- Obtain customer approval
- Continue process until entire design is implemented

The secret of decreasing the cycle time for that process is to use the 80–20 rule. The new time-savings sequence defined in the detailed design document should first be reviewed to determine if any module meets 80–20 rule specifications, i.e., 20 percent of the code base could result in 80 percent of the application's total functionality. If the hypothesis holds true, then the 20 percent of code base is coded and released first. The modules that are remaining are then prioritized and/or combined to realize better economies of scale.

PROTOTYPE

A prototype represents a piece (e.g., 20 percent) of an entire deliverable. Initially, a prototype might not consist of more than a drawing of a Web page, with an explanation of client/customer expectations. As functionality is identified, each new design should be reviewed in prototype format. This process will have a more logical flow than traditional sequential methodology.

Once code is completed on 20 percent of the design, a prototype is developed for customer review and acceptance. If the customer accepts the prototype, then delivery is arranged, resulting in more immediate customer satisfaction because that prototype represents most of the functionality outlined in the detailed design document.

The project team will be following these steps:
1. Subdivide the detailed design document into modules and schedule a prototype review date for each.
2. Walk customers through the functionality of each prototype.
3. Have customer agree on delivery.
4. Verify that delivery is working.
5. Develop a means of tracking customer problems.

Once the prototype's delivery and operations are verified, the development team moves on to a second prototype. One of the advantages of the RAD prototype module is that each module represents only a small percentage of the total development work effort. If the customer rejects any of the prototypes, time and cost savings were realized because only 20 percent of the total work effort (representing 80 percent of the design's functionality) was used before the project failed to meet customer expectations.

Prototype development usually results in a win-win scenario because the development process focuses on customer satisfaction versus a client-developer-customer approach. A sufficient audience of stakeholders should review and approve each prototype. Sign-off should occur after every prototype delivery, and customer comments should be documented. The "voice of the customer" should be infused into every step of the development cycle.

Eventually the series of prototypes evolve into a final deliverable. Because the deliverables were reviewed and scrutinized continuously throughout the prototype initiative, the customer is satisfied multiple times instead of only once with one deliverable.

TESTING STRATEGY

Testing is a critical part of the overall project cycle. The information systems infrastructure is the organization's bloodline. Most projects involve information systems in one way or another. Therefore, it's only logical to use the information systems infrastructure to test project deliverables. Adhering to testing-use cases, carefully monitoring progress, and clearly defining the characteristics of success will mitigate project risk.

The objective of testing is to prove that the business objectives for the project can be fully realized.

Testing is so important to verify accuracy of deliverables that every test case should be traced to project requirements:

- Test service and technical infrastructure that will support any current and future products in an integrated way.
- Test retention and sales goals that support strategic targets.
- Test speed to market with new products.
- Test productivity savings from database record keeping infrastructure.

Unfortunately, most projects don't fully utilize the benefits of testing, but it's the most appropriate way to verify that project deliverables achieve customer satisfaction. Organizations that believe their customers are their best testers have the wrong attitude.

LINKING TEST OBJECTIVES TO BUSINESS REQUIREMENTS

A project's objectives can be met by creating test cases based on business requirements and process pages. Each requirement contains use cases that translate it into actual test conditions. Each case should include expected results based on the designated criteria to match the requirement. A numbering system could also be incorporated to provide a direct audit trail and verification method between the requirements and the testing-use cases to ascertain that all project requirements have been tested. The objective can be met by verifying that the expected results match the actual results to ensure smooth implementation and ongoing maintenance. If the results don't match, then a defect is logged and analysis, recoding and retesting begins until success is met.

Phases are completed sequentially and must be deemed successful prior to moving into the next phase with appropriate sign-off. The testing approach begins by looking at specific code changes and ends with a big-picture view of how the new operations will run.

SETTING UP THE TEST CYCLE

The project team should look at specific production data and bring pertinent transaction data into the test environment. These data in turn are copied to the testing file and become the basis of the test bed. All team members—business, information technology, and the test team—are usually involved in creating plans. Test plans should represent business objectives that are within scope.

TEST CASES

A test case is a set of inputs, execution conditions, and outputs developed for the specific objective of exercising a particular program path or to verify compliance with a specific requirement. A use case fully describes a sequence of actions performed by a system to provide an observable result of value to a person or another system using the product under development.

Detailing test cases directly from use cases can highlight missing pieces or inadequate descriptions in the latter. In addition, if test cases are created immediately after use cases are, the test cases can be used to guide development so that additional out-of-scope requirements don't creep into code during development.

Fully detailed use cases can easily be transformed into test cases. The following technique is a three-step process for making this transformation. Because test cases are fully detailed, scenarios can be developed from the use cases. Then test cases are outlined using generic "valid" and "invalid" descriptors for the type of data necessary to execute each test case, along with the expected results of each. Finally, data are assigned to each test case.

Analysts who have developed the use cases, developers, or a specialized testing team can all develop test cases. Whichever group is chosen, it's important to involve the customer in this process so that appropriate data are used in testing, error messages are clear from a business perspective, and unusual or boundary conditions are included in the testing process.

Although this technique can quickly generate robust test cases, it can also verify the use-case specification's correctness and completeness. As a technique, it's readily understood and verified by the customer. It should be noted, however, that this technique won't result in test cases for nonfunctional requirements that haven't been captured as part of an individual user's requirements. For example, there might be performance or scalability requirements that must be tested that wouldn't fall within the scope of specification by a use case. However, in the situation where use cases are developed, this technique works quite well not only to specify test cases but also to verify the completeness of specification-of-use cases already developed.

This technique results in fully articulated test cases with test-case data defined. Further, the test cases relate directly to the use cases developed earlier in the project's life cycle. Because certain nonfunctional requirements (such as performance requirements) are unlikely to be defined as use cases, these must have test cases generated separately.

Project Management Excellence

The steps to transform a use case into test cases are:
1. For each use case, generate a full set of use-case scenarios. Identify each combination of main and alternate flows and create a scenario matrix. The basic flow will be the first scenario. Then, each of the remaining scenarios should be a combination of the basic flow plus alternative flows generated from the use case above.
2. For each scenario, identify at least one test case and the conditions that will make the test case execute. The test cases can be documented in a table format in which the first column contains the test case identifier, the second describes the scenario (or condition, if a scenario gives rise to multiple conditions that can be tested), and all the other columns except the last contain data elements that must be used when implementing the test. The last column describes the expected output for the test case. Note that a single scenario can result in multiple test cases.
3. For each use case, generate a full set of use-case scenarios. Identify each combination of main and alternate flows and create a scenario matrix. The basic flow will be the first scenario. Then, each of the remaining scenarios should be a combination of the basic flow plus alternative flows generated from the use case above. Note that some mathematically possible combinations aren't possible as scenarios.
4. For each scenario, identify at least one test case and the conditions that will make it execute. The test cases can be documented in a table format in which the first column contains the test case identifier, the second describes the scenario (or condition, if a scenario gives rise to multiple conditions that can be tested), and all the other columns except the last contain data elements that must be used when implementing the test. The last column describes the test case's expected output. Note that a single scenario can result in multiple test cases.

UNIT TESTING

The unit test is used to detect and correct logic errors as well as identify and resolve execution errors that cause the program to terminate abnormally. It will also uncover any differences or anomalies between design requirements and actual results.

SYSTEM TESTING

The system test is used to determine if information passes correctly from one program to another. Looking for process variations from expected results is very important. You use this test to ascertain data integrity as well as process flow. Also, at this stage you can verify that product or service modifications are functioning correctly.

DEFECT DETECTION

Once detected, all defects should be logged into the defect-tracking repository. Each should be assigned a number, status code, priority, and severity of defect rating. Each defect's status should be shown as either open, resolved, deferred, withdrawn, fixed in progress, retested, script error, under investigation, or work-around. The priority rating could be designated as high, medium, or low in conjunction with a severity of defect rating of critical, major, minor, or cosmetic.

REPORTING PROJECT STATUS

The process of reporting project status is critical; not only does the project's success rely on it but also continued support from project stakeholders. Reports can take various formats based on the recipients' expectations and the depth of detail the project manager wants to relay in the report. Sometimes it's best to provide a summary page up front, which consists of the most pertinent project information. In that manner, stakeholders, who have time constraints, don't have to read through every page of detail to determine the most important aspects of project status. Be sure to include:

- *Distribution list.* Make separate lists based on type of recipient.
- *Milestones.* Which milestones were and weren't realized
- *Accomplishments.* What major accomplishments were covered
- *Issues.* What are the most important issues that require resolution?

Reports can differ depending on the audience the project manager is targeting. There might be one format for the project teams, another suitable for the sponsor, and one specific to what the steering committee must know about project status. Regardless of which is used, it should be consistent so that, over time, the recipient will know exactly what has changed and understand which issues require resolution. In keeping pace with today's information speedway, many project managers send status reports by e-mail. In addition, they place a copy of the status file on the organization's intranet for internal review, and one on the Web for customer and supplier information. In any event, it's important to maintain a history of all status reports so periodic reviews can be conducted for best practices and postmortems.

Some of the more significant features of any status reporting system should include the following:

- The system is integrated, bringing together schedule, budget, and product rather than separate reporting systems for same.

Project Management Excellence

- It's structured to support, primarily, the work-package leaders and project managers. It can then provide roll-up summary information for more senior management.
- It includes a systematic procedure for updating plans for every control-period report.
- Exception reporting highlights real and potential problems.
- It provides a means of tracking problems, risks, and changes.

An amount of integration, cooperation, and support are required for a project to succeed. Status reports and project reviews are tools that allow the project managers to control those elements of project progress that require immediate resolution.

Project Review Meetings

Project review meetings are another method of assessing project status. Project managers usually schedule weekly status meetings with members of the team, less often with customers or stakeholders. Those reviews usually serve as catalyst to infuse cross-functional team integration into the project and assist the manager in uncovering problem areas before major corrective action is required. The information from the project status meeting can be summarized and placed in the project status report, enabling that critical information flow across organizational boundaries.

Quality Assurance

The American Society for Quality defines quality assurance as "All the planned and systematic activities implemented with the quality system and demonstrated as needed, to provide adequate confidence that an entity will fulfill requirements for quality." This means the quality plan should describe a systematic approach that allows product or service quality to be evaluated at various points throughout the project life cycle. The approach should be quantifiable and take into consideration the probability of delivering the product or service successfully, within the parameters of:

- Customer quality requirements
- Management quality standards
- Compliance standards
- Intellectual property standards
- Legal standards
- Industry standards

Quality assurance can be broken down into two major sections: review analysis and risk analysis. Review analysis is the initiative associated with the rigorous reviews of design, development, delivery, and product or service warranty. The resources assigned to this area of responsibility determine the measurement tools by which those areas are tested and verified. Such tools might include:

- Customer interviews
- Business value
- Project management methodology
- Technology
- Business management
- Project involvement
- Vendor support
- Project measurement

Risk analysis is used to determine the probability that something negative might happen at any point during the project life cycle. Some of the tools used during this effort are:

- Product- or service-life expectancy estimates
- Product- or service-failure mode analysis
- Product- or service-critical analysis
- Reliability predication
- Historical data
- Frequency distribution of failures
- Service strategy
- Mitigation strategy
- Corrective action analysis

Quality assurance is a critical process in any project. It improves the effectiveness of project execution.

PROJECT EXECUTION PHASE SUMMARY

According to the Project Management Institute's role delineation study, five tasks make up the project execution phase. They are:

- Apply resources in keeping with the project plan. Ensure that all activities are performed
- Execute the project plan
- Evaluate project progress to ensure the plan is followed and produces the required deliverables
- Report project status to appropriate stakeholders
- Perform project control activities

CHAPTER VIII

PROJECT CONTROL

Once the plan is approved and work begins, the project activities must be controlled. The method of project control described in this chapter covers a process that uses the work package plans to update and report status against product, schedule, and budget. At a minimum, control should include updating the plan, change and issues control, and management reporting shown in figure 8.1.

Using the control process and reporting status will ensure the collection and processing of pertinent data. It also must provide information that will define where the project is headed in relationship to its objectives. However, to be kept informed, the project manager shouldn't rely totally upon the project reporting system.

Good communication is fundamental to controlling the project. The manager must ensure that all parties are kept well informed of changes and events. He or she must know what's going on, be able to identify problems as they surface, and know whom to deal with to solve these problems.

CONTINUOUS IMPROVEMENT

Continuous improvement can be defined as the never-ending pursuit of process improvement. This means getting customers involved from the beginning of a project by having

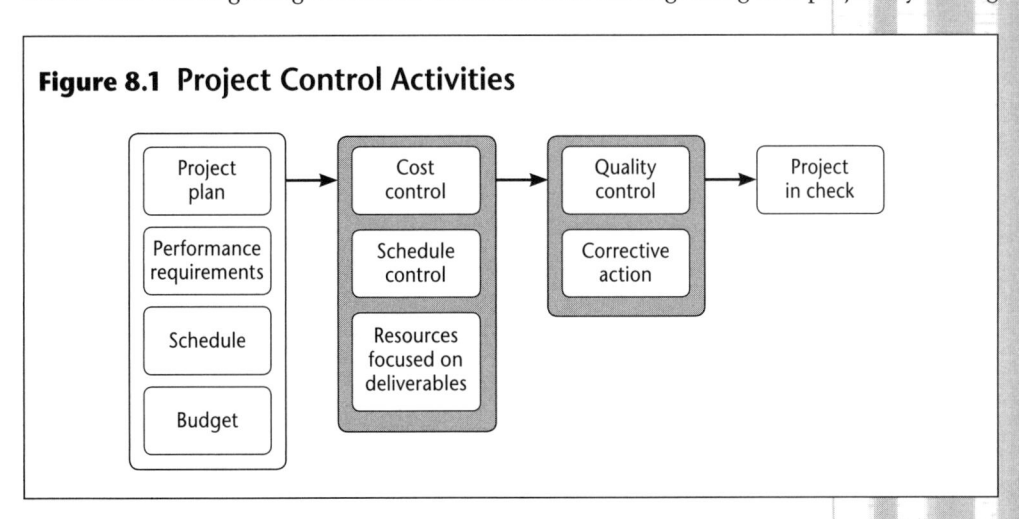

Figure 8.1 Project Control Activities

Project plan	→	Cost control	→	Quality control	→	Project in check
Performance requirements		Schedule control		Corrective action		
Schedule		Resources focused on deliverables				
Budget						

them define what they believe is required to change their perception of process quality, then following through to closure of customer transactions and ending with customer experience. Customer feedback should be used to eliminate process waste by realigning internal processes to customer needs. Customer efficiency and effectiveness are best realized by reducing cycle time, analyzing customer complaints, and taking actions to address customer concerns. It's important to examine not only internal process steps but also the process steps that are nonvalue-added to the customer. Every time a customer does business with your organization, you must understand what benefits the customer obtains and what might prevent the customer from doing business again. Therefore, you must:

- Identify customer problems
- Break down areas of concern into process steps
- Remove redundancy
- Eliminate nonvalue-added customer experiences
- List all possible solutions to improve process
- Implement the best solution
- Confirm that any new process works better than old processes
- Implement a customer feedback system (e.g., help desk)
- Use customer feedback for continuous process improvement

Clear and measurable process improvement can go a long way toward creating customer loyalty. Customer expectations and feedback serve as drivers toward continuous improvement. Variations from customer expectations should be analyzed and corrected as quickly as possible.

PROJECT CONTROL FRAMEWORK

Project control reviews are another essential tool for ensuring investments in projects generate the desired business results. The project manager, team, and senior management use the reviews to implement corrective action to help keep the project on track.

The project control review uses periodic project reviews to assess project execution, project quality, and risks, and to recommend corrective action that project leadership and senior management should take to improve project success. A key first step in beginning a project control review is upfront communication with the division management that a review is scheduled. As part of that dialog, an agreement is reached on what the review will entail and what team will serve as resources for the review from the division.

There are two review formats: an independent review conducted by an independent team, and a self-assessed review conducted by the project team itself. Both formats combine industry-best practices and experiences from across project management methodology.

The reviews use face-to-face project team interviews and documentary reviews to assess a project's health. Standardized checklists and questionnaires provide consistency between reviews. Results comprise both numerical and color ratings, as well as comments on positive findings, risks, recommendations, and opportunities for improvement. To prepare for an independent project control review, it's highly recommended that the project teams conduct a self-assessment first. That will enable them to determine if their idea of success is correct.

COST AND SCHEDULE CONTROL-VARIANCE ANALYSIS

A variance is a unit of measure that represents the difference between actual and planned requirements. Variances are used to determine if a project is on track or not. They're applied at specific times during the entire project life cycle to determine project efficiency and measure the following parameters of project success:
- Schedule completion
- Labor costs
- Material costs
- Overhead costs
- Costs to complete project
- Budget costs

Variances can be either favorable or unfavorable. A trend of unfavorable variances could be a red flag that the project is in trouble. Some variances will be within an acceptable range of performance, while others require corrective action immediately. Project managers should familiarize themselves with, and use, variance analysis regularly to assess the accurate status of a project. Project variances were originally described by Russell D. Archibald in his book, *Managing High-Technology Programs and Projects* (John Wiley & Sons, 1976). Since that time, project managers have used variances to determine when to take action to keep a project out of trouble.

Some of the terminology used in variance analysis as defined by the Project Management Institute follows:
- Actual cost of work performed (ACWP)—The actual cost of work expended within a given time period
- Budget at completion (BAC)—The budgeted cost to complete the project
- Budgeted costs of work performed (BCWP)—The budgeted amount of costs for completed work
- Budgeted costs of work scheduled (BCWS)—The budgeted cost of work scheduled for completion within a given time period

- Cost performance index (CPI)—BCWP divided by the ACWP.
- BCWP-earned value—The BCWS multiplied by the percentage of work accomplished
- Estimated cost to complete (ECC)—What the cost is expected to be at project completion
- Level of effort (LOE)—Number of person hours estimated divided by actual person hours completed
- Percent of budget spent (PBS)—ACWP divided by the BAC
- Percent complete (PC)—BCWP divided by the BCWS
- Schedule performance index (SPI)—BCWP divided by the BCWS

The cost variance (BCWP minus ACWP) measures deviations from the budget and doesn't necessarily provide an insight into the effectiveness of labor. Because we deduct the actual from budgeted measurements, a negative cost variance would represent a cost overrun. Depending on whether the variance is within an acceptable range or not, the project manager might want to investigate the situation to determine if corrective action would be required from the project team.

The schedule variance measures the difference between what was originally scheduled to happen (BCWS) against what the team actually accomplished (BCWP). A negative variance would indicate that the team was behind schedule. Depending on whether the variance is within an acceptable range, the manager would want to investigate the situation to determine if corrective action is required from the team.

The earned value provides insight into project control based on factors of scope, cost (BCWS), and schedule (percent complete). This measurement is the tool preferred by most project managers and is the calculation against which other measurements are compared. (See the more detailed discussion of earned value later in this chapter.)

Many project managers use the cost performance index as a method of forecasting the amount of gain against the amount spent.

- CPI = 1, anticipated cost performance
- CPI >1, better than anticipated cost performance
- CPI < 1, less than anticipated cost performance

Managers use the schedule performance index as a method of forecasting project schedule performance at a project's completion of the project:

- SPI = 1, anticipated schedule performance
- SPI >1, better than anticipated schedule performance
- SPI < 1, less than anticipated schedule performance

Variance analysis is an important aspect of every project. Project managers should use the project variation tools described here on a routine basis to determine if a project is on track.

QUALITY CONTROL

The American Society for Quality defines quality control as the "operational techniques that are used to fulfill requirements for quality." That definition can be interpreted as checkpoints established to verify a product's or service's conformance to standards of quality. If any area within the product or service doesn't conform, it's labeled as a defect. Usually this quality review is part of an inspection process that identifies defects as early as possible in the project life cycle. If they're identified in the project deliverable, a problem-solving technique should be used to analyze root causes of defects. The root causes can in turn be used to eliminate project inefficiencies. Root cause analysis usually consists of:

- Defect identification
- Defect categorization
- Defect analysis
- Defect resolution
- Resolution confirmation

With Six Sigma, areas of inspection are being phased out in favor of up-front vendor and process analysis. One best practice that's recently found favor with many companies is the system of tollgates. A tollgate review team is established and reviews a product or service at various points in the project's life cycle. If the project deliverable passes the tollgate, the team can proceed to the next level of project effort. Tollgate criteria should be derived from customer requirements and deliverable objectives.

INFORMATION AND REPORTING NEEDS

The project management information/knowledge system should be designed to meet many different people's needs.

Executive Managers' Needs

Executives require a knowledge system that will enable them to:

- Strategically rank and align project initiatives.
- Balance resource supply and demand.
- Monitor program risks, issues, and changes.
- Manage the decision-making process.
- Evaluate and track program team performance.
- Estimate, measure, and deliver project success.
- Capture and share program intellectual capital.

How do executives in your organization demonstrate business value?
- Easily access reports with minimal requisite learning
- View and rank all projects and programs, and define prioritizing criteria
- Generate, view, and print an array of canned, ad hoc, and customizable, executive-level project views and reports, such as:
  - ☐ *Department utilization.* Implement strategies for expansion based on increased utilization rates across one or multiple-pool domains and resource pools; increase profitability by monitoring status, utilization rates, productivity, and profits related to domain pools, across one or multiple projects, portfolios and programs.
  - ☐ *Project slippage.* Identify projects that fail to meet set quality standards and performance objectives, align their scopes with their stakeholders' requirements, and ensure that expected results are achieved.
  - ☐ *Project issues, change requests, risks (or triggers).* Ensure critical issues are addressed and adequate responses are instigated.
  - ☐ *Billable utilization.* Evaluate and optimize resource use.
  - ☐ *Client change requests.* Identify, qualify, and justify client-initiated amendments, evaluate their affect on profits and budgets, and, if necessary, implement measures to alter their occurrence.
  - ☐ *Engagement profitability.* Assess and optimize selection process of engagement opportunities.
  - ☐ *Earned value.* Evaluate, track, and optimize performance of teams, projects, programs, and business areas; initiate procedures to boost efficiency and limit productivity loss by tackling underlying issues.
  - ☐ *Project variances.* View and monitor any variants in projects, portfolios, and programs, and ensure high-priority initiatives comply with planned schedule, budget, and effort.

Project Manager's Information Needs

Acknowledging that less than 26 percent of information technology projects are successfully completed on time and on budget; that 46 percent are late, over budget, and fail to meet defined scope and quality; and that 28 percent are cancelled, how can project managers ensure that all their projects are delivered on time and on budget? By doing the following.
- Capture and share project intellectual capital.
  - ☐ Access, update, and store post-project process review reports, standard templates, sample projects, and best-demonstrated practices.
  - ☐ Respect formalized project management methodology and flow.

- Establish integrated project documentation management.
  - ☐ Control revision and changes.
  - ☐ Establish audit-trail project documents.
  - ☐ Author, modify, store, and retrieve templates.
  - ☐ Monitor concurrent access and modifications.

- Manage work breakdown structures top-down and bottom-up.
  - ☐ Track projects globally through a single database repository across multiple functions within the organization.
  - ☐ Request, negotiate, and accept resource scheduling (using generic profiles) in cooperation with the resource manager.
  - ☐ Roll up all budget, incurred costs, work effort, resource allocation, and schedule to project level, initiative level, and portfolio level.
  - ☐ Define links at multiple levels to reflect resource constraints or dependencies of deliverables and outputs.

- Identify and perform strategic trade-offs.
  - ☐ Analyze possible scenarios across multiple projects to forecast results on timing, resource allocation, and project status/progress.
  - ☐ Review projects' critical path, and identify project milestones and deliverables.
  - ☐ Report on performance against baseline at all levels.

- Quantify, qualify, and respond to changes, risks, and issues (CRIs).
  - ☐ Track CRIs by identification; responsible party, dates, classification, priority, and response tasks; evaluate effect and resolution.
  - ☐ Store CRIs in central database and retrieve at multiple levels.

- Ensure projects and portfolios are performing within budget.
  - ☐ Estimate budgets by building on readily available historical data.
  - ☐ Capture internal and external staff effort, procurement, funds, and nonpersonnel costs.
  - ☐ Allocate and charge back expenditures across business units, functional groups and cost centers, projects, and portfolios.
  - ☐ Plan, control, and monitor incurred and committed costs, payments, revenues, purchase orders, allocation of materials, and shipping/receiving of project materials.
  - ☐ Allow for fixed, unit costing, and amortization of capital expenditures.

- Report to management on project development.
  - ☐ Schedule predefined, automatically broadcasted reports.
  - ☐ Generate an array of performance, project status, and executive summary reports at multiple levels.

Resource Manager's Information Needs

Every percent increase in use after the 60 percent break-even point goes straight to the bottom line; the average use rate is 60–68 percent, and the optimal use rate is 75 percent.

To achieve the optimal use rate, your resource managers need to align the right resources with the right project initiatives at the right time all the time, eliminate time on the bench, develop strategies to secure and retain scarce resources, and capture and leverage valuable intellectual capital.

How do your resource managers ensure that their strategies will drive utilization up to improve bottom-line profits?

- Maintain an efficient and informative resource database.
  - ☐ Approve and complete employee resource information updates.
  - ☐ Assign cost and selling rates of skill sets, allowing for budget estimating prior to procurement.
  - ☐ Manage access privileges to views, reports, documents, and all other system data.
  - ☐ Track employees' time at project and task levels by requesting, accepting, modifying, or rejecting time sheets.
  - ☐ Provide individual resource performance-evaluation reports.
  - ☐ List outsourcing and hiring options for tasks and activities requiring skills that aren't available internally.
  - ☐ Calculate resource loading and forecast resource needs based on proposed and in-progress work.
  - ☐ Determine current total internal and external resource pool capacity, demand, availability, and use with generic and resource profiles.

- Strategically manage resource pool to achieve optimal use.
  - ☐ Assign resources across multiple programs, locations, and functional work areas.
  - ☐ Make assignment decisions in light of all relevant resource profile data, including:
    - Assigned resources across multiple programs, locations, and functional work areas
    - Availability for a given period and scheduled assignments across multiple projects
    - Qualified exhaustive list of competencies and skills, level of proficiency level, examples of experience as well as cost and selling rate per competency/skill
    - Background information (e.g., experience, area of expertise, personal preferences and interests, industry, work and project history, location preferences)
    - Location information (e.g., geographic, organizational, workflow group)

Project Control

- Project performance ratings by project manager for past completed tasks
- All related attachments (e.g., résumé, references)
- Calendar, status (including all assignments and exceptions)
- Billable use by resource

☐ Effectively balance supply and demand.
- Identify the type, quantity, and location where additional capacity is needed to undertake a new initiative.
- Ensure that proposed resources faithfully match profiles in the project managers demand list.
- Capture changing staffing requirements brought about by real-time project events.

☐ Secure and retain resources.
- Determine estimated effort, location, type of competency, skill, and proficiency required to perform a particular task.
- Effectively identify the optimum quantity and types of resources needed.
- Locate where the necessary availability of knowledge and skills can be found in the organization.
- Evaluate and improve resource effort for best schedule effect.
- Identify opportunities for reducing duration through effort splitting.
- Locate and leverage knowledge acquired by previous work assignments to improve current performance.
- Align most skilled resources with highest priority initiatives and projects.

Team Members' Information Needs

How do you get team members to effectively collaborate and communicate enterprise-wide?

■ Reduce waste and improve productivity through a smooth communication workflow.
  ☐ Abide by a standard method for accessing and manipulating common information, templates, and pertinent documents.
  ☐ Easily author, modify, attach, store, and retrieve documents (i.e., version-control tracking) related to a project or task.
  ☐ Receive notices for all relevant events (e.g., task assignments, overdue issues, issue assignment).
  ☐ Access to list of team members and contact info.
  ☐ Access to discussion threads of project team communications.

- Report systematically all pertinent events through a single point of entry.
  - ☐ Access customized views according to access privileges, role descriptions, and status.
  - ☐ Read only relevant part of the project database.
  - ☐ Enter work hours, costs, and comments against assigned projects, milestones, and tasks.
  - ☐ Update individual resource profile, customize calendar by pre-entering particular time (e.g., vacation, training), and review work packages and responsibilities.

Project Reporting Needs

Although some information can be obtained through monthly reports or various departments, management's challenge with projects is understanding the big picture from an enterprise perspective.

Among the most requested overall views required from managers by executives is exception reporting via an executive dashboard. What are the specific issues, risks, and changes that require executive intervention? The problem is in spotting the hot spots before they become full-blown crises.

Traditional structures tend to cover up pending problems until they can no longer be suppressed and end up involving senior management generally in damage control. The business context doesn't support a system where errors pile up and thus must authorize project managers and senior managers to "pre-act" rather than react.

Schedule vs. actual

Assuming projects have been broken down into smaller, traceable components, tracking both delays and remaining effort required will provide early warnings of negative trends. Further analysis of delays and overruns will also help identify root causes of delays (i.e., resource related, technology related, process related) so those lags can be eliminated in the future.

Budget vs. actual

Managers rarely go over their annual budgets, so executives rarely get the opportunity to understand why budgets are met but deliverables are late. The ability to drill down into specific projects will also help to identify which projects are the biggest drains on budgets and resources, and why.

Demand vs. supply

Biting off more than can be chewed is an endemic condition for IT and other projects. Projects always appear closer to completion than they actually are, and only when they're broken down into sufficient detail can managers assess the organization's capacity and skills availability to meet demand. Using automated systems for load balancing and sharing key resources across several projects is one solution; planning for specific contractors

Project Control

is another. Curtailing scope or outright pushing back on specific projects is another possibility. However, none of the preceding can be achieved or defended without knowing just what the organization's capacity is on a real-time basis.

Utilization and productivity

By using a centralized reservation and booking system for all your resources based on skills and availability, you can also track utilization (i.e., the percentage of time actually spent on a project doing productive work) by employee, function, or by staff knowledge and abilities (SKAs).

Turnover rate

Recruitment and retention remain a stiff challenge for knowledge organizations and is often symptomatic of other issues. According to Gartner Group, knowledge workers will interview potential employers so stringently that 40 percent of potential employers will miss recruitment goals by a substantial margin.

Return on projects

Knowing what's involved and then picking only projects that are "business imperatives" means determining up front what the expected return on each project is and then establishing measurements that define what it truly was. Certain projects are more painful than others, being late, expensive, or just plain failures. Having a global view of these situations coupled with an understanding of where the weaknesses occurred is paramount to avoiding those same issues in the future. Difficulties can crop up in technology issues, applications, managers, teams, or specific individuals. You might find recurring problems in certain project phases, such as scope or testing, and then take appropriate action.

Billing rates and costs per resource

As organizations rely increasingly on outside resources for e-business projects, and teams consist of blends of people, monitoring their costs and effectiveness becomes almost impossible. Using tools that segregate responsibility and then allow progress tracking becomes important when determining the effectiveness and efficiency of individual team members, whether they're employees or consultants.

Norbert Turek, e-business journalist and frequent contributor to *Business Week,* recommends that you buy a project management software package as you begin developing your organization's project management methodology. "If you wait until you've got a perfect project management process, no tool will fit perfectly," he observes.

(*Note:* See chapter five for a detailed discussion of project portfolio management.)

The biggest case study on project management comes from the world's biggest IT services organization, IBM Corp. Some 50 percent of IBM's revenues, about $40 billion, are generated annually through the delivering promised services in IT projects.

The global giant, called by *Business Week* the "biggest dot com of them all," manages literally thousands of projects and hundreds of thousands of people in fifty-two countries around the world, using Systemcorp's Project Management Office, a Web-based system.

The software was rolled out in 2002 to 350,000 IBM resources around the world, echoing industry consensus that IT in the new economy must incorporate Internet-based enterprise tools to run their e-businesses.

"Selecting a project management tool that fits an organization's requirements is critical in successfully managing e-business projects," states Margo Visitacion of Giga Information Group.

Systemcorp estimates that PMOffice can help organizations save a potential $12,000 per resource, per year. We believe that many other software packages will match these savings also.

EARNED VALUE ANALYSIS

Earned value analysis (EVA) is a method of measuring project performance. It compares the amount of work that was planned with what was actually accomplished to determine if cost and schedule performance is operating as planned.

Combining scope, cost, and schedule measurements, earned value analysis is one of the most frequently used approaches to evaluate a project's status. EVA makes effective use of three important values for each activity within the work breakdown structure.

- *Planned value (PV)*. This is the approved cost-estimate plan for a specific activity over a specific period of time. It's sometimes called "budgeted cost of work scheduled" (BCWS).
- *Actual cost (AC)*. This is the total of direct and indirect costs expended on an activity over a specific period of time. It's sometimes called "actual cost of work performed" (ACWP).
- *Earned value (EV)*. This the true value of work completed over a specific period of time. It's sometimes called "budgeted cost of work performed" (BCWP).

These three values are used to provide measures as to whether project work is being accomplished as planned. For example, they calculate:

- *Cost variance (CV)*. CV = EV – AC (negative variance indicates a cost overrun)
- *Schedule variance (SV)*. SV = EV – PV (negative variance indicates behind schedule for work by resources)
- *Cost performance index (CPI)*. Calculated by dividing the earned value by actual costs: (CPI) = EV/AC. This measure shows the dollar value the project is returning for every dollar spent.

Project Control

Figure 8.2 Plot of Actual Cost Versus Earned Value

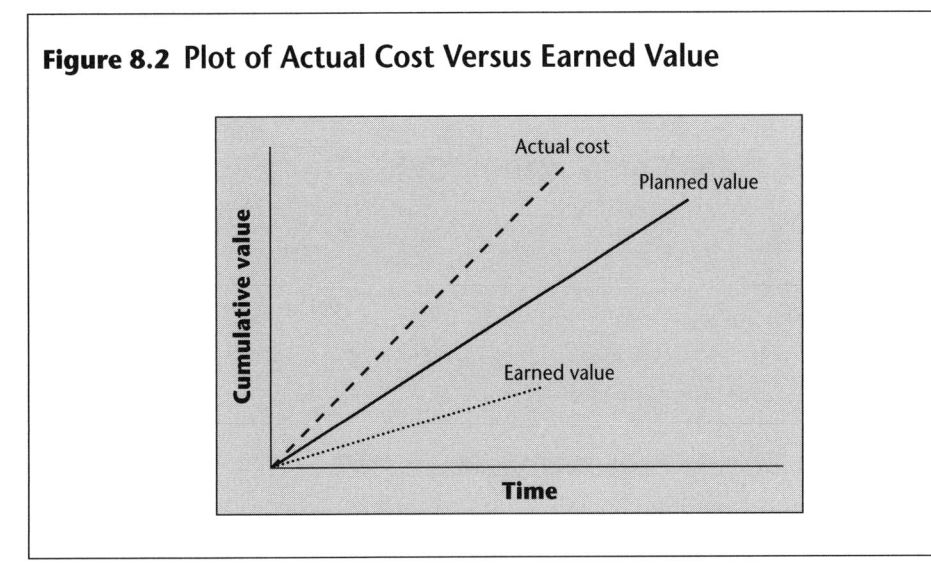

- *Schedule performance index (SPI)*. Calculated by dividing the earned value by planned costs: (SPI) = EV/ PC. This measure shows the value of work the project is returning for every dollar paid to resources.

The cumulative cost performance index (cumulative CPI) is calculated by adding all individual earned values (sum EV) and dividing by the sum of all individual actual costs (sum AC). Project managers use this calculation to forecast project cost at completion (CAC).

Figure 8.2 is a plot of the actual cost versus earned value.

Example 1: Calculating Earned Value (EV)

Task A, which was supposed to be completed today, is scheduled to cost $1,000 (BCWS). The project is 75 percent complete.
- EV = (percent completed) x (planned value)
- EV = 75 percent x $1,000 = $750

$750 is the true value of work completed for task A.

Example 2: Calculating the Sum of Earned Values (Sum EV)

This is sometimes called total earned value (TEV). Activity A is scheduled for completion today, but it's only 75 percent complete. Its planned value (PV) was $1,000. Activity B is 50 percent completed, and its PV is $500.
- Sum EV = EV A + EV B or
- Sum EV = (75% x $1,000) + (50% x $500) or

- Sum EV = $750 + $250 = $1,000

$1,000 is the true value of work completed for the two tasks.

Example 3: Calculating Cost Variance (CV)

Activity B is 50 percent completed, and its PV is $500. There has been $400 spent on that activity.
- CV = EV − actual costs
- CV = $250 − $400 = $−150

This negative variance indicates a cost overrun.

Example 4: Calculating Schedule Variance (SV)

Task C was scheduled to have $1,000 of work completed today. The earned value is $740.
- SV = EV − PV or
- SV = $740 − $1,000 = −$260

This negative variance indicates slow work progress.

Example 5: Calculating Schedule Variance Percentage (SVP) Using Example 4

- SVP = SV ÷ PV x 100 or
- SVP = −$260 ÷ $1,000 x 100 = 26 percent

The work progress is behind schedule by 26 percent.

Example 6: Calculating Cost Variance Percentage (CVP) Using Example 3

- CVP = CV ÷ AC x 100 or
- CVP = −$150 ÷ $400 x 100 = −37.5%

Spending is overrunning budget by 37.5 percent.

Example 7: Calculating Cost Performance Index (CPI) Using Example 3

- CPI = EV ÷AC or
- $250 ÷ $400 = $0.63

Every $1 spent on this project is worth only $0.63.

Project Control

Figure 8.3 Cumulative Effect of Earned Value on Project Work Packages

WBS work package	Budget (PV)	Earned value (EV)	Actual costs (AC)	Cost variance (CV)	% Cost variance CV x 100/ (AC)	Schedule variance (SV)	% Schedule variance SV x 100/ (PV)
Requirements	$10,000	$8,000	$9,000	-$1,000	-11.1%	-$2,000	-20.0%
Design	$60,000	$65,000	$63,000	+$2,000	+3.2%	+$5,000	+8.3%
Development	$100,000	$80,000	$110,000	-$30,000	-27.3%	-$20,000	-20.0%
Implementation	$80,000	$150,000	$100,000	+$50,000	+50.0%	+$70,000	+87.5%
Totals	**$250,000**	**$303,000**	**$282,000**	**+$21,000**	**+7.5%**	**+$53,000**	**+21.2%**

Example 8: Calculating Schedule Performance Index (SPI) Using Example 1

- SPI = EV ÷ PV or
- $750 ÷ 1,000 = $0.75

For every dollar spent on work, resource output is $0.75.

Example 9: Cumulative Effect of Earned Value on Project Work Packages

Overall, the project was successful. There were two areas—requirements and development—that require examination to understand why variances were realized. This information can be carried forward into future projects as lessons learned.

> "With the technologies that are available today, the standard should be set very high in terms of doing those things far more efficiently than you ever dreamed, with far, far fewer people, no paper, and with an incredible ability to get at the information with greatest of ease."
> —Robert J. Herbold
> Former COO,
> Microsoft Corp.

DASHBOARD REPORTING

Dashboard reporting is an essential management tool to keep management informed and promote action that supports project managers where necessary so that projects generate the desired business results. Dashboard reporting provides:

- Senior management visibility into project progress
- Project manager visibility into issues, risks, or obstacles
- Stakeholder visibility into analyzing and reviewing project status information

Project Management Excellence

Figure 8.4 Dashboard Reporting

Dashboards

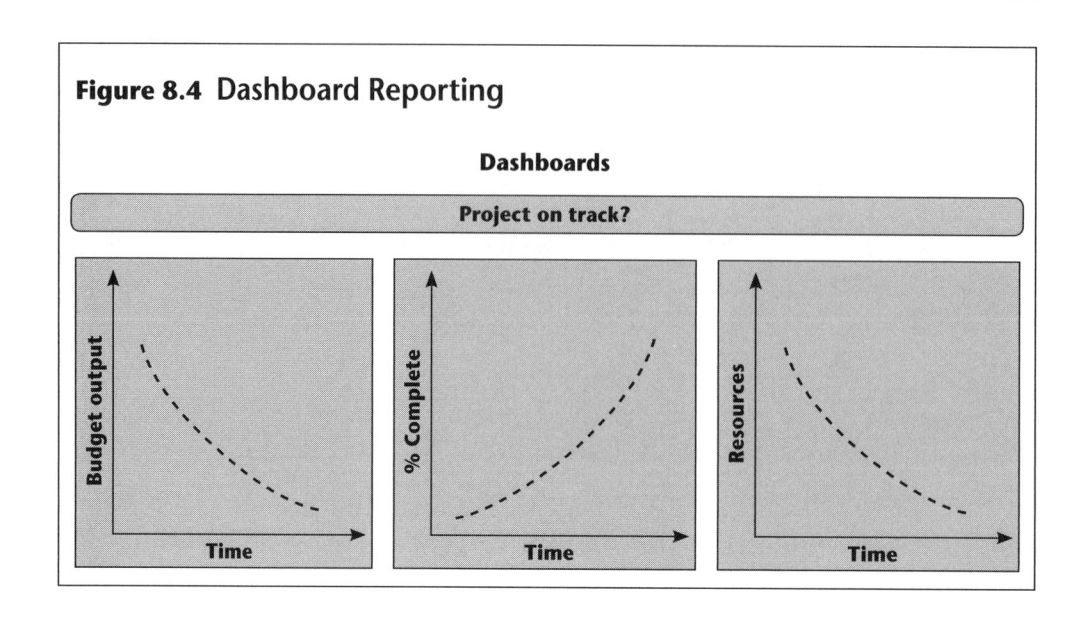

Project on track?

[Three graphs: Budget output vs Time (decreasing), % Complete vs Time (increasing), Resources vs Time (decreasing)]

Figure 8.5 Typical Dashboard Report

Portfolio A: Project Status View

Project name	Priority	Scope	Schedule	Budget	Index
Litton	900	■	▨	■	■
Bosch	700	■	▨▨	■	▨
BofA-S.F	800	■	▨▨	▨▨	▨▨
BofA-S.J.	800	■	▨▨	▨▨	▨▨
BofA-L.A.	800	▨	■	■	■
FAC	600	▨▨	▨▨	▨▨	▨▨
Ord. entry	300	■	■	■	■
Proj. mgt.	500	▨	■	▨▨	▨
Six Sigma	800	■	▨	■	■

Legend

	Scope	Schedule	Budget	Points	Index
■	0–2	0–less	0–less	0	0–3=G
▨	3–6	1–20%	1–20%	2	4–7=Y
▨▨	7+	20%+	20%+	4	8–12=R

What project information and metrics should be reported? Reporting has been streamlined and simplified through a red-yellow-green rating system and by focusing on five key project performance areas. They are:
- Financials/budget
- Schedule
- Resources
- Scope
- Quality

PROJECT CONTROL PHASE SUMMARY

According to the Project Management Institute's role delineation study, eight tasks make up the project control phase. They are:
1. Identify project trends and variances by continually measuring project status and comparing it to the plan.
2. Identify issues that need corrective action.
3. Identify the root cause of problems and take required corrective action.
4. Evaluate the effectiveness of the corrective action taken.
5. Monitor the response to change and alter the change management plan if necessary.
6. Conduct periodic reviews to ensure project control plans are effective.
7. React to risk-event triggers and implement appropriate actions as defined in the risk-management plan.
8. Audit the project process to ensure the project is progressing to plan and the plan is adequate. Identify any needed corrective action.

CHAPTER IX

PROJECT CLOSEOUT

Upon completing the project, the project management team begins the project closeout processes and report. (See figure 9.1.) The manager's closeout processes include administrative procedures to formally close out the project budget. He or she also conducts a project evaluation and assessment to include in the closeout report.

Once the project is closed, the organization then decides if the project will be given a post evaluation by someone other than the project manager.

REWARDS AND RECOGNITION

It's important to provide proper rewards and recognition to individuals and teams that accomplish difficult and/or important projects in a superior fashion. But when should you provide that recognition, and how do you decide what it should be? You should reinforce

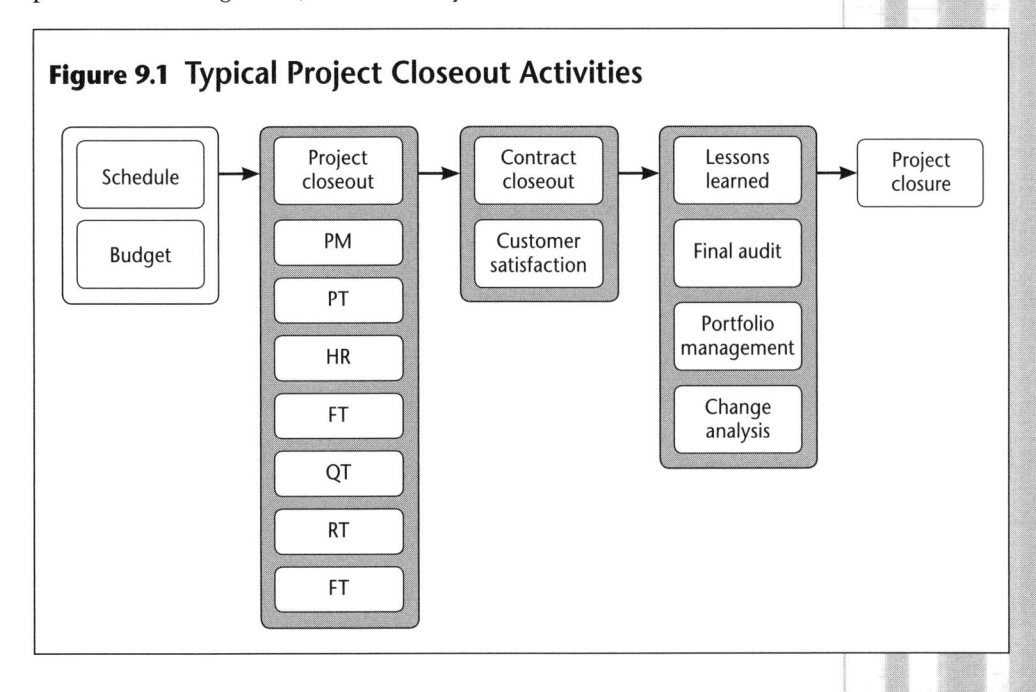

Figure 9.1 Typical Project Closeout Activities

Schedule → Project closeout → Contract closeout → Lessons learned → Project closure

Budget

Project closeout: PM, PT, HR, FT, QT, RT, FT

Contract closeout: Customer satisfaction

Lessons learned: Final audit, Portfolio management, Change analysis

Project Management Excellence

desired behaviors as soon as possible after they've been demonstrated. All teams that complete their projects below estimated cost and on schedule should be rewarded at project closeout. However, in many cases the project's true effect can't be measured until months after the project is closed out. When that happens, a small reward is given at closeout and another when the project's success has been measured.

Many factors influence the type of recognition given to the team. It can vary from a personal thank you from the sponsor to monetary rewards that amount to thousands of dollars. The amount of the award depends on factors such as:
- What new knowledge was added to the knowledge base?
- How much money did it save the organization?
- How critical was it to the business?
- How difficult was it to accomplish?
- How much of a competitive advantage did it give the organization?

But money isn't the only type of recognition that's used. Other things that work well include:
- Team awards
  - ☐ Articles about the team in the organization's newsletter
  - ☐ Team luncheons with upper management
  - ☐ Recognition family picnics
  - ☐ Attendance at a conference
  - ☐ Cake and coffee at a team meeting
  - ☐ Plaques
  - ☐ Team mementos (e.g., pen sets, computers)

- Individual awards
  - ☐ Promotions
  - ☐ Personal letter sent to the employee's home
  - ☐ Employee-of-the-month awards
  - ☐ Paper published in a technical magazine

> **"We still have Boy Scout merit badges and trophies gathering dust, and a medal or two from some insignificant ski race held decades ago. Nothing is more powerful than a positive reinforcement."**
> —**Tom Peters and Robert Waterman, Jr.**
> *In Search of Excellence*

If a group of employees did a good job and you want them to continue to do so, you must say "thank you" in a way everyone on the team will hear. The problem is that we all hear that in very different ways.

PROJECT CLOSEOUT PHASE SUMMARY

According to the Project Management Institute's role delineation study, five tasks make up the project closeout phase. They are:

- Obtain final formal acceptance of the deliverables to achieve closeout.
- Survey project team and relevant stakeholders to define lessons learned.
- Close out financial and administrative paperwork.
- Store project records as defined by legal and organizational requirements. Use good judgment in selecting things that are discarded.
- Release project resources as soon as possible so they can be applied to other activities.

We add two more tasks:

- Reward or recognize the individuals and teams that contributed to the project's success.
- Input relevant data into the organization's knowledge management system.

CHAPTER X

PROJECT MANAGEMENT LIFE CYCLE SUMMARY

"Good project management is a learned skill, not a personal trait."
—HJH

HOW THREE ORGANIZATIONS IMPROVED THEIR PROJECT MANAGEMENT

During the late 1980s, IBM's strategy changed. The company focused on growing its consulting services, which required greatly improving the existing project management process. The company created the IBM Project Management Center of Excellence, and one of its major goals was to develop a standard worldwide project management method (WWPMM). To accomplish this, the center established an expert panel of some 100 project managers and executives. To ensure the methodology's acceptance in all IBM divisions globally, the panel consolidated a range of project management methods and industrial standards. Some of them were:

- Project Management Body of Knowledge (PMBOK)
- IEEE/ACM
- ISO 9000
- IPD (brands)
- Euromethod
- Bird (CGI)
- PMM1
- Symeris (France)
- ADC (Japan)
- Software Engineering Institute

The end methodology was largely based upon PMBOK. It incorporated activities such as:
- Sponsor agreement management
- Event management

- Technical environment management
- Change management
- Project definition
- Work plan management
- Deliverables management
- Tracking and control
- Supplier management
- Quality management

The WWPMM contained thirteen knowledge areas that grouped 150 different processes. The IBM Project Management Center of Excellence defined successful operations by four factors:
- All project management professionals are knowledgeable, accountable, and part of a respected learning community
- Employees in all professions understand and practice their roles and responsibilities.
- All management systems, infrastructure, and staff organizations support project management with portfolio, program, and project views.
- Mechanisms are in place to sustain learning and continuous improvement of project management disciplines.

The center defined a five-level maturity model as follows:
- Level I—pilot phase. Ad hoc-type operation
- Level II—in deployment. The project management process is disciplined. Roles and responsibilities are specified in the project plan.
- Level III—functional. The project management process is standardized, consistent, and has defined practices.
- Level IV—integrated. The project management process produces predictable results. Monitoring and management tools are in place.
- Level V—world class. The project management process is continuously improving. A knowledge base provides continuous feedback and prompts upgrades that reflect best practices. Lessons learned are continuously included in the process design.

The center developed an education curriculum to provide the best project management education available in the industry. This curriculum translates education into effective business advantage through knowledge prerequisites, periodic testing, applied work experience, and a progressive course structure that builds upon previous classes. In 1992 IBM began certifying its project managers. The certification process provided the company with managers who could apply the latest technologies and methods. In addition, certified project managers were required to recertify every three years, thereby ensuring constant exposure to the most recent and advanced project management initiatives and experiences.

IBM conducted an extensive benchmarking study of project management software packages available around the world and selected two products:
- Microsoft Project Office
- Systemcorp PMOffice

The advantages and disadvantages of each of these are listed in figure 10.1.

As a result of its increased focus on project management, IBM greatly reduced cost, wasted effort, schedule overruns, and project failures throughout the organization.

Essex Electrical tried many combinations to make it's IT project successful. As the company president, Harold Karp, put it, "I've had teams that were headed up by just business executives, and I've had them headed up by just an IT executive. In both cases, the teams achieved only limited success." When they switched over to a project management approach, IT operating expenses dropped by 35 percent, and sales gained 1 percent, which translated into margins of 2.5 percent to 3 percent.

Figure 10.1 Advantages and Disadvantages of IBM's Project Management Software Selection

Project Office Software	PMOffice Software
■ Scope management ■ Communications management ■ Exception management ■ Knowledge enabled workflow ■ Time management	■ Scope management ■ Communications management ■ Exception management ■ Knowledge enabled workflow ■ Cost management ■ Quality management ■ Human resource Management ■ Integration management ■ Customized reporting
Advantages	**Advantages**
■ Lower cost ■ Less training ■ Minor organization change	■ More functionality
Disadvantages	**Disadvantages**
■ Less enterprise reporting capability ■ Less resource management capability	■ 3–6 months to implement ■ Significant organization change

Well-managed projects do make a difference, according to a December 2003 article in *CRM Magazine*: As a result of effectively implementing a customer relationship management project, Waters Corp. was able to:
- Achieve an overall ROI of 35 percent
- Nearly triple sales
- Increase e-commerce revenue by 300 percent
- Generate additional revenue of $2 million in the service department alone

Projects represent a significant investment of strategic importance to any organization. The investment is comprised of resources, capital expenditure, time commitment, and individual dedication to make and embrace a change that will enable the organization to improve business performance and strengthen its competitive position.

Because projects are so critical to an organization's continued growth, it's important to generate a project postmortem. This document consolidates and outlines essential project best practices and identifies any negative lessons learned so that other project managers don't have to make the same mistakes.

A postmortem verifies the following:
- Did the project realize business benefits?
- Did the project deliverables meet requirement objectives?
- What best practices could be passed on to other project managers?
- What lessons learned should other project managers look out for?
- Did the project result in customer satisfaction?
- Which resources excelled during this project?

Answering these questions for senior management will help them understand the project outcome. The information will also enable the organization to continue using its best resources on other projects.

The PMBOK and other standards define seventy-five different tools that a project manager should master. (These tools are listed in appendix B. Test yourself to see if you're ready to manage a project.) Few project managers I've met during the past fifty years have mastered all these tools. Today very few project managers are certified as such by their peers. The Project Management Institute has an excellent certification program that we highly recommend. As an executive, you should select certified project managers to run your projects.

"Project management is one of the most important improvement tools available but also one of the most misused. It's as if we're trying to use a hammer to remove a screw."

—HJH

APPENDIX A

DEFINITIONS

- **Activity definition**—Identifying and documenting specific activities that must be performed to produce the deliverables and subdeliverables identified in the work breakdown structure.
- **Activity duration**—The best estimate of the time (e.g., hours, days, weeks, months) necessary to accomplish the work involved in an activity, considering the nature of the work and resources needed.
- **Activity-on-arrow (AOA)**—A method of depicting a network plan that indicates work is performed on the lines between nodes (i.e., events).
- **Activity-on-node (AON)**—A method of depicting a network plan that indicates work is performed on the nodes with lines connecting the nodes to show the network's logic.
- **Actual cost of work performed (ACWP)**—Total costs incurred (direct and indirect) in accomplishing work during a given time period.
- **Agreement**—Step in contract negotiation in which the final agreement is documented.
- **Alternatives identification**—Using various methods to determine which risk events might affect the project and documenting their characteristics.
- **Analogous estimating**—Using the actual duration of a previous, similar activity as the basis for estimating the duration of a future activity; a form of expert judgment.
- **Architecture**—A cohesive and consistent solution framework for achieving business objectives. Every solution architecture is composed of business process, data, technology infrastructure, application, and organizational architectures.
- **Asset**—Any tangible piece of equipment, hardware, or software that's purchased, leased, used, maintained, and tracked by the project team.
- **Asset management**—The process of acquiring, building, maintaining, and disposing of assets.
- **Assumptions**—Factors that will be considered true, real, or certain for planning purposes.
- **Assumption analysis**—A technique used to explore the accuracy, consistency, or completeness of an assumption.
- **Balanced matrix**—Organizational structure in which some staff is involved in project work as coordinators or expeditors while other staff is involved full-time, as for example the project manager.

Project Management Excellence

- **Benefit-cost ratio**—Comparative analysis of benefits versus costs that can be used to determine potential returns from a project. If the ration is greater than one, benefits exceed costs; if it's less than one, it's not profitable because costs exceed benefits; if it equals one, benefits equal costs.
- **Benefit-measurement method**—Method of project selection that includes items such as cost-benefit analysis, present value, payback period, return on investment, and internal rate of return.
- **Bottom-up estimate**—An approach that estimates cost starting at the lower levels of the work breakdown structure (WBS) and then summing up to successively higher WBS levels.
- **Budget at completion (BAC)**—The estimated total cost of the project when done.
- **Budgeted cost of work performed (BCWP)**—The sum of the approved cost estimates (including any overhead allocation) for activities, or portions of activities, completed during a given period (usually project to date).
- **Budgeted cost of work scheduled (BCWS)**—The sum of the approved cost estimates (including any overhead allocation) for activities, or portions of activities, scheduled to be performed during a given period (usually project to date).
- **Business risk**—The inherent chances for both profit and loss associated with a particular endeavor.
- **Business system analyst (BSA)**—A project team member. Serves as the primary point of contact with the information technology organization and is accountable for business integration.
- **Change control**—The project management function of monitoring and dealing with changes to the scope of a project or its objectives.
- **Change control board (CCB)**—A formally constituted group of stakeholders responsible for approving or rejecting changes to the project baselines.
- **Closure**—Step in contract negotiation in which positions are summarized and final concessions are made.
- **Communications management plan**—A document that provides a collection and filing structure that details what methods will be used to gather and store various types of information; a distribution structure that details to whom information will flow and methods to be used.
- **Configuration management**—Any documented procedure used to apply technical and administrative direction and surveillance to identify and document the functional and physical characteristics of an item or system; control any changes to such characteristics; record and report the change and its implementation status; and audit the items and system to verify conformance to requirements.
- **Constraint**—Factors that limit the project management team's options for planning purposes.

- **Contingency allowance**—Provision to mitigate cost and/or schedule risk.
- **Contingency plans**—Predefined action steps to take if an identified risk occurs. An active risk acceptance response. Identifying alternative strategies to be used if the risk occurs.
- **Continuous risk management**—An approach to software risk management developed by the Software Engineering Institute with processes, methods, and tools for managing risks in a project. It provides a disciplined environment for proactive decision making to continuously assess what could go wrong (i.e., risks), determine which risks are critical enough to warrant taking action, and implement strategies to deal with them.
- **Contract**—A mutually binding agreement that obligates the seller to provide the specified product and obligates the buyer to pay for it. A legal relationship subject to remedy in the courts.
- **Contract work breakdown structure (CWBS)**—Describes the total product and work to be done to satisfy a specific contract.
- **Cost-benefit analysis**—Comparative analysis of cost versus benefits that can be used to determine net returns from a project.
- **Cost performance index (CPI)**—The ratio of budgeted costs to actual costs (BCWP/ACWP). CPI often is used to predict the magnitude of a possible cost overrun using the following formula: original cost estimate/CPI = projected cost at completion.
- **Cost risk**—(1) Failure to complete tasks within the estimated budget allowances. (2) The degree of uncertainty associated with system acquisition life cycle budgets and outlays that could negatively affect the project.
- **Cost variance (CV)**—(1) Any difference between the estimated cost of an activity and its actual costs. (2) In earned value, the numerical difference between budgeted cost of work performed (BCWP) less actual costs (ACWP).
- **Critical path**—In a project network diagram, the series of activities that determine the earliest completion of the project. It's the path with the greatest duration. The critical path usually is defined as those activities with float less than or equal to a specified value, often zero.
- **Design of experiments**—Used in quality planning to identify the variables with the most influence on the overall outcome.
- **Duration**—The number of work periods (not including holidays or other nonworking periods) required to complete an activity or other project element.
- **Earned value analysis (EVA)**—A method for measuring project performance. It compares the amount of work that was planned with what was actually accomplished to determine if cost and schedule performance is functioning as planned.
- **Empowerment**—People doing the work have the authority and responsibility to carry it out and are able to make decisions concerning it.

- **Estimate**—To make a judgment as to the likely or appropriate cost, quality, or duration. To evaluate a rough calculation, a preliminary calculation of cost of work to be undertaken, or an opinion.
- **Estimate at completion (EAC)**—The expected total cost of an activity, group of activities, or the project when the defined scope of work has been completed. A forecast of total project costs based on project performance.
- **Estimate to complete (ETC)**—The expected additional cost needed to complete an activity, a group of activities, or the total project. Most techniques for forecasting ETC include some adjustment to the original estimate based on project performance to date.
- **Estimated cost to complete (ECC)**—What the cost is expected to be at project completion.
- **Exception report**—Used for a specific decision on the project; reports are distributed to individuals who are involved or must know. Report issued when a decision is made on an exception basis and it's desirable to inform other managers.
- **Expected monetary value**—The product of an event's probability of occurrence and the gain or loss that will result.
- **Exposure**—The susceptibility to loss, perception of a risk, or a threat to an asset or asset-producing process, usually quantified in dollars. An exposure is the total dollars at risk without regard to the probability of a negative event. A measure of importance.
- **External risks**—Risks that are beyond the control or influence of the project team; addressed in risk identification.
- **Fifty-fifty approach**—In earned value analysis, the fifty-fifty rule or approach is used to estimate the amount of each task that has been completed. As soon as a task has started, it's assumed that half the effort is completed and half the budgeted cost of work-scheduled value associated with the task is entered into the project accounts book. Only after the task is completed is the remaining half of the BCWS value entered into the accounts.
- **Finish-to-finish (FF)**—A relationship in a precedence diagram method network that indicates a preceding activity must be completed before a succeeding activity can be finished.
- **Finish-to-start (FS)**—A relationship in a precedence diagram method network that indicates one activity must be completed before the succeeding activity can be started.
- **Forward-looking view**—A principle of continuous risk management that requires thinking toward tomorrow, identifying uncertainties, and anticipating potential outcomes and managing project resources and activities while anticipating uncertainties.
- **Guess**—To predict or assume (an event or fact) without enough information to be sure; to suppose; to judge.
- **Impact**—The loss or effect on the project if the risk occurs.

- **Independent cost estimate**—An estimate of project costs conducted by individuals external to the normal project management structure.
- **Indirect costs**—Part of the overall costs of doing business in the organization that are shared by all projects underway. Examples include receptionists, security guards, insurance, taxes, etc.
- **Information technology manager (ITM)**—Serves as primary manager of the information technology organization participants and is accountable for coordinating and oversight of IT effort across the project. Provides subproject(s) status to project manager by rolling up project statuses provided by information technology teams leaders.
- **Interface management**—Identifying, documenting, scheduling, communicating, and monitoring interfaces related to a project's product.
- **Internal rate of return (IRR)**—Measure of a project's expected profitability. Average rate of return for the project. The interest rate that makes the present value of costs equal to the present value of benefits. The higher the IRR, the better the project.
- **Internal risks**—Risks under the control or influence of the project team; addressed in risk identification.
- **Kickoff meeting**—A meeting conducted to acquaint participants with the project and each other; the project kickoff meeting presumes the presence of the customer, facilitates an initial review of project scope and activities, and usually is conducted after contract award.
- **Known/unknown (risks)**—Risks that are identified, assessed, and qualified and for which plans can be made.
- **Late finish date (LF)**—In the critical path method, the latest possible point in time that an activity can be completed without delaying a specified milestone (usually the project finish date).
- **Late start date (LS)**—In the critical path method, the latest possible point in time that an activity can begin without delaying a specified milestone (usually the project finish date).
- **Law of diminishing returns**—As more is put into something, less is received from it proportionately.
- **Leveling**—The practice of constraining resource use to practical limits and applying these constraints to the project schedule after completing the building of the unconstrained schedule.
- **Level of effort (LOE)**—Number of person hours estimated/actual person hours completed
- **List reduction**—A simple approach used to deal with a large number of risks, strategies, or other ideas and especially the results of a brainstorming session to help clarify opinions and reduce the list to a more manageable number.

- **Major risk**—A risk that has a high or medium likelihood of occurring with a significant adverse effect on the affected item(s).
- **Mandatory dependencies**—Hard logic; they involve the physical or technological limitations of the work to be done.
- **Milestone**—(1) A significant event during the project, usually completion of a major deliverable. (2) A clearly identifiable point in a project or set of activities that commonly denotes a reporting requirement or completion of a large or important set of activities. (3) A task with a duration of zero that's used to measure a project's progress or signify completion of a major deliverable.
- **Milestone chart**—A scheduling technique that depicts the start and completion of tasks through the use of events (or milestones) on a time-scale chart.
- **Minor risk**—A risk that doesn't cause significant problems and represents a relatively small financial amount.
- **Mitigation**—In project risk management, taking steps to lessen risk by lowering the probability of a risk event's occurrence or reducing its effect should it occur. Mitigation deals with a risk by developing strategies and actions for reducing or eliminating its impact, probability, or both to an acceptable level. It might also involve shifting the time frame when action must be taken.
- **Mitigation plan**—An action plan for mitigating risks. It documents strategies, actions, goals, schedule dates, tracking requirements, and all other supporting information needed to carry out the mitigation strategy.
- **Monitoring**—Capturing, analyzing, and reporting project performance, usually as compared to planned performance.
- **Most likely time**—In PERT estimating, a term used for the modal value of the distribution of the value that will occur most frequently. (If it's based upon the past experience it would be the average when the current conditions are concerted.)
- **Monte Carlo analysis**—A type of simulation in which a distribution of probable results is defined for each activity and is used to calculate a distribution of probable results for the total project.
- **Opportunity cost**—The cost of choosing one alternative over another.
- **Order of magnitude estimate (-25 percent, +75 percent)**—This is an approximate estimate made without detailed data, usually produced from a cost-capacity curve, scale-up or -down factors that are appropriately escalated, and approximate cost capacity ratios. This estimate is used during the formative stages of an expenditure program for initial project evaluation.
- **PDM finish-to-finish relationship**—This relationship restricts the finish of the work activity until some specified duration following the finish of another work activity.

- **PDM finish-to-start relationship**—The relationship where work activity can start just as soon as another work activity is finished.
- **PDM start-to-finish relationship**—This relationship restricts the finish of work activity until some duration following the start of another work activity.
- **PDM start-to-start relationship**—This relationship restricts the start of work activity until some specified duration following the start of the preceding work activity.
- **Percent complete (PC)**—An estimate, expressed as a percent, of the amount of work that has been completed on an activity or group of activities, typically based on resource use. Used in calculating earned value.
- **Performance reviews**—Meetings held to assess project progress.
- **Performance risk**—The degree of uncertainty in the development and deployment process that might keep the system from meeting its technical specifications or that might result in the system being unsuitable for its intended use.
- **Phase-gates**—(See tollgates.)
- **Predict**—To state, tell about, or make known in advance; foretell.
- **Present value**—Translates future flows of money to the current value to evaluate a project against today's value of money rather than a future value. Also known as the discounted cash flow. Consider a project for possible selection if the sum of its net present values of all estimated cash flows is positive.
- **Process owner (PO)**—A project team member who serves as primary point of contact to the business, develops service level agreements (SLA), and ensures that authorizations, funding, and engagement personnel are in place. The project manager coordinates with the PO when providing status to the project sponsor.
- **Program**—A program is a group of projects managed in a coordinated way to obtain benefits not available from managing them individually. Many programs also include elements of ongoing operations.
- **Program evaluation and review technique (PERT)**—An event-oriented and probability-based network analysis technique used to estimate project duration when a high degree of uncertainty exists with the individual activity duration estimates. PERT applies the critical-path method to a weighted average duration estimate.
- **Project**—A temporary endeavor undertaken to create a unique product or service.
- **Project audit**—Review of the project to provide an impartial objective appraisal and identify any potential problems or positive practices for use on other projects.
- **Project charter**—A document that formally recognizes a project's existence by senior management and provides the project manager with the authority to apply organizational resources to project activities.

- **Project closeout**—A process that involves completing various project records, making the final revisions on documentation to reflect the "as-built" condition, and issuing and retaining essential project documentation. The project sponsor also accepts the project during closeout.
- **Project control**—Systems and methods that assist the project manager and team in managing the project.
- **Project cost management**—A subset of project management that includes the processes required to ensure the project is completed within the approved budget. It consists of resource planning, cost estimating, cost budgeting, and cost control.
- **Project human resource management**—A subset of project management that includes the processes required to effectively use the people involved with the project. It consists of organizational planning, staff acquisition, and team development.
- **Project life cycle**—A collection of generally sequential project phases whose names and numbers are determined by the control needs of the organization(s) involved in the project. Defines the project's beginning and end. Each phase is marked by the completion of a deliverable.
- **Project management**—The application of knowledge, skills, tools, and techniques to project activities to meet or exceed stakeholder needs and expectations from a project.
- **Project Management Body of Knowledge (PMBOK)**—An inclusive term that describes the sum of knowledge within the profession of project management. As with other professions such as law, medicine, and accounting, the PMBOK rests with the practitioners and academics that apply and advance it. PMBOK includes proven, traditional practices that are widely applied as well as innovative and advanced ones that have been used on a limited basis.
- **Project management information system**—Provides information on projects to support decision making. It involves tools and techniques to gather, integrate, and distribute information from other project management processes. It can be automated or manual.
- **Project Management Institute (PMI)**—A nonprofit organization dedicated to advancing best practices in the profession of project management.
- **Project management processes**—Processes concerned with describing and organizing the work of a project.
- **Project manager**—The individual responsible for managing the overall project and its deliverables. Acts as the customer's single point of contact for services delivered within the project's scope. Controls scope planning and executing of activities and resources to meet established cost, time, and quality goals.
- **Project network diagram**—Any schematic display of the logical relationships of project activities. Always drawn from left to right to reflect project chronology. Often incorrectly referred to as a "PERT chart."

- **Project plan**—A formal, approved document used to guide both project execution and project control. The plan primary uses are to document planning assumptions and decisions facilitate communication among stakeholders, and document approved scope, cost, and schedule baselines. A project plan can be a summary or detailed report.
- **Project procurement management**—A subset of project management that includes the processes required to acquire goods and services from outside the performing organization. It consists of procurement planning, solicitation planning, solicitation, source selection, contract administration, and contract closeout.
- **Project quality management**—A subset of project management that includes the processes required to ensure the project will satisfy the needs for which it was undertaken. It consists of quality planning, assurance, and control. It includes all the activities of the overall management function that determine the quality policy, objectives, and responsibilities and implements them through quality planning, control, assurance, and improvement within the quality system.
- **Project review**—Periodic monitoring of the project activities and tasks. Can be either periodic or topical. A tool used to monitor and control projects.
- **Project risk**—The cumulative effect of the chances of uncertain occurrences that will adversely affect project objectives. It's the degree of exposure to negative events and their probable consequences. Project risk is characterized by three factors: risk event, risk probability, and the amount at stake.
- **Project risk management**—A subset of project management that includes the processes concerned with identifying, analyzing, and responding to project risk. It consists of risk identification, quantification, response development, and response control.
- **Project schedule**—The planned dates for performing activities and the planned dates for meeting milestones.
- **Project scope management**—A subset of project management that includes the processes required to ensure that the project includes all the work required, and only the work required, to complete the project successfully. It consists of initiation, scope planning, scope definition, scope verification, and scope change control.
- **Project selection method**—A process that places weighted scores against project deliverable so the project selected is in alignment with organization strategic plans
- **Project sponsor**—An individual in an organization whose support and approval is required for a project to continue.
- **Project stakeholder**—Individuals and organizations who are actively involved in the project or whose interests might be positively or negatively affected as a result of project execution or successful project completion.
- **Project team**—The group of people who share responsibility for accomplishing project goals and who report either part-time or full-time to the project manager.

Project Management Excellence

- **Project time management**—A subset of project management that includes the processes required to ensure a project's timely completion. It consists of activity definition, sequencing, and duration estimating, and schedule development and control.
- **Proposal**—Submitted by sellers in response to a solicitation.
- **Quality function deployment**—Used to help provide better product definition. Through a series of matrices, the customer's requirements are related to a product's technical requirements, component requirements, process control plans, and manufacturing operations.
- **Quality management plan**—Describes how the project management team will implement its quality policy. It provides input to the overall project plan and must address the project's quality control, assurance, and improvement.
- **Rapid application development (RAD)**—A term used to describe parallel efforts associated with developing information systems. The coding process takes project requirements and translates them into specific language constructs. The step prior to coding is usually completing a detailed design document, where requirements are broken down into modules of impacted code.
- **Ranking**—The process of establishing the order or priority.
- **Request for proposal (RFP)**—Used to request a proposal from a seller, usually for complex or nonstandard items of higher monetary value.
- **Request for quotations (RFQ)**—Used to request a proposal from a seller for low monetary purchases, usually for commodity items.
- **Residual risks**—Risks that remain after a response action has been taken. Also includes minor risks that have been accepted and addressed by, for example, adding contingency amounts to the cost or time allowed.
- **Resource leveling**—Any form of network analysis in which scheduling decisions (i.e., start and finish dates) are driven by resource management concerns (e.g., limited resource availability or difficult-to-mange changes in resource levels). Offers approaches for evening out the peaks and valleys of resource requirements so that a fixed amount of resources can be used over time.
- **Resource planning**—Determining the physical resources and quantities of each one required to perform project activities.
- **Responsibility assignment matrix (RAM)**—A structure that relates the project organization structure to the work breakdown structure to help ensure that each element of the project's work scope is assigned to a responsible individual. Assigns roles and responsibilities for specific activities to particular individuals.
- **Risk**—The possibility of suffering harm or loss. A measure of uncertainty. An uncertain event or condition that, if it occurs, might have a positive or negative effect on the project's objectives.

- **Risk assessment**—Performing a qualitative analysis of risks and conditions to prioritize their affects on project objectives.
- **Risk baseline**—A "snapshot" of all currently known risks to a project, used to begin the process of implementing continuous risk management on a project.
- **Risk categories**—Sources of possible risk that could affect the project for better or worse, typically organized in terms of technical, quality, or performance risks; project-management risks; organization risks; and external risks.
- **Risk event**—A discrete occurrence that might affect the project for better or worse.
- **Risk identification**—Determining which risk events might affect a project and documenting their characteristics.
- **Risk management plan**—A plan that documents the procedures to be used to manage risk throughout the project. It covers who's responsible for managing various areas of risk, how the initial identification and quantification outputs will be maintained, how contingency plans will be implemented, and how reserves will be allocated. It's a subsidiary element of the project plan.
- **Risk metric**—A standard way of measuring an attribute of the risk management process.
- **Risk monitoring and control**—Monitoring risks, identifying residual risks, executing risk reduction plans, and evaluating their effectiveness in the project life cycle.
- **Risk probability**—Determining how likely a risk event is to occur.
- **Risk response planning**—Developing procedures and techniques to enhance opportunities and reduce risks to the project's objectives.
- **Risk symptom**—Trigger or indirect manifestation of a risk event.
- **Risk threshold**—Level of risk acceptable to the organization.
- **Schedule baseline**—The approved project schedule to provide the basis for measuring and reporting schedule performance.
- **Schedule change control system**—Defines the procedures by which the schedule can be changed. It includes the paperwork, tracking systems, and approval levels necessary for authorizing changes.
- **Schedule management plan**—Defines how changes to the schedule will be managed. It's a subsidiary element of the project plan.
- **Schedule performance index (SPI)**—The ratio of work performed to work scheduled (BCWP/BCWS). SPI <1 indicates a project is behind schedule.
- **Schedule variance (SV)**—(1) Any difference between the scheduled completion of an activity and its actual completion. (2) In earned value analysis, it's the BCWP less BCWS. SV < 0 indicates that the project is behind schedule.
- **Scope change**—Any modification to the agreed-upon scope as defined by the WBS.
- **Scope change control**—Controlling changes to project scope; influencing the factors that create scope changes to ensure that changes are beneficial; determining that a scope change has occurred; and managing the actual changes when and if they occur.

- **Scope creep**—The project's scope increases gradually such that the project management team or customer doesn't notice it. This occurs because the customer adds additional requirements, but when several minor changes are added together, they can collectively result in a significant change in cost and budget over-runs.
- **Scope definition**—Subdividing the major project deliverables as identified in the scope statement into smaller, more manageable components.
- **Scope management plan**—A document that describes how project scope will be managed and how scope changes will be integrated into the project. It also should include a clear description of how scope changes will be identified and classified.
- **Secondary risks**—Risks that arise as a direct result of implementing a risk response.
- **Smoothing**—Conflict resolution approach that de-emphasizes or avoids areas of difference and emphasizes areas of agreement.
- **Sponsor**—Individual or group in the performing organization who provides the financial resources, in cash or kind, for the project.
- **Stages**—A set of prescribed and concurrent activities that should incorporate best practices. (Also known as "phases.")
- **Stage gates**—(See tollgates.)
- **Stakeholder**—Individuals and organizations that are involved in or might be affected by project activities. Anyone who has a vested interest in the project.
- **Statement of requirements (SOR)**—Variation on the statement of work used for a procurement item that is presented as a problem to solve.
- **Statement of risk**—A description of the risk typically defined in terms of condition-consequence format to show the conditions causing concern for a potential loss to the project followed by a description of these conditions' potential consequences.
- **Statement of work (SOW)**—A narrative description of products or services to be supplied under contract.
- **Status reviews**—A meeting used to determine where the project stands compared to its schedule.
- **Strength-weakness-opportunity-threat (SWOT) analysis**—A risk-identification tool and technique used to examine the project in terms of its strengths, weaknesses, opportunities, and threats to increase the breadth of risks examined and considered.
- **Task**—(1) A well-defined piece of project work that appears at the lowest level of the project's work breakdown structure. Each task accomplishes a discrete work item. (2) An activity that is composed of input and output, has an owner, and is performed within a specified duration.
- **Team charter**—Serves as a mission statement for the project team and describes the roles and responsibilities of team members. Describes the team's operational ground rules.
- **Teamwork**—A sustaining principle of continuous risk management that requires working cooperatively to achieve a common goal and pooling talent, skills, and knowledge.

- **Threat**—Negative outcomes as a result of risk.
- **Time frame**—The period when action is required to mitigate a risk; an attribute of a risk.
- **Tollgate**—A template, or road map, for driving projects from idea to launch or install and beyond. A decision point that allows for sponsor review. Called or "phase gates" or "stage gates." (The latter term developed by Dr. Robert G. Cooper.)
- **Top-down estimate**—An approach to cost estimating that starts at the top level of the WBS and then works down to successively lower levels.
- **Total float (TF)**—The amount of time (in work units) that an activity might be delayed from its early start without delaying the project finish date. Total float is equal to an activity's late start minus its early start.
- **Trigger**—Thresholds for indicators that specify when an action, such as implementing a contingency plan, might need to be taken. Triggers generally are used to provide warning of an impending critical event, indicate the need to implement a contingency plan to preempt a problem, and request immediate attention for a risk.
- **Unacceptable risk**—Exposure to risks that can jeopardize an organization's strategy and/or present dangers to human lives and/or represent a significant financial exposure.
- **Unknown (risk)**—Risks that aren't yet identified or are impossible to predict.
- **Value analysis**—Identifying the required functions for a product, establishing values for the required functions, and suggesting an approach to provide the required functions at the lowest overall cost without performance loss to optimize cost performance. Product analysis technique.
- **Variance analysis**—Comparing actual project results to planned or expected results.
- **Virtual team**—A project team that isn't collocated but works across organizational boundaries, relying primarily on technology for communications. Team members can be distributed across buildings, states, and countries.
- **Workaround**—A response to a negative risk event. Distinguished from a contingency plan in that a workaround isn't planned in advance of the risk event's occurrence.
- **Work breakdown structure (WBS)**—A deliverable-oriented grouping of project elements that organizes and defines a project's total scope. Each descending level represents an increasingly detailed definition of a project component, which might be a product or service.

Note: Most of these definitions are excerpts from an extensive list of project management terms and definitions created by Ginger Levin.

APPENDIX B

PMBOK TOOLS AND TECHNIQUES

Some of the more commonly used project management tools and techniques (as recommended by the Project Management Institute and others) are listed below. Evaluate yourself to determine your project management maturity level. For each one, check off your present level:
- Do not know it
- Know it but have not used it
- Used it
- Mastered it

If you would like a more information on these or other improvement tools, visit the Harrington Institute Web site: *www.harrington-institute.com.*

Using the sum of the individual point scores, the following is your project manager maturity level.
- Excellent project manager.. 175–225
- Acceptable project manager...................................... 125–174
- Acceptable project team member 100–124
- Unacceptable project manager 50–100
- Unacceptable project team member 0–50

Any project managers who have a point score below 125 need project manager training.

Project Management Excellence

Figure AppB.1 PMBOK Tools

	Don't know it	Know it, but haven't used it	Used it	Mastered it
1. Arrow diagramming method (ADM)				
2. Benchmarking				
3. Benefit-cost analysis				
4. Bidders conferences				
5. Bottom-up estimating				
6. Change control system				
7. Configuration management				
8. Checklists				
9. Communications skills				
10. Computerized tools				
11. Conditional diagramming methods				
12. Contingency planning				
13. Contract change control system				
14. Contract type selection				
15. Control charts				
16. Control negotiation				
17. Cost change control system				
18. Cost estimating tools and techniques				
19. Decision trees				
20. Decomposition				
21. Design of experiments				
22. Duration compression				
23. Earned value analysis				
24. Expected monetary value				
25. Expert judgment				
26. Flowcharting				
27. Human resource practices				
28. Information distribution tolls and techniques				
29. Independent estimates				
30. Information distribution systems				
31. Information retrieval systems				
32. Interviewing techniques				
33. Make-or-but analysis				
34. Mathematical analysis				
35. Negotiating techniques				
36. Network templates				
37. Organizational procedures development				

Figure AppB.1 PMBOK Tools (continued)

	Don't know it	Know it, but haven't used it	Used it	Mastered it
38. Organizational theory				
39. Parametric modeling				
40. Pareto diagram				
41. Payment system analysis				
42. Performance measurement analysis				
43. Performance reporting tools and techniques				
44. Performance reviews				
45. Pre-assignment technique				
46. Precedence diagramming method (PDM)				
47. Procurement audits				
48. Product analysis				
49. Product skills and knowledge				
50. Project management information system (PMIS)				
51. Project management information system, organizational procedures				
52. Project management software				
53. Project management training				
54. Project planning methodology				
55. Project selection methods				
56. Quality audits				
57. Quality planning tools and techniques				
58. Resource leveling heuristics				
59. Reward and recognition systems				
60. Schedule change control system				
61. Scope change control system				
62. Screening system				
63. Simulation modeling				
64. Stakeholder analysis				
65. Stakeholder skills and knowledge				
66. Statistical sampling				
67. Statistical sums				
68. Status review meeting				
69. Team-building activities				
70. Trend analysis				
71. Variance analysis				

(continues)

Figure AppB.3 PMBOK Tools (continued)

	Don't know it	Know it, but haven't used it	Used it	Mastered it
72. Weighting system				
73. Work authorization system				
74. Work breakdown structure templates				
75. Workarounds approaches				
Total				
Times weight	0	1	2	3
Point score				
Sum of point scores				

INDEX

A

ABT/NIKU 77
activity 155
activity-on-arrow (AOA) 155
activity-on-node (AON) 155
actual cost of work performed (ACWP) 131, 140, 155
agreement 155
alternatives identification 155
American National Standard Institute (ANSI) 11
American Society for Quality xxxiii, 126, 133
analogous estimating 155
ANSI/PMI 99-001-2000 11
Archibald, Russell D. 131
architecture 155
Artemis International Solutions 77
asset management 155
assumption analysis 155
audit 80

B

balanced matrix 155
balanced scorecard 114
BCWP-earned value 132
benchmarking xxxiii, 3, 89
benefit-cost ratio 156
benefit-measurement method 156
best practices 9, 20, 30, 37, 38, 40, 69, 95, 102, 154

billing rates 139
bottom-up estimate 156
break-even point 136
budget 144
budget at completion (BAC) 131, 156
budgeted cost of work performed (BCWP) 131, 132, 140, 156
budgeted costs of work scheduled (BCWS) 131, 132, 140, 156
burning platform 68, 113
business case 92, 96
Business Engine 78
business intelligence 77
business objectives 122
business plan xxvi, xxix; eleven documents of xxx; *see also* planning
business risk 156; *see also* risk
business strategy 7
business system analyst (BSA) 117, 156
Business Week 140

C

Cap Gemini Ernst & Young 76
Carrow, John 71
Case, Ken xxxiv
Champy, James 3
change xxv, xxxi, 10, 22, 29, 30, 37, 46, 48, 68, 80, 96, 106; agents 40; control 14, 18, 26, 45, 156; environmental 86–87; management 3, 20, 21, 113, 145, 152; process flow 112; strategy 111–113

173

change control board (CCB) 156
change management excellence xxi, xxv–xxvi
change request (CR) 46, 47, 48, 49, 80, 134
Changepoint 78
changes, risks, and issues (CRI) 30, 135
Chaos Report xxiv, 1, 4
closeout review 39
closure 156
communications management plan 156; *see also* planning
conceptual design 108–109
configuration management 156
conflict resolution 32
constraint 156
contingency plan 157; *see also* planning
continuous improvement xxiii, xxxi, 7, 10, 52, 63, 86, 97, 129, 152; *see also* Six Sigma
continuous risk management 157; *see also* risk
contract administration 68
contract work breakdown structure (CWBS) 157; *see also* work breakdown structure
Cooper, Robert G. 55, 68
corrective action 69, 73, 127, 129, 130, 132, 145
cost 14, 25, 28, 30, 34, 36, 39, 49, 50, 51, 55, 58, 69, 72, 78, 86, 98, 106, 108, 135, 140, 148; of actual vs. earned value 141; control of 13–132; cumulative performance index of 141; independent estimate of 159; indirect 159; management of 19, 21, 43; of project 64–65
cost at completion (CAC) 141
cost-benefit analysis (CBA) 17, 22, 48, 55, 83, 87, 89, 93, 94, 105, 106, 157; per resource 139; risk 157
cost performance index (CPI) 132, 140, 157

cost variance (CV) 140, 143, 157
Covey, Stephen R. xix, xxiii
critical chain method (CCM) 61
critical path 157; project reviews 30
critical path method (CPM) 61
CRM Magazine 154
crushing 61
cumulative cost performance index 141; *see also* cost
customer xxxi, xxxiv, 4, 9, 10, 17, 23, 26, 28, 32, 44, 60, 86, 121, 122, 123, 129, 147; expectations 88–89; external 72, 115; needs 88; satisfaction 48; tools for profiling 88
cycle time 9, 44, 61, 69, 89, 120, 130; decreasing 120

D

dashboard reporting 138, 143–145
data integration 44
defect 133
deliverables 30, 32, 42, 46, 52, 53, 56, 57, 61, 65, 81, 88, 94, 96, 98, 99, 102, 103, 107, 110, 121, 122, 129, 133, 135, 149, 152, 154
design 17, 48; of experiment xxiii, 157
detailed design document 109–110
discretionary dependency 58
document control xxiii, 33
document reviews 11
documentation 17, 20, 21, 39, 47, 49, 58, 67, 80–81, 104, 110, 149
duration 157

E

earned value (EV) 132, 134, 140, 143; analysis of 140–143, 157
80–20 rule 120
Eisenhower, Dwight D. 53

employee xxvii, xxviii, 34
empowerment 157
engagement model 116
enterprise resource planning (ERP) 2, 76
Essex Electrical 153
estimate 50, 72, 158; definitive 53; independent 159; of budget 53; of cost 64–65; of task effort 58–59; order of magnitude 160; top-down 167
estimate at completion (EAC) 158
estimate to complete (ETC) 158
estimated cost to complete (ECC) 132, 158
exception report 58, 175
executive team 38
expected monetary value 158
exposure 158
external customer 72, 115; *see also* customer
external dependency 58
external resource 34; *see also* resource
external risk 158; *see also* risk

F

fast tracking 61
feedback xxiii, 10, 130
Feigenbaum, Armand V. xxii
Feigenbaum, Donald xxii
fifty-fifty approach 158
finish-to-finish (FF) 158
finish-to-start (FS) 158
five pillars of organizational excellence xix, xx–xxii, xxi, xxxiv
five Ps xix
forecast 66, 71
forming 100, 101
Fortune 6
forward-looking view 158
future-state model 111

G

Gantt chart 63
Gartner Group xxv, 1, 2, 4, 7, 8, 78, 139; Research 35, 36, 38, 40, 56, 66, 67
GE xxix
Giga Information Group 140
Girdler, Zena 78
graphical evaluation and review technique (GERT) 61
guess 158

H

Hammer, Michael 3
Herbold, Robert J. xxxiii, 143
Horizon Blue Cross Blue Shield 73
Hubble telescope 2
Huey, John 6
human resource 14, 20, 21, 34, 43, 66, 70, 72; *see also* resource

I-J

IBM xxiv, 3, 4, 6, 76, 139, 140, 151, 152
IEEE/ACM 151
impact 158
information technology (IT) xxiv, xxvii, 1, 3, 4, 8, 29, 36, 69, 83, 116, 119, 138, 139, 153; engagement models for 116
information technology manager (ITM) 117, 159
innovation xxii
input 11, 44, 59, 61, 62, 110, 114, 123; requirement statement xxiii
intellectual capital 5, 133, 134
interface management 159
internal rate of return (IRR) 90, 159
internal resource 34; *see also* resource
internal risk 159; *see also* risk
Internet xxvii, 9, 76, 97
interrupt-driven work strategy 89

ISO 9000 6, 151
ISO 9001:2000 xxiii, xxxi, xxxii, xxxiii
ISO 14001 xxxii
just-in-time xxiii

K

Kellogg School of Management 69
kickoff meeting 159
Kinikin, Erin 27
Knight, Phil 4
knowledge 35; capital 5; explicit xxvii; management 75, 119; networks xxviii; resource planning 76; six phases of xxvii–xxviii; system xxvii, 72, 149; tacit xxvii
knowledge management excellence xxi, xxvii–xxviii
known/unknown risk 159; *see also* risk

L

late finish date (LF) 159
late start date (LS) 159
law of diminishing returns 159
Lawson Software 78
leadership skills 29
lean 10
level of effort (LOE) 132, 159
leveling 159
life cycle 25, 28, 46, 52, 83, 92, 94, 95, 96, 99, 116, 133; phases of 16; product 6; of project 21; six phases for project 22–23
list reduction 159

M

macro-level integration 45
major risk 160
Malcolm Baldrige National Quality Award xxxiii
mandatory dependency 58, 160
Manhattan Project 9

measurement xxiii, 28, 32, 33, 52, 64, 66, 92, 94, 130, 131, 132, 140, 145, 148
Microsoft Corp. 3, 78
Microsoft Project Office 77, 153
milestone 160; chart 160; plan 55
Miller, Pamela 9, 73
minor risk 160; *see also* risk
mission statement xxx
mitigation plan 160
monitoring 160
Monte Carlo analysis 160
Morrison, Ian 6
most likely time 160

N

net present value (NPV) 71, 90
Nike 4
norming 100, 101

O

operational integration 44
opportunity cost 160
order of magnitude estimate 160
organizational change management (OCM) 20, 43, 68, 113
organizational excellence xxxi–xxxiv
output 6, 7, 11, 12, 25, 30, 44, 50, 58, 60, 61, 62, 123, 135; requirement statement for xxii
outsourcing 7, 34, 36, 43, 67, 86, 98, 136

P

Pacific Edge 78
payback period method (PPM) 90
PDM finish-to-finish relationship 160, 161
PDM finish-to-start relationship 160, 161
peer reviews 49
percent complete (PC) 132, 161
percent of budget spent (PBS) 132

performance 100, 102; integration 44; reviews 30, 161; risk 161
PERT: *see* program evaluation and review technique
Peters, Tom xxxi, 8, 25, 148
phase gate 55, 73, 83, 161
phase review 37
planned value (PV) 140
planning xxix, 5, 9, 10, 15, 16, 17, 18, 19, 20, 21, 22, 28, 31, 48, 83, 87; business xxvi, xxix; contingency 157; communication management 156; five-step process for project 106–107; improvement 63; project 50–63, 105–117; seven tasks of 117; strategic xxix; *see also* business plan
PlanView 77
PMBOK: *see* Project Management Body of Knowledge
portfolio 5, 25, 26, 30, 37, 39, 96, 97–98, 119, 135; management of 20, 21, 43, 147; review team 73; management of 68–79
predict 161
present value 161
Primavera Systems 77
PRINCE: *see* projects in controlled environments
problem solving 32
process xxii, 44, 66, 67, 86, 108, 110, 130; capability xxiii, 33; engineering xxxiii; five iterative groups 15, 16, 17; improvement 10, 97, 129; management xxiii; nonvalue-added steps in 10; redesign 3; reengineering xxxi, 3, 97; refining of xxiii–xxiv; team 115
process management excellence xx, xxii–xxiv
process owner (PO) 32–33, 117, 161
process-improvement initiatives 86
product and/or service scope 46; *see also* scope

product cycles 6; *see also* life cycle
product development 57
program 1, 161
program evaluation and review technique (PERT) 62, 161
project xxiv, 1, 4, 7; audit of 161; benefit monitoring of 94; budget for 29, 30, 38; charter 26, 40, 41, 95, 99, 105, 106, 162; closeout 147–149, 162; communications management for 66; constraints 53, 93; control 129–145, 162; control review 130–131; cost of 3, 13, 49, 64–65, 71, 162; cost management of 64–65, 162; cost of lost revenue 8; cycle 12, 72; database 33; definition 52; document management 80–81; effect of earned value on 143; environmental effect on 86–87; estimating methodology 36, 50–52; evaluating importance of 72, 89–90; execution of 119–127; extension phase activities of 119; failure of 3, 4, 45, 49; five-level maturity model for 152; human resource management of 66, 162; information needs for 133–140; initiation 95–104; investment in 22; integration management of 20, 21, 43–45; leaders 44; life cycle 20, 21, 22, 25, 28, 46, 54, 58, 119, 123, 131, 162; milestone 53–54; network diagram 162; on-time 30–31; over-budget 7; performance chart 74; phases 45; phase reviews 37, 38; planning 31, 47, 45, 50–63, 105–117, 163; portfolio 5, 20, 21, 25, 26, 30, 37, 39, 43, 68–79, 96, 97–98, 119, 135, 147; portfolio management software 75–79, 153; outsourcing of 7; phases of 21; postmortem 15; procurement management 20, 67, 163; quality management 65, 163; reporting 138; requirements 107, 108; review 32, 93, 126, 163; review team 40; risk manage-

177

ment of 67, 163; scheduling 2, 58, 59–63, 163; scope 13, 19, 21, 27, 33, 45–49, 55, 67, 163; selection 22, 25, 83–94, 95–96, 163; senior management's role in 93; slippage 134; sponsor 22, 27, 28, 29, 31, 40, 41, 47, 49, 54, 57, 66, 83, 92, 94, 98, 99, 105, 107, 114, 115, 117, 161, 163, 166; stakeholder 163; status report 31, 125–127; structure 115; subphases 85; success rate of 4; suppliers 40; target board 103–104; team 9, 12, 14, 27, 29, 33, 36, 37, 38, 47, 51, 52, 54, 57, 66, 73, 83, 89, 99, 100, 102–104, 115, 122, 131, 163; testing of 121–124; time management 64, 164; tollgate 26; typical structure of 114; types of 97–98; work breakdown structure 54–55
projects in controlled environments (PRINCE) 18
project management 1, 75, 119, 162; center of excellence model for 38, 39; function model for 38, 39–40; information center model for 38–39; information system 162; innovations in 9–10; knowledge areas 43–81; life cycle 151–154; methodologies 37, 39; nine knowledge areas of 19; office 35–40, 94, 114, 115–116; PRINCE 18; processes of 11, 162; process model for 17; six phases of 84; software for 75–79, 153; system 7, 11; team 18, 20; three Cs of 36
project management body of knowledge (PMBOK) 11–17, 19, 21, 50, 51, 68, 151, 154, 162, 169
project management excellence xx, xxiv–xxv
Project Management Institute (PMI) 3, 10, 19, 43, 53, 104, 117, 127, 149, 162,
project manager (PM) 12, 17, 20, 21, 22, 23, 25, 26, 27, 28–31, 32, 33, 35, 38, 39, 40, 41, 46, 48, 49, 52, 53, 55, 57, 58, 83, 92, 95, 96, 98, 99, 100, 101, 105, 107, 108, 111, 114, 115, 117, 125, 126, 129, 132, 134, 137, 143, 147, 151, 152, 161, 162
proposal 164
prototype 121

Q

quality 18, 106, 152; assurance 126; circles xxiii, xxxiii; control xxxi, 14, 133; function deployment 164
Quality Council of Indiana 88
quality management 19, 21; plan 164; for project 65; techniques xxxiii

R

ranking 164
rapid application development (RAD) 120, 121, 164
recognition 147
reengineering 4
request for proposal (RFP) 164
request for quotations (RFQ) 164
requirement 107, 109, 122; integration of 44; specifications 48; statement of 166
residual risk 164; *see also* risk
resource xxviii, 4, 5, 13, 22, 26, 28, 29, 30, 35, 37, 39, 43, 44, 47, 57, 58, 59, 68, 73, 89, 103, 105, 106, 136, 137, 144, 145, 149, 154; and skill requirements 70; database 34; estimates of 37; external 8, 34; human 20, 21, 43, 66, 70; internal 34; leveling 164; manager 34–35, 136; planning 64, 164
responsibility assignment matrix (RAM) 164
return on investment (ROI) 26, 39, 73, 89, 103

Index

return on projects 139
review analysis 126
rewards 147
Rifkin, Jeremy 6
risk 11, 27, 37, 39, 57, 58, 59, 62, 90, 97, 103, 108, 126, 164, 167; analysis 14, 106, 111, 126, 127; assessment 165; baseline 165; business 156; categories 165; continuous management of 157; event 165; external 158; identification 165; internal 159; known/unknown 159; management 11, 13, 18, 20, 21, 43, 67, 165; metric 165; minor 160; monitoring and control of 165; probability 165; residual 164; response planning for 165; secondary 166; statement of 166; symptom 165; threshold 165; unacceptable 167
Robbins-Gioia 7, 36
root cause analysis xxiii, 133
Ruggles, William 12

S

scenario analysis 30
schedule 59–63, 64, 106, 135, 140, 144, 145, 148; baseline 165; change control system 165; estimating 36; management plan 165
schedule performance index (SPI) 132, 141, 165
schedule variance (SV) 140, 165
Schwarz, William J. xxiii
scope 39, 47, 50, 51, 52, 57, 62, 76, 98, 99, 103, 104, 108, 110, 123, 140, 144, 145; analysis 80; change 45, 46; change control 165; creep 5, 166; definition of 166; management 43, 45–49, 166; planning 14; product 46; review 47; statement, 17, 106

secondary risk 166; *see also* risk
Shewhart's cycles xxiii
simulation modeling 62
SIPOC: *see* supply, input, process, output, customer
Six Rules for Self-Examination xxix
Six Sigma xxiii, xxxi, xxxii, xxxiii, 51, 74, 133; *see also* continuous improvement
Smith, Fred xxx
Smith, Ted 2
smoothing 166
software 153; for portfolio management 75–79; integration 44
Software Engineering Institute 151
staff knowledge and abilities (SKAs) 139
stage gates 12, 55–57, 166
stakeholders xxvii, xxxiv, 26, 48, 49, 53, 56, 66, 87, 92, 96, 104, 121, 125, 143, 166
Standish Group International xxiv
statement of requirements (SOR) 166
statement of risk 166; *see also* risk
statement of work (SOW) 166
status reviews 166
steering committee 25, 26, 27, 32, 49, 54, 86, 92–93, 95, 96, 99, 114, 115, 125
storming 100, 101
strength-weakness-opportunity-threat (SWOT) analysis 166
suggestion system xxiii
supplier xxxiii, 67, 152
supply and demand 35, 137
supply chain 120
supply, input, process, output, customer (SIPOC) 110
system testing 124; *see also* testing
Systemcorp 77, 78, 119, 140
Systemcorp PMOffice 153

T

Tapscott, Don 7
task 166; duration 58–59; effort 58; sequencing 58; structure 5
team xxxii, 2, 20, 28, 31, 44, 48, 49, 52, 53, 55, 57, 63, 65, 101, 105, 108, 109, 137, 147, 148; charter 101, 106, 166; data design 116; implementation 116; leader 32, 58; members 32; planning 106; process 115; product 116; project 9, 12, 14, 27, 29, 33, 36, 37, 38, 47, 51, 52, 54, 57, 66, 73, 83, 89, 99, 100, 102–104, 115, 122, 131, 163; stages of development 100; testing 116; virtual 102–103
testing 123–124; cycle 122–123; self-assessment 130–131; strategy 121–122; of system 124; of unit 124
threat 167
time frame 167
Toffler, Alvin 6, 68
Toffler, Heidi 6
tollgate 55–57, 67; review 133
tool 4, 7, 8, 11, 20, 37, 55, 88, 126, 143; management xxv
top-down estimate 167; *see also* estimate
total earned value (TEV) 141
total float (TF) 167
total improvement management xxxii; *see also* continuous improvement
total quality management (TQM) xxxi, xxxii; *see also* quality
traceability matrix 111
tracking 138
training 5, 17, 28, 29, 65, 113
trigger 167
Tuckman, Bruce W. 100
Turek, Norbert 69, 75, 139

U

unacceptable risk 16; *see also* risk
unit testing 124; *see also* testing
use case 123, 124
utility curves 88

V

value analysis 167
variance 131, 134, 145; analysis 131–132, 167
virtual companies 86
virtual team 102–103, 167; *see also* team
vision statement xxvi, xxx
Visitacion, Margo 140

W

Wall Street Journal 2, 38
waste xxviii, 137; elimination of 90–91; reduction of project 33
Waterman, Robert Jr. 148
Waters Corp. 154
weighted-selection method 93
weighting factor 71, 72
Welch, Jack xxix, xxxiv
Woolard, E. S. xix
work breakdown structure (WBS) 46, 48, 52, 56, 77, 105, 106, 117, 135, 167; contract 157
work plans 32; *see also* planning
workaround 167
workforce xxx, 36
worldwide project management method (WWPMM) 151

Z

zero defects xxxi
Zollars, Bill 5